S0-ABR-955

OTHER BOOKS BY WILLIAM DRAKE

*

Sara Teasdale, Woman and Poet

Mirror of the Heart (Editor)

The
FIRST
WAVE

The FIRST WAVE

Women Poets in America 1915-1945

WILLIAM DRAKE

MACMILLAN PUBLISHING COMPANY * NEW YORK

COLLIER MACMILLAN PUBLISHERS * LONDON

Copyright © 1987 by William Drake

All rights reserved. No part of this book may be reproduced or
transmitted in any form or by any means, electronic or mechanical,
including photocopying, recording or by any information storage and
retrieval system, without permission in writing from the Publisher.

Macmillan Publishing Company
866 Third Avenue, New York, N.Y. 10022
Collier Macmillan Canada, Inc.

Library of Congress Cataloging-in-Publication Data
Drake, William.
The first wave.
Bibliography: p.
Includes index.
1. American poetry—Women authors—History and
criticism. 2. American poetry—20th century—History
and criticism. 3. Women and literature—United States.
I. Title.
PS151.D7   1987   811'.52'099287   87-12243
ISBN 0-02-533490-5

10 9 8 7 6 5 4 3 2 1

Designed by Jack Meserole
*

Macmillan books are available at special discounts for bulk purchases
for sales promotions, premiums, fund-raising, or educational use.
For details, contact:

Special Sales Director
Macmillan Publishing Company
866 Third Avenue
New York, N.Y. 10022

PRINTED IN THE UNITED STATES OF AMERICA

Permissions and Acknowledgments appear on
pages 305–308.

For

ELIZABETH, LYNDA, AND JANE

*

C O N T E N T S

*

*

A C K N O W L E D G M E N T S

*

Countless tributaries have flowed into the stream of this book, and there is not enough space to express my thanks for every one. Above all, I am indebted to Lynda Marin for her remarkable combination of critical skills, insight into female creativity, and ability to articulate her perceptions. She borrowed time from her own work to read every word of this book, and saved me from many an unfortunate blunder as well as contributing to the testing and elaborating of ideas. I am grateful, too, to Susan Gevirtz, poet, for her discerning comments on my work in progress and for many stimulating discussions about women's creativity, particularly regarding modernism and experimentation. I thank Jane Drake for her unfailing interest and encouragement, for insights from her own experience, and just for being there. My gratitude goes also to Philomena Drake for valuable assistance. Simon Bockie has been an indispensable friend, always willing to listen to me talk my way through problems and obstacles and showing me that things are never as bad as they seem. This book owes far more than is apparent to my late wife, Elizabeth, who opened all the important doors; and to the late Margaret Conklin, her friend, who also helped to reveal the meaning of friendship among creative women. My thanks, then, to all friends, seen and unseen.

I am particularly appreciative of the generous cooperation of the children and friends of some of the poets who appear in this book. Allyn Asti-Rose offered reminiscences and a wealth of family records concerning her grandmother, Marjorie Allen Seiffert, and shared her own creative aspirations and beliefs. Her brother, John C. Pryor, also provided important, often witty, insights into a remarkable family. Chauncey Spencer conducted me through his mother's home in Lynchburg, Virginia, with inimitable charm and hospitality, answering my questions and offering his candid observations, while giving me complete freedom to form my own impressions; Anne Spencer "belongs to the ages," he said. Marcia D. Liles painstakingly reviewed my presentation of her mother, Genevieve Taggard, correcting my errors and those that have crept into the public record, and offering important insights while generously allowing me my own emphasis. Adam Yarmolinsky welcomed my questions about his mother, Babette Deutsch, and responded to my many requests for his help with promptness and thoughtful consideration. Kenton Kilmer kindly provided copies of correspondence between his mother, Aline Kilmer, and other poets, and shared his recollections of the poetry scene between the wars. Penny Lehman talked to me of her long friendship with Margaret Conklin and of her own memories of Marianne Moore.

Special thanks are owing to May Sarton for a greater contribution to this book than she realizes: not only an interview and telephone calls and letters in which she probed her friendship with Louise Bogan, but the spiritual depth and example of her work, her profound understanding of the meaning of friendship, that cast light on all the themes this book is concerned with. All of these women and men who once shared intimacy with the poets have without exception striven conscientiously to honor the truth, even when it involved pain. Their truth comes filtered through me; I therefore take responsibility for any distortions, oversights, or failures of perception.

Other scholars have been generous in sharing their own researches and ideas. Without Elaine Sproat's help I could not have written about Lola Ridge at all, a figure central to this book. Elaine Sproat's biography of Ridge will be a major contribution to our understanding of women's poetry between the wars. Gloria Bowles allowed me to read her study *Louise Bogan's Aesthetic of Limitation* in manuscript and helped guide me through the difficulties of interpreting Louise Bogan's life and work. I was delighted to find that Gloria Bowles had anticipated my own approach to modernism. I thank her for a stimulating exchange of ideas and for reading the manuscript of this book. I thank Carol Schoen for letting me read her book *Sara Teasdale* in manuscript and for discussions of Teasdale that have helped me modify my views. I have benefited from discussions with Glenn Ruihley about the women poets of Teasdale's generation, and from his work on Amy Lowell. I also thank Myra Cohn Livingston and Sandra Whipple Spanier for assistance generously given when needed.

Librarians too numerous to mention have given me access to manuscript materials and often pointed out sources I might have overlooked. While I cannot thank each individually, I wish to acknowledge some of those who went beyond the call of duty in helping me with special requests: Diana Haskell, of the Newberry Library, Chicago; Nora Quinlan, of the University of Colorado; Margaret Fusco, of the University of Chicago; Melanie Yolles, of the New York Public Library; Minnie H. Clayton, of the Atlanta University Center; Susan Boone, of Smith College; Patricia C. Willis, of the Rosenbach Museum and Library, Philadelphia; and the staff at the Moorland-Spingarn Research Center of Howard University, particularly Wilda Willis, who assisted me in sorting through the Angelina Weld Grimké Collection. I also thank the reference staff at the Moline, Illinois, Public Library; and Sallie Hassler, librarian at Dunbar School in Lynchburg, Virginia, who directed me to the sources on Anne Spencer.

I am most grateful to my editor, Alexia Dorszynski, for seeing the possibilities of this book even before I did, for believing in it, for her acute and reliable judgment, and for steering it through countless difficulties with a firm hand; and to her very competent assistant, Jessica Berman.

I thought, I am a Poet, one of them.
—LOLA RIDGE

*

F O R E W O R D

*

The written story of any life can never be a final word. When I had finished a biography of Sara Teasdale in 1979, I found new letters, new information, continuing to come to light, even after ten years of searching. But more important than that, Teasdale's close friend and literary executor, Margaret Conklin, began to remember things she had forgotten, brought back now by her own shifting perspective. She herself had been changed by the emotionally charged task of exploring a relationship central to her life, a friendship filled with both joy and pain, that she had fixed in her mind over the years as a kind of myth. Myths not only enshrine a meaning: They protect against reality. Margaret likened the experience of exhuming the disturbing contents of the past to undergoing psychoanalysis. A different, more human, Sara emerged from the one she had idealized in her youthful admiration, the Sara she had fiercely guarded for nearly half a century against the vulgar curiosity of an insensitive world.

Although Margaret Conklin attempted always to divert my

attention away from herself to her much-loved Sara, it was evident
that she herself had been a central player in Teasdale's life and
imagination. The story of their friendship, so precious and vulnerable to Margaret, opened out in widening ripples, revealing a pattern of relationships with other women in Teasdale's life. It was
not the men whom Sara Teasdale admired, or loved, or married,
that fostered and fed her creativity; it was rather women who for-
tified her courage and confirmed her identity. And Teasdale was
not alone in this. Margaret Conklin had also served, I found, as a
catalyst to Marianne Moore, a friend of hers for over forty years.
The connections among the women poets formed a kind of web,
almost never spoken about—for their attention was on their professional struggle for recognition, on the rules set by the male world—
but a web of consciousness nevertheless essential to their creative
growth and survival. Yet the inner history of the women poets in
that period remained as silent and invisible as Sara Teasdale's life in
Margaret Conklin's keeping. One faced a gallery of dim and clouded
portraits, consigned to rooms where viewers seldom strolled, while
certain likenesses—mostly of men—hung in the glare of endless
examination and praise.

This book is, in part, an effort to revive memory, to restore
some of those portraits to their original freshness—not as a series
of isolated portrayals, but in the context of interrelationships with
family, friends, husbands, and lovers that nourished or obstructed
their creative will. This is not a survey, however, or an inclusive
chronology of the women poets who flourished in America between
the two world wars. For those modes of storytelling always carry a
hidden hierarchy of values and assignments of status. One needs to
escape the arrogance of condescension and rule-giving that fixes the
lives of others in patterns serviceable to oneself. The women poets
were struggling to free themselves from exactly that kind of pat-
terning. They sensed that they were creating a new history and
wanted to live in the fluidity of time rather than in the prison of
prior definition. "The minute you or anybody else knows what you
are you are not it," Gertrude Stein wrote. "As everything in living

is made up of finding out what you are, it is extraordinarily difficult really not to know what you are and yet to be that thing."[1] Or, as Nikki Giovanni has said more recently, "You only define a thing when it's on the way down. . . . As long as it's traveling, you're only guessing."[2]

"Finding out what you are": That was perhaps the central task the women poets undertook, and it led them from the very outset in a different direction from that of the male poets of the modern period. "At present most of what we know, or think we know, of women has been found out by men," Helen Hoyt wrote in the avant-garde magazine *Others* in 1916. "We have yet to hear what woman will tell of herself, and where can she tell more intimately than in poetry?"[3] While male poets and critics treated women's focus on self as evidence of restricted capacities and intellectual inferiority, the fact is that women were laying the groundwork for their own future development.

The surge of women's creativity beginning around World War I and cresting in the mid-1920s was one of the phenomenal developments of a revolutionary age, and was acknowledged as such in its time. Publishers rushed to the opportunity to discover and issue women's poetry. Women themselves moved into editorial positions on influential magazines, not only the cluster of women surrounding Harriet Monroe at *Poetry*, but Lola Ridge at *Broom*, Elinor Wylie at *Vanity Fair*, Marianne Moore at the *Dial*. Edmund Wilson wrote in 1926, "I find [the women poets] more rewarding than the men. Their emotion is likely to be more genuine and their literary instinct surer."[4] The atmosphere was suffused with a spirit of success: "Isn't it wonderful how the lady poets are coming along?"[5] Edna St. Vincent Millay exclaimed in 1923. Sara Teasdale had published the first twentieth-century anthology of poetry by women in 1917, and in an enlarged edition of 1928 wrote, "The decade since 1917 has produced more good poetry by women than any other in the history of the language."[6] Genevieve Taggard's *May Days: An Anthology of Verse from Masses-Liberator* (1925) included forty-nine women out of a hundred and sixteen poets, or forty-two percent. The female contributors to Harriet Monroe's *Poetry* ran at about the same percent-age in the early 1920s. These figures are far above the token fourteen percent of women included in most anthologies after 1945.

The distinguishing characteristic of this new wave of women poets, in contrast to those of the nineteenth century, was their professionalism, their arrival on the scene as the first career women in the field of poetry. Elizabeth Barrett Browning had written in a well-known passage in *Aurora Leigh,*

> Am I such indeed? The name
> Is royal, and to sign it like a queen
> Is what I dare not.

The women of the 1920s did not hesitate: Their foremost ambition was to claim the name of poet with as much right as men did.

I have borrowed the term "first wave" from historians of femi-nism who have used it to describe the suffragist movement of the late nineteenth and early twentieth centuries in contrast to the "sec-ond wave" of feminist activism in the 1970s. I do not mean to iden-tify the women poets of the 1920s with the suffragists, but only to use the term in a parallel sense, suggestive of the two major surges of women's poetic creativity in the 1920s and the 1970s. These two waves of creativity were doubtless grounded in forces generated by the major feminist movements. To trace such connections, how-ever, is outside the scope of this book. The dates of 1915–1945 have been arbitrarily selected to enclose a generation of women's work, the period of a wave that crested rapidly and slowly subsided.

Because my aim is to explore the dynamics of a movement rather than to assess importance and merit, I have included a number of little-known or forgotten figures along with some whose reputa-tions are well established. I have made no attempt at comprehen-siveness, but have focused on lives that seem particularly relevant to the questions pursued herein. Many interesting figures who would also have yielded valuable insights, such as Mina Loy, Gertrude Stein, and Laura Riding, have had to be omitted, and others, like H.D. and Moore, have been touched on somewhat tangentially.

I am acutely aware of the difficulties I face as a man writing about women poets—the unconscious biases and assumptions of authority that have traditionally blocked men's capacity to comprehend and empathize with female creativity—and cannot hope to have fully succeeded. Nevertheless I have tried to be guided by Nikki Giovanni's sobering admonition, "I have not created a totally unique, incomprehensible feat. I can understand Milton and T. S. Eliot, so the critic can understand me."[7]

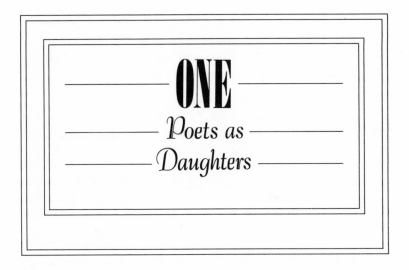

ONE
Poets as
Daughters

*E*MILY DICKINSON'S remark, "I never had a mother," reflects the disappointment of an imaginative child in not being able to project her own ideal selfhood upon a parent of the same sex. They are words that reverberate with loneliness, and with an expanded meaning: the lack not only of a literal mother, but of a community of creative women, a presence of ancestors.

The creative child yearns to find itself through another, not the "role model" of contemporary jargon, a figure whose behavior one can copy, but someone who can carry a projection of idealized strength, beauty, intelligence, or prestige, possibilities that are seen in oneself, that transcend role–playing. In a child's love for the person so enhanced, a door of consciousness opens to reveal a life purpose, a sense of what one is and may become.

A rare glimpse of the dawn of consciousness through a mother, a spiritually–directed consciousness that would drive a lifetime's work, is provided by Lola Ridge—born in Ireland in 1873, migrating to

Australia and New Zealand as a child, and then to New York in 1908, where she remained. She began a diary in the last year of her life, and her first entry, on January 17, 1940, describes a moment in her mother's arms nearly seventy years before: [1]

> I remember clearly my first sight of the stars—or at least the first time I noticed them. In my mother's arms—she had been walking the floor with me, I screaming in one of my rages, these early rages I remember. . . . I remember struggling in her arms, that sensation of fury that was to be more familiar than hunger and almost as punctual.
>
> Mama stepped out on the balcony overlooking the gardens. I suppose she was distraught with the small ungovernable thing in her arms. I think I remember the feeling that she was controlling her own exasperation enduring me (thus for the moment alien; no longer the one comforting certainty in my bewildered mind) and that this goaded me to a further rage. Anyway, as I strove in her face upturned to the sky, I caught sight of the stars. It was a clear night. Those still points of light. All the anger died in me. I lay looking up at them, feeling a sweet peace that was somehow more than peace, a relief and a gladness. All was very well. No doubt my mother shared this relief. . . . I believe rage is simply the frenetic desire for equilibrium, or for the restoration of a disrupted harmony.

This rhythm of rage and separation from the maternal source followed by rejoining, which brings peace and transcendence, became a fundamental pattern of her life. "Speak or write from the citadel," she told herself, "—To which the way always has to be rediscovered for the circle about it is pathless as the air. It is the place where all is very well, there is no hate, no vindictive quiver of being. . . . There is no *farther* of distance, no further to go. . . . One reaches this place, not during, but immediately after, life-shaking moments— and one is always surprised to find there a sweetness—better a purity—in which there is no place for resentment."[2] The beginning of a lifelong feeling of having such a center was associated with being carried in her mother's arms to be put to bed.

Indeed, the consciousness of her own identity flowed from an intense realization of her mother's beauty and the heightened, idealizing aura surrounding her. She had been lying in her cradle, she wrote,[3] beside a table or chiffonier, my mother seated gazing into the mirror before her. She was doing something with her hair. Watching her, I suddenly became aware of her beauty (she was very lovely in her youth).

Now, this luminous moment yet lives in me, her face in profile then turned toward me, the delicate, finely structured face and head, the sweet proud mouth, the large turquoise-blue eyes. The image hangs, the mingled sweetness and pride that was almost hauteur on her face—but there the unnamable haunting thing that is beauty. The light streaming on her and on my cradle—I suppose sunlight through a window.

Of course I could not name this feeling for myself—I had no symbols, for I was at the pre-symbol age—I could not speak. But the sense of beauty was there and I distinctly remember a feeling of pleasure—a contentment in knowing that the beautiful object was in some way attached to me, was *mine*. The experience was so intense it automatically recorded itself on consciousness—the lighted moment, a perpetual oval, to be recalled at will, sometimes to reappear spontaneously, a soft serene shining.

It must have been at that precise moment I first became conscious of my own identity, I lying watching from my cradle the mirror, glimpsed obliquely, my mother's face, aglow in the instreaming light.

Lola Ridge dedicated her second volume of poems, *Sun-Up* (1920), to her mother, in effect attributing the life of the book to the revivified presence of her mother:[4]

> Let me cradle myself back
> Into the darkness
> Of the half shapes . . .
> Of the cauled beginnings . . .
> Let me stir the attar of unused air,
> Elusive . . . ironically fragrant
> As a dead queen's kerchief . . .
> Let me blow the dust from off you . . .
> Resurrect your breath
> Lying limp as a fan
> In a dead queen's hand.

"Mother," the first in a series of poems titled "Portraits," defines how the idealized image of the mother transfigures and empowers a child with qualities she cannot otherwise see in herself:

Your love was like moonlight
turning harsh things to beauty,
so that little wry souls
reflecting each other obliquely
as in cracked mirrors . . .
beheld in your luminous spirit
their own reflection,
transfigured as in a shining stream,
and loved you for what they are not.[5]

Ridge's poetry is marked both by rage at injustice and by a fiercely maternal urgency, as if the disorder of the world arose out of a separation from the spiritual center that the mother represents. The perverted violence of this dislocation is luridly dramatized in "Lullaby," from her first volume, *The Ghetto and Other Poems* (1918). She appended an explanatory footnote: "An incident of the East St. Louis Race Riots, when some white women flung a living colored baby into the heart of a blazing fire." "Lullaby," written in mock Negro dialect, contrasts with savage irony the brown child's unsuspecting trust in the white hands that hold it, and the carnival of awaiting flames:

Rock-a-by baby—higher an' higher!
Mammy is sleepin' an' daddy's run lame . . .
(Soun' may yuh sleep in yo' cradle o' fire!)
Rock-a-by baby, hushed in the flame. . . .[6]

Lola Ridge's derivation of feminine power from maternity makes it clear that "power" is not something women would like to borrow from men, imitating male attitudes; but that there is authentic female power to be drawn by women from their own resources, from their own experience. Echoes of this realization can be seen in Ridge's interest in pre-Hebraic female divinities followed by "Abraham, the first concept of the male, the mateless God, who was to topple from their pedestals so many goddesses."[7] Her own spiritual striving was fed by "some immeasurable presence" which vanished, however, as soon as she tried to picture it in human, especially patriarchal, form: "It is as though some intangible but powerful current were suddenly cut off. The image of Jehovah can do this more completely than any other."[8]

Few poets of Ridge's generation shared her intuitive grasp of the distinction between power as oppressive in men and liberating in women, with radical political implications. But mother-daughter relationships without such revolutionary connotations could be equally indispensable to a poet's self-confidence and ability to maintain a high level of professionalism over the years. Marianne Moore and her mother, for example, religious and political conservatives, were virtual collaborators on Moore's poetry.

Marianne Moore, who was as guarded in self-revelation as Lola Ridge was open, would speak engagingly of her mother, with whom she lived all her life, but without exposing the powerful emotional bond that seemed to make them one person. Moore, born in 1887 in Kirkwood, Missouri, a western suburb of St. Louis, grew up without a father. John Milton Moore abandoned his wife and children after a business failure and nervous collapse and returned to his own family in Portsmouth, Ohio. Mrs. Moore took Marianne and her brother John to live with her father, Rev. John Riddle Warner, minister of the First Presbyterian Church in Kirkwood.

The influence of a patriarchal religious tradition upon Moore through her family background is one of the most important factors in her work. Her early childhood years were spent in the shadow of the church, and according to Donald Hall she "attended church regularly every Sunday of her life and [took] an interested and active part in church activities."[9] Bryher, H.D.'s companion and friend, visiting Marianne Moore and her mother for dinner in 1934, was discomforted by a lengthy saying of grace and a discussion of religion. Moore's brother John, to whom she frequently appealed for advice on her poems, became a Presbyterian minister like his grandfather. It seems likely that Moore's mother, a minister's daughter and mainstay of the family, was a forceful transmitter of her father's faith.

Those who observed Marianne Moore and her mother together at home were struck by their remarkable unity of outlook and speech. Marguerite Young commented that the two conversed in a language much like Moore's poetry. This is confirmed by Margaret Conklin, a lifelong friend, who worked in the publicity department at Macmillan in the early thirties when she first met Moore, often visiting the Moore household in Brooklyn. Marianne was not inclined to invite people home, Conklin thought, but did so because her mother wanted to meet the people Marianne had talked about. Mrs. Moore was a "great talker" with an eye for the significant detail, and could pick up some mundane topic, like a windowshade, and discourse on it wittily for a quarter of an hour, employing the kind of verbal virtuosity and precision so impressive in Moore's poetry. "Marianne Moore's mother was the guiding force of her life," Conklin believed. Moore's poetry could almost have been written by her: "I think that's where [it] came from."[10] Although Marianne Moore could also be a fluent, even dazzling, conversationalist in her mother's style, she was often quiet and retiring around her mother, allowing her center stage. Moore depended on both her mother and her brother for criticism of her work, considering their judgment more reliable than her own. She told Donald Hall, "I said to my mother one time, 'How did you ever permit me to let this be printed?' And she said, 'You didn't ask my advice.'"[11] Moore was a sensitive, inconfident child who could thrive only under the cover of her mother's protective strength: "I seemed to need very humane handling [in college], mothering by everyone—the case all my life, I think."[12] She confessed to having been fearful of her teachers, easily intimidated and uncertain of her abilities. Critics have noted that Moore's imagery of self-armored, defensive animals corresponds to the tight, glittering surface of her work, which serves as a shield to protect personal emotion rather than a medium for exposing it. Safety lay in the language she and her mother invented and shared.

The family religion is an unseen hand in all this. Christian faith and the shield of language, compressed into hardness, have similar uses, as suggested by her poem "Bulwarked against Fate." The meek survive, paradoxically, by admitting weakness, by being crushed into firmness:

Affirmed. Pent by power that holds it fast—
a paradox. Pent. Hard pressed,
   you take the blame and are inviolate.
   Abased at last;
     not the tempest-tossed.
Compressed; firmed by the thrust of the blast
   till compact, like a bulwark against fate.[13]

Marianne Moore's Christian humility and good works were genuine. She protested in all sincerity that her writing could be called poetry "only because there is no other category in which to put it."[14] "Marianne was our saint—if we had one," William Carlos Williams remembered. "Everyone loved her."[15] Margaret Conklin's first meeting with her was characteristic. Margaret, on that busy day, had not eaten lunch. Moore, who had come into the office at Macmillan, observed her and said, "You look hungry." She disappeared, returning shortly with a sandwich and an apple. "She was one of the best people I ever knew," Margaret recalled. "She was *good*—always trying to help someone and not thinking of herself."[16] In spite of her own poverty, Moore felt a duty to help others in misfortune, and more than once, according to Conklin, gave away prize money she had won. On hearing of this, Margaret Conklin, who was Sara Teasdale's literary executor and heir, one year sent Moore the royalties she had received from the Teasdale estate.

Moore's self-effacing goodness seems to have grown out of her devoted submersion in her mother's personality. Bryher, visiting Moore in 1947, wrote to H.D.:

She terrified me, she was so queer about her mother. The mother was thought to be dying of cancer and in such agony Marianne wanted the Dr. to do something, as the mother could neither eat nor speak, and could eat nothing because she could not eat if Mother could not eat, and thus got rashes and kidney trouble and pains. Now she will only eat her mother's diet—raw vegetable juice. Really I was frightened about Marianne. But she is upset over the worldliness of her niece![17]

In the patriarchal Christian tradition women have generally borne the burden of humility, diffidence, and charity, while men attended to matters of power. Moore faithfully fulfilled her duty as a Christian woman, even denying herself the power of the title of poet, but made the most of the "compression," the "abasement," by converting it to a kind of captive strength and toughness in alliance with her mother. There is nevertheless a wistfulness in "O To Be a Dragon":

> If I, like Solomon, . . .
> could have my wish—
> my wish . . . O to be a dragon
> a symbol of the power of Heaven—[18]

A poet's deeply admired mother, like Moore's, becomes a contemporary, an equal, a friend. As Kay Boyle wrote, "I had the most satisfactory of childhoods because Mother, small, delicate-boned, witty, and articulate, turned out to be exactly my age." In the fond appreciation of her delicacy and smallness, one senses, as with Lola Ridge's mother, that the daughter finds strength and pleasure in a reciprocal, maternal feeling toward her own mother. Boyle's mother was refreshingly free-spirited, mentally adventurous, and principled. "Owing to continuous bad health, she had had barely any education, and so her spirit had remained fervent and pure. She alone, with her modest but untroubled intuitions about books and painting, music and people, had been my education. Everything she took into her awareness she poured out again to me."[19] Her mother ran for a seat on the Cincinnati Board of Education on the Farmer-Labor ticket in an attempt to put her social ideals into practice. Associating the avant-garde in art with social advance, she read from *Ulysses* to union organizers. Besides Joyce, her literary tastes included Gertrude Stein, Dreiser, Shaw, and a host of other contemporaries.

Kay Boyle, having had secretarial training, went to work for Lola Ridge in early November 1922 in the New York office of the international little magazine *Broom*, where Ridge was American editor; there she sat in on Ridge's famous Thursday-afternoon tea parties for poets and intellectuals held in the basement of the East Ninth Street house. She recognized immediately that Lola Ridge belonged in the company of ground-breaking women of principle whom her mother admired. Ridge's passionate devotion to the downtrodden, her daring freedom of thought, her profoundly maternal concern for human suffering, awakened Boyle's affection: "It was Lola who spoke the vocabulary I wanted to hear." Through the ensuing years abroad she found steadiness, whenever she was troubled, in holding in mind the images of Ridge and her own mother: "I did not doubt that Mother's and Lola's presence would be there forever."[20]

These women also provided her with a liberating alternative to the dogmatic disposition of her grandfather, who presided over the family with "winning, gracious tyranny," and his "stringent" wife, who "had come close to effacing my father from the scene." One finds again here the elements that so often seem to contribute to a daughter's creative empowerment: a weak or absent father, and an independent, imaginative mother who successfully circumvents male domination. "Because of my mother, who gave me definitions," she wrote, "I knew what I was committed to in life; because of my father and my grandfather, who offered statements instead of revelations, I knew what I was against."[21] Like Ridge and her mother, Boyle was always stirred to rebellion against oppressive authority.

There emerges a clear tendency of these poets to reproduce in later years the emotional pattern of childhood relationships. This is no doubt true in some sense for all persons, men and women alike. But the particular form it takes is of interest here, because women's place then was defined as the family circle rather than the workplace. Relationships vital to creativity and professional success were therefore likely to be modeled after the family rather than in resistance to it, or apart from it, as is the case with men, at least until women could create a new and self-assured status in the outside world.

Edna St. Vincent Millay's life illustrates how the powerful grip of the childhood family pattern could be both life-giving and disabling. Millay's mother, a forceful, independent woman, ousted her husband from the household when Edna was seven, for his gambling habit and general irresponsibility. In the isolation of a Maine small town the mother and three daughters formed a cheerful, self-sufficient unit, blithely indifferent to the ways of conventional family life. Mrs. Millay, a practical nurse, suggests the familiar type of hard-working, self-sacrificing mother who came out of rural or frontier America, overwhelmed by domestic responsibilities but determined that her children should have the education and culture she thirsted for but had been denied. On her mother's death Cora Millay had raised her five younger brothers and sisters and then become the sole support of her own three daughters. Still, she found time to play the piano and copy out parts for the local orchestra, and to write sketches and poems, sometimes even longer pieces for serialization, in the newspapers. Unable to fulfill her ambitions personally, she encouraged her daughters to take up poetry, drama, and music, played and laughed with them like a fourth sister, pushed their talent like a stage mother, and gave them plenty of freedom and praise. The result, of course, was that they did not want to leave her.

Millay's letters to her mother and sisters swarm with terms of endearment: "darling," "sweetheart," "dearly beloved." Edmund Wilson's perceptions were doubtless colored by his own disappointed love for Edna St. Vincent Millay, but he remembered that "she did not . . . give the impression that personality much mattered for her or that, aside from her mothers and sisters, her personal relations were important except as subjects for poems; and when she came to write about her lovers, she gave them so little individuality that it was usually, in any given case, impossible to tell which man she was writing about."[22] Millay, writing her mother from Paris in 1921, poured out her tribute of love and gratitude:[23]

Mother, do you know, almost all people love their mothers, but I have never met anybody in my life, I think, who loved his mother as much as I love you. I don't believe there was ever anybody who did, quite so much, and quite in so many wonderful ways. I was telling somebody yesterday that the reason I am a poet is entirely because you wanted me to be and intended I should be, even from the very first. You brought me up in the tradition of poetry, and everything I did you encouraged. I can not remember once in my life when you were not interested in what I was working on, or even suggested that I should put it aside for something else. Some parents of children that are "different" have so much to reproach themselves with. But not you, Great Spirit.

In another letter from Paris she asked, "Do you suppose, when you & I are dead, dear, they will publish the *Love Letters of Edna St. Vincent Millay & her Mother?*"[24]

Cora Millay performed the pioneering work of lifting herself above her own origins, in a pursuit of freedom that would be continued in her daughter, whom she chose for that role. Edmund Wilson, meeting Mrs. Millay on Cape Cod in 1920, recalled: "She sat up straight and smoked cigarettes and quizzically followed the conversation. She looked not unlike a New England schoolteacher, yet there was something almost raffish about her. She had anticipated the Bohemianism of her daughters; and she sometimes made remarks that were startling from the lips of a little old lady."[25]

Edna Millay's spirited, unconventional life in Greenwich Village, where she became a national byword for Flaming Youth, was not a revolt against a stultifying family background but rather the fulfillment of a trend already established in her life. She continued to keep herself as close as she could to her mother and sisters, bringing them with her to New York and involving them in her work with the Provincetown Players. Her mother sewed costumes and even acted a role in a play. Millay's taking numerous lovers only to reject them flippantly may have been influenced by the ambiguous family feeling about marriage, which posed a threat to talented women.

When Millay married Eugen Boissevain in 1923 at age thirty-one, she retired with him shortly to a farm at Austerlitz, New York, placing herself in his hands like a child-genius under the management of a parental guardian, with no demands whatever made on her for the conventional domestic duties of a wife. The instability and flamboyance of her brief bohemian period in New York, which may even have affected her health, were followed by an orderly life sustained by a husband possessing the nourishing, maternal qualities of a woman. John Peale Bishop visited her not long before the couple left New York City, and reported,

I found her drinking gin and reading William Morris on the top floor of her house, all alone and with really an air of having allowed herself at last to be attended to and put away and forbidden to see people. Her husband takes good care of her and her lousy rout of followers has been banished.— She is calmer than she used to be—and I really felt for a moment as if I were visiting a sort of voluntary prisoner who had crept away and given herself up to other people's kindness.[26]

Millay's mother had taught her to cherish and guard her talent as the central commitment of her life. But it was a responsibility she could not handle alone, without someone to provide conditions equivalent to home and family. The voice of her poetry is that of an actress, and her volatile temperament is reminiscent of the Hollywood stars of the thirties. But as she played to the audience and devoured its applause, she also shrank from it and clung to her guardian; acquaintances noted that she could alternate between regal imperiousness and little-girl timidity. Her marriage reproduced the pattern of her childhood, while shielding her vulnerability.

*

But not all mothers served their poet-daughters as a source of empowerment. There were some who haunted their daughters' lives with a deep disappointment, an unsatisfied longing for connection. Such mothers, by and large, were not necessarily to blame for the fact that fate foisted on them an offspring whose needs they were not prepared to meet. Still, that connection had to be sought with someone, for it is essential to creation. "The mind of the artist," Virginia Woolf wrote, "in order to achieve the prodigious effort of freeing whole and entire the work that is in him, must be incandescent, like Shakespeare's mind. . . . There must be no obstacle in it, no foreign matter unconsumed."[27] For this condition to prevail, there must be an inner sense of liberation, of released power, that depends on the conviction that one is totally accepted, is able to accept and love oneself, that no barriers, no failure of understanding, no anger or belittlement, can constrain the exercise of that power. The prospect of such empowerment is glimpsed in the possibility of unconditional love, for which the mother is usually the source. When social controls or prejudice deny one's full "power to be"—as they do women and minorities—the necessity of liberating love becomes more urgent. If the foundation and prototype for such love cannot be established with a mother, the person nearest and most like herself and most different from depowering male authority, a creative woman may well be baffled all her life by a frustrating struggle to set free her creative energies.

If the mothers of Kay Boyle and Edna St. Vincent Millay offered a clear alternative to patriarchal attitudes, Sara Teasdale's mother devoted herself to upholding them. Teasdale, born in St. Louis in 1884, was the late-arriving child of a wealthy wholesaler of dried fruits and nuts whose wife, by the age of forty, had grown fiercely dedicated to her notions of middle-class prestige and propriety. Instead of feeling a contemporaneity, a comradeship, with her mother, the child felt an immense gulf. Her parents were always old, admonishing, solicitous. Their continual apprehensiveness over her health—which was actually normal—their swaddling her in protective care, keeping her always under their anxious, controlling gaze, almost seem like deliberate efforts to ensure that a child displaying dangerous signs of originality and boldness will not do anything unseemly or out-of-the-ordinary. It is probable that Mrs. Teasdale had submitted to this same kind of systematic control, for she also had been sickly, "frail," lacking in energy, until the age of eighteen, when she abruptly changed, becoming a brisk, driving wife, mother, and manager of a household. This transformation would seem to be the result of first resisting and then accepting her designated place as a woman, with a determination to make the most of it. Sara felt she maddened everybody with her irritable and commandeering attitudes.

Sara Teasdale received no initiation into the love of language or the arts from her parents, who were unswervingly pious Baptists with a solid grip on property, business acumen, fine furnishings, and fine horses. It was not the oriental rugs her mother proudly collected that awakened her sense of the beautiful, but the poems of Christina Rossetti read to her by her older sister Mamie. The connection with Rossetti lasted all her life. At the time of her death she was writing a biography of Rossetti, whom she took for her spiritual ancestor, finding in the poet the pattern of her own psyche, a woman's volatile impulses "held in check" by a forbidding religion while her brother's were allowed free rein.

Teasdale made her fame with a prodigal outpouring of youthful poems that cry out of loneliness for love. The restless dissatisfaction, the dreaming of perfect love, the pain of failure, were themes that resonated to the experience of a large public. But there is a disturbed note of overwrought emotion in her love lyrics that she learned to keep publicly under control:

> I am a wave beneath the tempest's rod,
>   Voicing the lost mid-ocean's shaken cry,
>   I am a woman who will live and die
> Without the one thing I craved of God.
> I am a harp with over-tightened strings,
>   Where all the lonely winds of heaven come . . .[28]

She was assumed to be entreating the love of a man, for her poems are usually couched in the language of traditional romantic love. Indeed, she apparently did try her best to direct her longing into conventional channels, for this is what the weight of her background pressed her to do.

But the virtue of Teasdale's poetry is that emotional honesty keeps breaking through, as in this very early poem (1910):

> For though I know he loves me,
>   To-night my heart is sad;
> His kiss was not so wonderful
>   As all the dreams I had.[29]

Contradicting the apparent yearning for a man's masterful love is the actual malaise glimpsed in many of her poems, that finds repellent the very thing she presumably desires. People who knew Teasdale commented that she was "in love with love," not with persons, as she confessed in "Sappho," a poetic monologue about the legendary figure into whom she projected herself:

How should they know that Sappho lived and died
Faithful to love, not faithful to the lover . . .
I asked for something greater than I found . . .[30]

While some might consider this the disillusion of a self-centered romanticism, it actually reveals the creative artist's need for empowering, unconditional love, the kind of love Teasdale groped for but which she had missed in the life given her. Looked at this way, her love poems have a hidden message, crying out for a kind of love quite different from the romantic heterosexual union they supposedly refer to.

Teasdale's mother had effectively depowered Sara, sincerely believing she was doing the right thing. Because of her mother's perverse and overwhelming protectiveness, Sara was required to beg permission to do anything on her own until almost the age of thirty. Feeling trapped in the home of her aging parents, she tried to isolate herself from the force of her mother's personality, as she wrote to a friend in 1911:[31]

I am ill and very much in the dumps generally. It seems to me as tho' the whole creation, and myself in particular, were pretty much of a failure. My mother, who is a sort of super-woman, nearly drives me mad. . . You have no idea how utterly selfish and restless and jealous she is. I keep saying to myself, "You must not grow like her, you must not grow like her." I don't know what is to become of her. She is sixty-seven and has as much strength in her little finger as I have in my whole body. She has nothing to do in the world but to worry and fret people. There, do you think me horrible and unnatural to speak so?

Sara Teasdale's entire life was ruled by a craving for love she found impossible to satisfy, because nothing could ever fill the original emptiness. Her creative genius rested on a void, struggling against an annihilation that threatened continually to swallow her—as eventually it did, in suicide. "You see her exchanging her gold for the brass of other people," her friend John Hall Wheelock said, "making such tremendous efforts because she wanted so much to have people like her."[32]

Louise Bogan, also unable to derive her tools for empowerment from the original source, found love and friendship difficult, and was plagued by anger, resentment, and jealousy. More than once women friends appeared to her in her dreams as violent and spiteful, shaking her so deeply that she was temporarily estranged from them. Like Teasdale, whom she admired, Bogan sought her salvation in poetry, the chosen means of transmuting suffering into something orderly and beautiful. Teasdale had discovered how to do this in early childhood, when she lay frightened in bed and told herself tales in order to get to sleep. In later years she composed most of her poems in the long insomniac hours of the night. "As soon as a thing is nicely arranged in rhyme and meter," Teasdale wrote a friend, "it ceases to bother one." [33] Bogan wrote, "The repressed becomes the poem." [34]

Louise Bogan traced her psychic misery to an appalling childhood and to a mother she could not accept or love. She seemed to feel that if she could only forgive and detach herself from that blighted figure, she could free herself from the destructive emotions that drove her twice to commit herself to a mental hospital. At sixty-two she wrote in her journal, "We must not bring back and describe 'the bad mother'—'the Dragon mother'—in order to justify ourselves. Only to understand.—To hold the portrait of this evil figure unresolved, into age, is madness. It should be resolved in youth. . . . The artist must resolve it into art." [35]

In her early thirties, and again in her fifties, Bogan determined to set down in dispassionate prose the scenes of her childhood that had always loomed with horror, as if the exorcism of pain through her poetry was not enough. "Actually, I have written down my experience in the closest detail," she said in reference to her poems. "But the rough and vulgar facts are not there." [36] The effort to describe the "rough and vulgar facts" proved, however, to be more than she could handle. "Forgiveness and the eagerness *to protect:* these keep me from putting down the crudest shocks received from seven on. With my mother, my earliest instinct was to protect—to take care of, to endure." [37]

Emily Dickinson's one sad sentence about her mother breathes the air of finality, a closed page. But Louise Bogan raged like a disappointed lover. She recorded in fond detail her mother's "large, beautiful hands," that could peel an apple "like no one else. . . . They were incapable of any cheap or vulgar gesture. The fingernails were clear and rather square at the tops. The palms of her hands were pink."[38] They were hands that could give, could create order and pleasantness. They suggested the refinement that Louise yearned for in contrast to "the incredibly ugly [New England] mill towns of my childhood" and the lumpish people who "bore ugly scars— of skin ailments, of boils, of carbuncles—on their faces, their necks, behind their ears."[39] One sees again the imagination's need for a figure who can carry the child's projection of its ideals of self.

But "the hands that peeled the apple and measured out the encircling ribbon and lace could also deal out disorder and destruction. They could tear things to bits; put all their soft strength into thrusts and blows; they would lift objects so they became threats and missiles."[40] Bogan's parents sometimes quarreled violently. Once Louise was hurriedly packed up and carried to another place on one of her mother's flights. May Bogan was secretive, had affairs with other men, and could disappear for intervals. "A terrible, unhappy, lost, spoiled, bad-tempered child. A tender, contrite woman, with, somewhere in her blood, the rake's restlessness, the baffled artist's despair."[41] Louise Bogan could not forgive her mother for failing as the object of her love, a love necessary to her own validity of being. "For half my life," Bogan said of herself, she was only "the semblance of a girl, in which some desires and illusions had been early assassinated: shot dead."[42] Bogan in her sixties tried— unsuccessfully—to write an end to the churning misery that could have no end: "Finished. Over. The door is open, and I see the ringed hand on the pillow; I weep by the hotel window as she goes down the street, with *another* . . . but it is long over. And forgiven."[43]

The mothers of Sara Teasdale and Louise Bogan, although both forceful women, spent their rebellion against male authority in futile ways, one by fulfilling her duties with a kind of violent obedience, the other by self-demeaning faithlessness. In either case, the result was to turn their daughters against them, and against the conscious thought of rebellion as well, since their only example of revolt had been repugnant. Indeed, the daughters seem to have disliked their mothers for violating a sense of loyalty and fairness toward men, and so tended to feel sorry for their fathers. The romanticizing of femininity seen in Teasdale and Bogan is common to women lacking an adequate grounding in feminine power and therefore tending to identify themselves with male attitudes toward women.

*

The problem of empowerment for a creative woman grows even more difficult and inward when the mother disappears from the scene entirely, and the father becomes both a figure of patriarchal authority and the mainstay of love and nurturance. This was the case with Angelina Weld Grimké, a black poet born in Boston in 1880 but living much of her life in Washington, DC, where she was an English teacher at Dunbar High School.

Grimké was descended from the prominent white abolitionist family of South Carolina and named after her father's aunt, Angelina Grimké, and her activist husband, Theodore Weld. Their brother Henry had fathered three sons by a slave woman, Nancy Weston, one of whom, Archibald, became Angelina's father. The black branch of the family were freed and the boys sent to a school in Charleston run by liberal whites for the children of free blacks. After the Civil War, Archibald Grimké and his brother Francis were sent north to Lincoln University in Pennsylvania, where they earned BA and MA degrees. Archibald Grimké went on to Harvard Law School, supported financially by his aunts, who had settled in Massachusetts, and graduated with an LLB degree in 1874, the second black to receive that degree from Harvard. He shortly afterward set up a law practice in Boston.

Archibald Grimké's friends were centered in the old Boston abolitionist community. Through them, apparently, he met a student, Sarah Stanley, daughter of a liberal white minister from Ann Arbor, Michigan. They were married in 1879.

The marriage seems to have been in trouble from the outset.

Sarah's father, though an advocate of racial equality, drew the line at mixed marriages. The limited evidence suggests that Sarah was a dutiful daughter, often in severe conflict over her own willfulness, hoping to please her father, and probably anxiety-ridden over the marriage. She was described later by her husband as sickly and under treatment for a nervous condition before he met her. From his point of view, she was excessively overreactive, suspicious and accusatory, always living "under the shadow of the injury she thinks she has received." She in turn called him an "oppressor," though he claimed to see no basis for this other than his refusal to do housework. Her side of the story is not well documented. The record does show that she was secretive, changeable, and given to surprising moves.

Their daughter Angelina, "Nana," was born on February 27, 1880. Some two years later, in June 1882, Sarah Stanley Grimké left with her child to join her family in Michigan, ostensibly for a summer vacation on Mackinac Island. She stayed for an entire year, probably with no intention of returning. In May of 1883 she asked her husband to ship them a trunkful of clothes and books.

Archibald Grimké tried to negotiate her return and pleaded futilely for help with her father, who apparently wished to remain neutral. In 1884 Sarah was demanding a legal settlement, including two hundred dollars a year, to which Archibald agreed. Her chief anxiety, however, was that he might interfere with her possession of their child. She wrote him from Detroit, "I wish to be assured that you fully relinquish your claim to her person, and freely trust her care and education in my hands." She was "a child of unusual promise,"[44] whom a mother could bring up best. She also demanded guarantees that he would not attempt to snatch Angelina away from her. On that condition, he could visit his daughter or have her stay with him from time to time. But as for herself, she never wished to see him again.

For the next several years she moved about the Midwest, occasionally demanding changes in the agreement and reheating her accusations. Then, on April 25, 1887, she wrote her husband an astonishing letter from St. Louis:[45]

Dear Archie;

Within the past few weeks I have been obliged to suspend all work, and I now realize that it is for the best good and happiness of little Nana that she should go to you at once. She is so very *happy* at the prospect of going to see her papa that I am quite reconciled to resign her to you (at least for the present). She is really much more like you than myself and you can control her better than I have been able to do. In many ways I have been too strict—in others, not strict enough. But just now I am both physically and mentally unfit to have the care of her at all.

She needs that love and sympathy of one of her own *race* which I am sure her father still has for her, but which it is impossible for others to give. My own family, kind and anxious as they are to do right, do not, neither is it possible for them to give her the *love* she requires to make her *good* and *happy,* and a child cannot be good unless it is also happy. It is almost impossible for her to be happy with me, try as I will, because she is now getting old enough to see and feel the *thoughts* of others, which the difference in race and color naturally engender regarding her. My present plan is to send her on to you by express from St. Louis or Cleveland. I will telegraph to you the moment she starts so there will be no mistake, and this letter will reach you a few hours ahead of her, so that you may understand how matters are. . . . I am thinking of spending the season upon the northern Lakes or in Canada—my health demands a radical change. . . . I am in hopes to resume my work of teaching in the Fall and may visit Hartford, Ct. [where a sister lived] during the season. Still I leave the *future* to take care of itself, only trying to do the *very best possible* for the *present*.

Angelina was bundled back to her father with only a few hours' warning, when her mother's nerves collapsed under the strain of facing a white world with her black child. The evidence suggests that mother and daughter never saw each other again. Angelina's father sent her to several girls' schools, including Carlton Academy in Minnesota and the Girls' Latin School in Boston, during the ensuing years when he rose to prominence as a publisher, civil rights lawyer, and activist. The scholar Gloria Hull describes her in a school photograph at the age of ten as "a tiny East Indian-looking girl with large sad eyes. The thousand conflicts and contradictions of her identity and position followed her through life."[46]

Angelina Grimké was eighteen when a letter came from her mother's sister in October 1898 informing her of her mother's death. "She was hoping to see you once more," Emma Toller wrote, "and was trying so hard to make a little house to which you could come and visit. She never ceased to love you as dearly as ever and it was a great trial to have you go away from her, how great God alone knows; but it was the only thing to do."[47] She was implying, of course, the undesirability of a racially mixed household. Angelina passed the news on laconically to her father, then just completing a four-year term as American consul to the Dominican Republic. He acknowledged his wife's death in a casual sentence at the end of a cheerful, newsy letter. The impression is unavoidable that the two had long since turned their backs on a woman who had allowed social prejudice to destroy bonds of love that should have grown stronger under strain.

The hidden resentment of Angelina Grimké for the rejection by her mother, an unwillingness to excuse her weakness, emerged vehemently in a play she wrote in 1916. The heroine is a young black woman who, after several years of demeaning encounters with race prejudice, despairingly renounces marriage and having children. The play troubled some black viewers, who felt that Grimké was preaching "race suicide" as a response to racism. Jessie Fauset, reviewing *Rachel* in the *Crisis,* found it as "terrible, as searching, and as strong"[48] as contemporary European drama, but excessively morbid and defeatist. In a reply, Grimké stated that "the appeal is not primarily to colored people, but to the whites." And in particular, to white mothers.[49]

Now the colored people of this country form what may be called the "submerged truth." From morning till night, week in and week out, year in and year out, until death ends all, they never know what it means to draw one clean, deep breath free from the contamination of the poison of that enveloping force which we call race prejudice. Of necessity they react to it. Some are embittered, made resentful, belligerent, even dangerous; some are made hopeless, indifferent, submissive, lacking in initiative: some again go to any extreme in a search for temporary pleasures to drown their memory and thought, etc.

Now my purpose was to show how a refined, sensitive, highly-strung girl, a dreamer and an idealist, the strongest instinct in whose nature is a love for children and a desire some day to be a mother herself—how, I say, this girl would react to this force.

The majority of women, everywhere, although they are beginning to awaken, form one of the most conservative elements of society. They are, therefore, opposed to changes. For this reason and for sex reasons, the white women of this country are about the worst enemies with which the colored race has to contend. My belief was then that if I could find a vulnerable point in their armour, if I could reach their hearts, even if only a little, then perhaps instead of being active or passive enemies they might become, at least, less inimical and possibly friendly.

Did they have a vulnerable point and if so what was it? I believed it to be motherhood. Certainly all the noblest, finest, most sacred things in their lives converge about this. If anything can make all women sisters underneath their skins, it is motherhood. If, then, I could make the white women of this country see, feel, understand just what their prejudice and the prejudice of their fathers, brothers, husbands, sons were having on the souls of the colored mothers everywhere, and upon the mothers that are to be, a great power to affect public opinion would be set free and the battle would be half won.

Behind this statement is the poignant realization that the rift with her mother, because of race, had deprived her of shared "sisterhood" and "motherhood" with the one person she most needed. Lola Ridge at about the same time was writing "Lullaby," a poem that drives home a related point: The failure of white women to place motherhood and sisterhood above racial hatred is a betrayal of the spiritual values of which women are supposedly the guardians. And it is black children who pay the price; the ultimate extension of racism is genocide.

Rachel was first presented by the NAACP in Washington, DC, in April 1916 at the Myrtill Miner Normal School. The play was performed again in May 1917 at St. Bartholomew's Church in Cambridge, Massachusetts under the direction of Rev. Walter D. McClane. Angelina Grimké, in Washington, was not able to attend, but friends wrote of its success, the troubling impact of its negative climax, and of the fifty or more whites who were there. *Rachel* was her experience at Vassar: In *Against the Wall,* a young woman leaves her college in disillusionment for the brighter lights of New York and freedom. The reviewers were widely offended at what they felt was a kind of immature, hysterical antagonism toward women's colleges and a desire to shock with sensational exploitation rather than offer serious analysis. It was another attempt to follow Edna, this time as a bohemian mocking bourgeois proprieties.

Kathleen Millay's poems are steeped in loneliness and unsatisfied wants. What she might have had to offer is overshadowed by her painful consciousness of what she lacked. The poem "Moth" surely describes herself:

> They have wondered at my wings
> Till I can no longer fly;
> Here I beat upon the wall—
> *Let me, let me by!*
> *Here is not for such as I!*[7]

She writes of stone walls rising around her, of dead birds, a "little brown girl" with "your sorry tears and your hungry eyes"[8] with whom she identifies herself; of "the chill of winter in my soul."[9] She is a caged wild thing, with no place for her in this world; she is "queer," an outcast.

Dazzled by an example she could never hope to duplicate, Kathleen Millay made her chief theme the incapacity to live in her own right. The self-dramatizing that the Millay sisters took to be the posture of an artist led, in the case of Kathleen, to a mournful, self-pitying display of personal pain:

> I am a shell down underneath the sea,
> An emptiness that twists and turns and writhes
> Unceasingly beneath the ceaseless tide,
> Forever lonely and forever free;
> A drifting death no one may ever know . . .[10]

The poems suggest that beyond their alarming self-devaluation lay a further level of misgiving; maybe the poems themselves, in their hoped-for deliverance, are failures. "Oh, my little crying songs," she wrote, "What is to become of you?"[11] She could not build an audience, create the rapport, the magical appeal, on the basis of complaint. As she wrote in "The Little Daughter of Doom,"

> Hers was a light that only burned
> To mark a shadow passing by[12]

—not the incandescence of her sister.

Nevertheless, the family unity forged by the mother and fired by her ambition to make a mark on the world seems to have endured in spite of its inner stresses. There was a remarkable suppression of rivalry. When Kathleen collapsed and died unexpectedly in 1943 at the age of forty-seven, Edna's compassion was stirred more deeply than by the sense of her own loss alone. Remembering silver rings from their childhood engraved with their nicknames, she cried to Norma, "Oh, poor little Wumpty Woons,"[13] summing up the sadness of Kathleen's life, her failed bid for success as well as her early death.

*

Sara Teasdale's patriarchally centered family was almost exactly the opposite of Millay's in its structure of power relations. The household was organized around the dominant, conservative figure of her father, a respected St. Louis businessman and Republican with close ties to the Third Baptist Church. Teasdale, in choosing sides against her mother, formed a close attachment to her much esteemed father. And so she blamed her mother's ill temper for her own unhappiness rather than the benign patriarchal domination of both their lives.

Teasdale had an intense aversion to the conventional domestic responsibilities that were the center of her mother's life. While her mother's vigorous, noisy activity overseeing the household continually irritated her and disturbed her quiet for composing poetry, Teasdale seems never to have expressed any word of criticism of her father. In 1909, at twenty-four, writing to a young poet named John Myers O'Hara, she exclaimed, "Please don't say that you hate Christianity. . . . I wish you knew my father who is one of my

ideals and *is* a Christian."[14] As a young woman rehearsing love in
countless sonnets and lyrics, she depicted herself as falling at her
lover's feet—"I shall kneel before you, oh my King"—in the kind
of worshipful posture she took toward her father. A woman friend
titled one of these poems "The Door-Mat."[15] In an unpublished
poem, "The First Thing I Remember," she refers to her father as
"my first lover" and describes her peace at being held in his arms
as an infant.[16] (One recalls Lola Ridge's similar memory of being
held by her mother.)

When complaining in a letter, previously quoted, that her mother
"nearly drives me mad," Teasdale concluded, "If it were not for my
father I should— Oh I *will* stop."[17] In the last resort, it was always
the thought of her father that saved her. When she suffered a violent shock from rejection by the first man she had fallen in love
with, she wrote to Louis Untermeyer, "I think if I hadn't a father
and were courageous (which I'm not in the least) I'd get out of this
messy world."[18] Her father's death in 1921, when she was thirty-
seven, depressed her profoundly. "I think of him so very, very often,"
she wrote her sister-in-law many months afterward, "and dream of
him far too often for my own good—but I don't seem to be able
to break off."[19]

Sara Teasdale's infatuation with the patriarchal image gave her
character both strength and self-defeating contradiction. Her willing submissiveness manifested itself in countless acts of acquies-
cence to social convention: a wish to be at all times a "lady," a
compulsion to marry and be supported by a man, to prolong the
woman-as-child relationship throughout her life; a horror of mis-
behavior, of reflections on her reputation.

But any idealization, as we have seen, even when it incurs negative consequences, also inspires and gives form to the drive for
creativity. This requires drawing on strengths of the person idealized, and so for Sara Teasdale these were the strengths of her father.
The weak, fainting side of Teasdale, the anxiety to please, was surprisingly contradicted by executive toughness. Her early St. Louis
friend Williamina Parrish wrote: "In the scheme of life she carved
out for herself, many people could not possibly fit—she never allowed

herself to burn her candle at both ends. . . . Her life was a fixed and orderly entity, into which other lives had to fit, if they entered hers at all. It never entered her head to fit herself to others."[20] Friends throughout her life were required to make appointments before visiting her. She had an entrepreneur's objective grasp of what she sometimes called the "writing game" and would never offer a poem to a magazine that didn't pay. Undaunted by rejections, she submitted her work repeatedly until it was accepted, welcoming criticism and applying it when it was useful. She recorded the history of the submission and publication of each poem in a little account book along with what she had been paid. At the back of these books she also kept a running account of her investments, dividends, and profits. Teasdale was well aware of the double nature of her life, the public image of a romantic poet of love, the private reality of a disciplined, businesslike craftswoman.

Teasdale's obsession with neatness suggests that the influence of her mother's furious housekeeping gave a cast of feminine obedience to her labor. Both she and her mother reveal the pressure of perfectionism upon women ambitious to perform outstandingly. "Perhaps if Miss Sadie were less methodical," she said of herself in the third person, when young, "and if she could keep her bureau drawers in disorder and her life at loose ends, she would be a better poet."[21] Her favorite adjective for the kind of emotional eruptions that lead to divorce, marital infidelity, or other improprieties was "messy." This is not merely evidence of prudery. Her pursuit of a professional career seemed to her to demand the sacrifice of feeling and the maintenance of rigorous self-control.

Sara Teasdale derived from her father the ambition and business skills that enabled her to be a disciplined and productive poet, and it fitted nicely with the new economic position of women. While her feminine social graces were becoming outmoded—she continued to dress in long gowns after World War I and never cut her hair short—her skillfully engineered commercial success was in tune with women's emancipation in the marketplace.

But by following the male style of empowerment Teasdale also internalized the male's superior, competitive attitude toward women, the male's disapproval of a woman seeking power. The greater her success, the more she shrank from it as undeserved; as the proof of her genius mounted, the more she felt she was nothing. The guilt-ridden, self-destructive conflict, however, was too deeply imbedded to be resolved, for the one thing she could not do was to turn against the authority and the values of the father she loved. She chose to live with a concealed inner disaster:

> Shut your heart, though it be like a burning house,
> Keep it shut on the shuddering cries and the roar;
> There is nothing new about this fire in your heart,
> It has all gone on for long and long before.[22]

*

Sara Teasdale's plight epitomizes, to an extreme, the difficulties faced by women who were not prepared to differentiate the power they needed for full self-realization from that of the men who exercised some degree of control over them. The problem was most acute for women like Teasdale whose affluent families were closer to the currents of financial and political power that drove American life, in her case further reinforced by religious conservatism.

Among other upper-middle-class women caught and wrenched in the self-contradicting pursuit of success, one of the most gifted and by far the most interesting is Elinor Wylie. Born Elinor Hoyt in 1885, a year after Teasdale—professionally she kept the surname of her second husband, Horace Wylie—she was descended like Teasdale from old families dating back to seventeenth-century New England. Teasdale's ancestors had included judges, distinguished clergy, and enterprising money-makers who pushed westward with the frontier. Wylie's forebears moved only as far as Philadelphia, where from the eighteenth century on they gradually became prominent in politics and finance. Teasdale and Wylie both held their distant New England backgrounds accountable for a lingering Puritan chill, though the pressure of patriarchal authority offers a more realistic explanation.

The chief difference between their families lay in the provincial, pious narrowness of the Teasdales compared with the more sophisticated and worldly Hoyts, who operated on a grander scale. One grandfather, Henry Martyn Hoyt, had been governor of Pennsylvania. The other grandfather, Morton McMichael, was a wealthy Philadelphia banker whose father had been a newspaper publisher and mayor of the city, and presumably something of a power broker. Wylie's own father, Henry Hoyt, was appointed assistant attorney general of the United States under President McKinley in 1897 and later solicitor general. President Theodore Roosevelt attended Elinor's wedding in 1906. Elinor Wylie's closeness to national concentrations of power through money, politics, and social standing shaped all the important actions of her life, and lies implicit in her poetry.

As one might expect from someone so exposed to the public gaze, she was acutely conscious of appearances. "I am tremendously proud of such a handsome, distinguished looking father,"[23] Elinor wrote at eighteen on receiving a photograph of her father while she was traveling abroad—homage to the patriarchal ideal. It was a family attractive, rich, and favored, enjoying its superior social status, with a retinue of nursemaids, "colored" cooks, and servants. Elinor's youthful letters evoke the leisurely world of Henry James: shopping for fashions in Paris or London; flowers, fêtes, theaters, afternoon teas and walks under a parasol; passing self-assured judgments on architectural monuments and paintings in museums. While visiting the area of Gray's Inn in London, near the law courts, Elinor "saw the most beautiful tall young lawyer there who would have done admirably for the hero of a novel."[24] It was a style of life in which roles were tinged self-consciously with the artificiality of fiction.

Behind the facade of power, privilege, and respectability that families like the Hoyts and McMichaels assiduously maintained, all, however, was not as idyllic or enviable as outsiders might think. Among the upper classes of Philadelphia and Washington, DC, a family which failed to keep up sanctioned appearances was ruthlessly brought in line by gossip, often published in the newspapers, and by the threat of ostracism, of being "cut." This effectively crushed the open expression of any troubled individual's tendency to deviate, particularly a woman's. There was not the tolerance and cultivation of foibles or eccentricity found in the English aristocracy of the same period, which gave Virginia Woolf a certain latitude. Elinor's mother responded to the pressures of this rigorously controlled world by retiring into chronic invalidism after an early attack of typhoid fever and heart trouble, using her sickliness as a means of manipulative control. Nor was Elinor's father the vigorous, commanding male idealized by his social class, in spite of an influential position and a distinguished appearance. He suffered two nervous breakdowns, having to isolate himself in New Mexico and Canada for periods of recuperation. Both parents responded to the built-in stress of their lives by becoming ill. Most of their five children suffered even more severely from personality conflicts; two committed suicide, and a third is believed to have tried. It was a life of splendid surfaces and troubled inner actualities.

Elinor was a spirited child, who once said defiantly of her brother's attempt to control her, he "will find it harder to keep this squirrel on the ground than he knows." Her admiration for men who cut a bold and interesting figure was probably a reaching out to validate the freedom-loving, assertive qualities in herself; the women of her class, such as her mother, certainly offered few examples. Given the highly structured world in which she lived, her adventurous spirit could flourish only by breaking free. One sees it foreshadowed even in small things. Writing to her mother from Paris in 1903, where she had gone with her grandfather McMichael and her sister Connie, she chafed against restraint: "The only thing which really irritates me is the half-witted convention which makes it impossible for me or two young girls to take walks by themselves—for I love to walk and some of these wide tree bordered avenues look very delightful and alluring—much like Washington only new and unexplored. It makes me furious."[25] Better to follow the hunt, "the sound of the silver horn," as she later wrote in "Madman's Song," "than to sleep with your head on a golden pillow."[26]

Elinor was an intellectually gifted, hard-working student, but was discouraged from attending college. Incessantly reminded that she was a beautiful girl, a beautiful woman, she was groomed chiefly for display as a proud female ornament of her class. In the tranquil Edwardian years when the order of society seemed, at least to the privileged, to be permanently fixed, this gilded debutante appeared destined to follow the path of any other rich young woman, marrying well and upholding the family's social standard. The transformation of a flesh-and-blood woman into a lifeless objet d'art was a theme central to some of the fiction she later wrote.

The rebellion that made Elinor into a poet instead of a porcelain doll was not planned, however; it burst spontaneously out of the failure of her first marriage, as a kind of overwhelming urge for sheer survival. The marriage, a few months after her twenty-first birthday in 1906, was evidently entered upon without serious thought, perhaps on the rebound from a disappointed love affair, perhaps to gain some independence from her family. Elinor's mistake—which she learned never to repeat—was to base her decision on the kind of superficial appearances she had been taught to value. Philip Simmons Hichborn II was the son of a rear admiral in the US Navy and a descendent of Paul Revere: a Harvard graduate, a sportsman with charming social skills and some literary ambition, tall, elegantly handsome. Elinor's mother was quite taken and later remembered him as a "Rudolph Valentino."[27]

In actuality, Philip Hichborn's surface attractiveness masked rather mediocre talents and a psychotic condition that was alarmingly stirred up by his marriage. Elinor's compulsive emotional intensity, the baffled driving force which she saw as being "excitable," others as a tendency to hysteria, was a challenge which he lashed back at defensively. "I think he's crazy," Elinor eventually told her mother. His violent rages and threats of suicide frightened her. "I think he simply hates me . . . and being married at all, at least that is what he always says." Matters were complicated by her becoming pregnant almost immediately after the wedding. Philip was jealous of the baby and soon began to exhibit more pathological behavior: "He says we cannot ride in the streetcar, or take a taxi, or go to the country club, because all the men employed by all three insult him, or despise him, because they believe he is unmanly . . . They don't, really, they never do or say anything, it is simply an *idée fixe.*"[28]

Philip Hichborn's paralyzing doubt about his masculinity when having to cope with fatherhood and a forceful wife curiously echoes the projection of sexual stereotypes along class lines by radical male writers of the period. Hichborn attributed "real" manliness to the working classes, but saw them as contemptuous of his own inability to live up to the image of his father and the power class to which he belonged.

The marriage dragged along a few more years, though it was acknowledged to be a disaster. After a fall from a horse in 1908, Philip's mental derangement became so pronounced he was institutionalized for a time with the diagnosis of dementia praecox, or schizophrenia. Elinor's father began gathering evidence for a divorce action, though her mother considered such a course a disgrace. But Elinor meanwhile had met a millionaire lawyer and lover of books and poetry, Horace Wylie, whose friendship offered an escape from the grim life with her husband and the tedious, stultifying round of bridge parties, dinners, and afternoon teas. Horace Wylie was also married and had two children. They began to meet secretly for luncheons and trysts in Rock Creek Park, and in October 1910, after the death of Elinor's father, Wylie proposed that they elope, even though they could not be married. On December 16, 1910 they fled to Canada in such great secrecy their exact movements have never been known, and sailed to England. They left behind a public uproar that prostrated both their families.

Only three days earlier, Philip Hichborn had written to Elinor's mother, "Someday, perhaps not right away, and yet perhaps not so far away either I shall find myself and then the little things that have upset Elinor and me will seem very trivial and cease to be."[29] His words betray the air of unreality of their marriage. Fifteen months later he shot himself to death, leaving a note: "I am not to blame for this. I think I have lost my mind."[30] Elinor, of course, was blamed.

Elinor Wylie's development as a poet is understandable only in terms of the enormous cost of defying the forces of conformity arrayed against her. The public outrage over the elopement shows how important it was for her social class, the self-appointed guardians and examples of conventional morality, to uphold the appearances of faithful wife and mother. To such minds, Elinor's abandonment of her husband and three-year-old son was a sordid act of sexual profligacy and selfishness. Even President Taft sent condolences to Elinor's mother, offering to help if he knew where Horace Wylie had hidden with Elinor: "I might use the diplomatic or consular corps to try to bring him to a sense of the awful course he is pursuing. I'll talk with Secretary Knox about the matter."[31] Detectives were put in pursuit, friends abroad were alerted. The couple were forced to live like felons in exile.

Ironically, sexual passion had very little to do with Elinor's action: she had found the person who could awaken her mind and creative intelligence. Horace Wylie, a socialite with a known weakness for pretty young women, at first found Elinor "hard to talk to & thought her mind rather empty & not clever. My Lord! what an Ass I was!"[32] She pressed him to teach her what he knew of history, philosophy, and literature, to give her the education she had missed. "The amount I learn from him . . . is without end,"[33] she wrote her mother from their hideaway in rural England. While the storm raged about them, their capacity for a selfless, sustaining relationship developed steadily. Elinor's birth as a poet coincided with her daring escape from a life that had predetermined the pattern of her mind and emotions, with her finding a genuine relationship that encouraged her to develop freely in her own direction.

In 1912 Elinor Wylie published privately her first small collection of poems, *Incidental Numbers,* consisting of twenty-five pieces she had written from the age of seventeen until the previous year, when she was twenty-six. None were substantial enough to be included in her later volumes, but her line of development had been laid out, and Horace Wylie continued to provide the conditions of personal freedom under which growth was possible. Eventually he was able to obtain a divorce, long withheld by his embittered wife, and the couple could marry and live openly, though socially shunned, in America.

It was to men that Elinor Wylie turned for the kind of liberating love that would engender her creative work—men who were attracted by the exciting power of her personality as well as her physical beauty, men appreciative of her gifts. Wylie's precise orientation to men, however, has puzzled her biographers and critics. She found it offensive to be cast in the stereotyped role of femme fatale, the reputation that always preceded her into the drawing rooms and parties where she was a guest. On acquaintance, people described her personality, like her poetry, as "cold fire," lacking the sexual fervency that many had inferred from her actions. Her surface was coolly, elegantly beautiful, like the apartments she decorated or the antiques and objets d'art she gathered around her. She had an aesthete's exquisite taste for the artificial, which she displayed to the world and yet mocked at the same time, knowing its unreality. That beautiful surface was the femininity instilled in her by wealth, class, and male insistence, and it was "cold" because her passion was centered in the thrust of freedom and adventure denied her as a woman. Her relations with men were therefore a kind of exchange, in which she could give her beauty in return for contact with their power.

*

The sense of having to play a masquerade is strong in women of the affluent classes, who were under particularly heavy pressure to present a conformist's face to the world while pursuing unconventional goals. Marjorie Allen Seiffert, a Midwestern poet from a family whose wealth doubtless greatly exceeded that of Elinor Wylie's, was not only highly conscious of role-playing in the society she moved in, but even created other personalities under pseudonyms. These other voices relieved her of the obligation to cater to her own reputation and allowed her to speak with a certain satirical abandon. In the early thirties, she contributed sophisticated light verse to the *New Yorker,* commenting cynically on love and marriage, under the pseudonym of Angela Cypher (a pun on the name Seiffert). A cipher is both a secret code and a zero, or nonentity.

Earlier, in 1917 and 1918, Seiffert had participated in a famous literary hoax, the creation of the "Spectra" school of poetry. The Spectrists were Witter Bynner's idea, to con gullible critics and a public confused by the wild profusion of avant garde movements in the arts—imagists, vorticists, futurists, surrealists. Bynner drew Arthur Davison Ficke, a lawyer-poet from Davenport, Iowa, into the scheme, and they published a vague manifesto on mystical premises, followed by examples of Spectrist poetry. The Spectra school was supposed to be centered in Pittsburgh, a mundane city they thought most unlikely to give birth to anything either spectral or new in poetry. Bynner took the name Emmanuel Morgan, and Ficke wrote as Anne Knish (probably in an attempt to satirize Amy Lowell, the chief publicist of imagism). The two began composing parodies of "modern" poetry and looked around for a third person to join in the hoax, finally settling on Marjorie Seiffert, a friend of Ficke's in nearby Moline, Illinois.

As "Elijah Hay," Marjorie Seiffert produced a body of poems caricaturing the tendency of the new poetry to juxtapose discordant, "unpoetic" elements. The opportunity for an underlying, serious irony was not to be missed, however, and many of her pieces expressed the frustration of a woman rebelling against domestic life and longing to fly free before it was too late. "Night," in spite of its attempted absurdity, is akin to Marianne Moore's "O To Be a Dragon" in both its imagery and its yearning for power:

> . . . years ago night was a python
> Weaving designs against space
> With undulations of his being . . .[34]

The Spectrist school was taken quite seriously and enjoyed a brief success until the truth began to leak out and Bynner made a public confession in 1918. Marjorie Seiffert, posing as Elijah Hay, had carried on a correspondence with William Carlos Williams, among others. Williams had caught the humor, supposing Spectrism to be a joke, though he didn't question the poets' identities. He wrote to Marjorie Seiffert (as Elijah Hay) complaining that he preferred the work of Morgan and Hay to that of Anne Knish, because "she" took the Spectrist affair too seriously. "The cream of the whole thing," Seiffert told Bynner, "is that Arthur [Anne Knish], who especially scorns the whole business, is criticized as taking it too seriously! And what a wonderful argument for the feminist cause that we poor women cannot take our work in a lighter vein!"[35] Williams greatly enjoyed the hoax when the truth came out, and struck up a friendship with Marjorie Seiffert that lasted long afterward.

Born in 1884, in the decade that produced so many remarkable women, Seiffert was the only child of a wealthy manufacturer of farm implements, Frank Gates Allen of the Moline Plow Company. Marjorie's mother, Minnie Stephens, was a forceful, imposing woman, wealthy in her own right, and a member of the first class to graduate from Smith College. Three more generations followed her in attending Smith College, a line of interesting, talented women extending to the present day.

Minnie Stephens's life also established the conflict each subsequent generation had to struggle with: how to reconcile her desire for a career in the arts with marriage and conventional family life, which to a woman of her social class made very heavy demands. Minnie Stephens had wanted to be a concert pianist but was forced to choose between a career or marriage; she married. But her ambitions descended to her daughter, Marjorie, who also went off to Smith College to study piano and composition. And she, like her mother, was also deflected into marriage and a social life that cut off any hope of a musical career. She fortunately possessed a literary talent that could be exercised in the quiet hours between child-rearing and hosting dinner parties—the factor that historically has allowed women greater achievement in literature than in the other arts. "Many ideas come to her in the morning or in the night,"[36] a local interviewer wrote.

One of Marjorie's student composition-books in 1905 shows her writing not only conventional love lyrics to set to music ("Oh night of love . . .") but scribbling occasional satirical verses that aim gleeful, deadly shafts at males:

> Freddie and some other brats
> Ate up all the rough on rats
> Father said, when mother cried,
> "Don't you care they'll die outside." [37]

Marjorie Seiffert poised herself between her conventionality and scorning it, carrying on a virtual double life, with one set of literary friends to whom she wrote and spoke candidly of herself, and another of local society people. When she spoke before women's clubs, she mesmerized them with her charm, leaving the impression that she was not overly serious about her poetry, just as with William Carlos Williams, Morton Dawen Zabel, or her editor John Hall Wheelock she reversed the emphasis and mocked the triviality of the social life that engulfed her. The truth is, as her grandson John Pryor has observed, she was "immensely spoiled," [38] was never refused anything by her parents, and frankly enjoyed a life of luxurious indolence. She was too bred in her way of life to consider breaking from it, regardless of her aspiration for a more authentic self. Allendale, the family home in Moline, was a three-story, half-timbered, English-style mansion with curving drive and porte cochere; White Ledge, the summer home in Michillinda, Michigan, was also a showpiece, bearing a resemblance to the White House. When Marjorie Allen married a successful businessman, Otto Seiffert, in 1910—perhaps a degree or two below her social level, and not entirely approved by her parents, for he was the son of German immigrants—she continued the style of life to which she was accustomed, for she probably could not have endured any other. Otto Seiffert built her an impressive mansion with Italian marble steps and columns, and filled it with Italian antique furniture, which he and Marjorie went abroad to buy. Here, overseeing her cooks and servants, she became a legendary hostess, staging frequent parties, entertainments, and sit-down dinners for as many as seventy people at a time.

It is a difficult feat, however, to remain suspended for a lifetime between irreconcilable alternatives. These were vividly stated in an early poem, "Maura." "Maura [the name suggests 'Marjorie'] dreams unawakened—"; she is a woman in "rapt seclusion," "in a quiet room, her soul unstirred." Two possibilities for arousal and fulfillment are offered:

> The call of a silver horn floats by,
> A lover tosses flowers into her hands.

That is, love of a man or the call of the imagination in pursuit of its quarry. Unable to break from her trance, she joins the dance of the other women and gives herself to her lover, fulfilling biological necessity: "Earth draws her close." The "note of a horn" dwindles to an echo, and then it is too late:

> Who knows the mountain where the hunter rides
> Winding his horn?
> Maura who heard it in her dream
> Wakens forlorn,
> Too late to catch the tenuous thread
> Of silver sound
> Which in the troubled, intricate fugue of earth
> Is drowned.

Maura is trapped: "Her youth is landlocked in a hidden pool/ Where thirsty love drinks deep." She has lost the "silver call," but for compensation has a kind of comfortable unconscious existence, "The simple mysteries of sleep and death,/ Of love and birth," the unawakened earthbound life that men have reserved for women. "And over the hill lies music yet unborn." In the end, Maura lies dead, having given her body "to child and lover"; but her spirit "has followed the silver horn/ Over the distant hill."[39]

The archetypal portrayal goes back as far as Diana, the goddess who, like a man, followed the hunt and avoided entanglement in love. Here it suggests the difficult way of spiritual birth for a woman, calling as it does for resistance to the massive inertia of conformity to male expectations. And the musical imagery hints at Marjorie Seiffert's disappointed career plans, which might have meant her own liberation. A newspaper interviewer in the mid-thirties referred to how "fifteen years before . . . the duties of marriage, motherhood and management of a home had smothered a career in music composition and driven her genius for expression to poetry . . ."[40] This assessment probably came from Seiffert herself. Ironic suspense between accepting her life and the sometimes caustic, almost morbid, defiance of it as a death to her spirit was not a very satisfactory solution in the long run. Yet she maintained her balance through a problematic marriage and a term of psychoanalysis that almost destroyed the dissatisfied poet in her.

*

To those like "Maura," who faced the contradiction between their impulse for power and freedom and the massive regimentation of women's lives, to say nothing of the temptation to remain safely within it, death was not only a haunting symbolic image but a real possibility. Sara Teasdale killed herself at the age of forty-eight; Elinor Wylie died of a stroke at forty-three, after years of high blood pressure aggravated by continual stress. To their company must be added one of the most poignant cases of all, that of Gladys Cromwell. She found intolerable the empty life of playacting assigned to upper-class women and made a bold and tragic attempt at authenticity.

Gladys Cromwell and her sister Dorothea were identical twins. "Neither ever used the singular pronoun," a friend wrote, "and those who knew them fairly well often doubted to which sister they were speaking." They were born in Brooklyn in 1885, the last of five children, when their parents were middle-aged. "We were an afterthought,"[41] Gladys said. Her father, Frederic Cromwell, descending from a branch of the family of Oliver Cromwell, had graduated from Harvard at twenty, amassed a fortune, and settled down unostentatiously in New York, where he served as director of many corporations and supported political reform and the arts. The twins, however, considered their parents' taste to be shallow and uncritical. Like that other late arrival, Sara Teasdale, the girls were sheltered to a degree inconceivable today, virtually deprived of normal

contact with the world outside the family circle. They were educated at a private school, the Brearley, and were "dragged around
Europe," as they told Mary Colum, with "lonely days and weeping
nights spent in hotels in Constantinople, Vienna, Venice, and such
places."[42] There was no thought, of course, of college education or
any kind of career. They made their formal debut into New York
society, where they gave the impression of beauty with a certain
"strangeness," shrinking from conventional social life with the over-
sensitivity, perhaps fear of contact, that had been bred into them
by their isolation.

Gladys had begun writing poetry and Dorothea short stories at
an early age. The family, it seems, did not take their work seriously
and were alarmed when Gladys, the more articulate one, later began
to publish her poems and to attract publicity they considered an
unwelcome invasion of family privacy. Writing poetry was a suitable pastime for young ladies, like painting watercolors or playing
the piano, as long as it did not turn into a serious professional
commitment along male lines—i.e., toward publication. Discouragement of women's creativity leads usually, as we have seen, to
their forming supportive alliances. What is so remarkable here is a
bond of empowering love, usually sought with a mother or older
sister, between twin sisters. They seem to have created their own
private world apart from the other family members, with whom
they may never have felt as though they entirely belonged.

The twins' mother died when they were twenty-four, their father
five years later. The rapid flowering of Gladys's talent coincided
with their release from the restrictive family atmosphere, which
Gladys frankly described as "the cloud/ That held my spirit."[43] The
sisters took a fashionable apartment at 535 Park Avenue. Gladys began
to publish in *Century, Poetry,* and other magazines that gave her
professional standing, and in 1915 she published a volume of her
work, *Gates of Utterance.* "When it was suggested to Gladys that
[the book] should be dedicated to Dorothea," according to a friend,
"she answered that poets were not in the habit of dedicating their
verse to themselves."[44] They developed several close friendships with
other young women and ventured somewhat timidly into literary

life through an acquaintance with Padraic and Mary Colum, who helped promote Gladys's work with publishers.

A taut, uneasy sense of strain lies over Gladys Cromwell's poetry. It rises from her feeling of having been kept from normal development: "I wonder when . . . I shall be completed."[45] Without the rough, shaping hand of experience in the world, she was ethereally idealistic, unworldly, as all observers noted. In the most important area of their lives—experience—the twins could not supply one another with what was missing. The poems reflect walks in the secluded New Jersey countryside or the White Mountains of New Hampshire, where the family had country estates. The romantic tradition provided, as it did for Emily Dickinson, the symbolic imagery for a lonely, isolated poet's inner states of being. The landscape of her own soul was small, Gladys Cromwell wrote in "The Poet's Thrift," for she was "unprepared for the sublime":

> I find enough in scant elusiveness
> Of springs and little brooks.[46]

She accepted the challenge of having to find beauty in wintry deprivation:

> We like red weeds and branches blackly drawn,
> And the white snow embroidered with brown roots.[47]

But while measuring the small-scale introspective prison of her experience, she reacted against it with a violence of spirit that recalls Emily Brontë:

> Confined within the walls of a grey world,
> And never from that iron realm allowed,
> My powers were wasted; I was broken, bowed;
> Throughout the years my strength and will were furled.[48]

The tension in Cromwell's work is that of a woman who knows the power of which she is capable, but who is driven to despair by her deprivation at the time when she might have learned to handle it. She was one of many women to use the imagery of a caged animal to describe herself, as she wrote in "The Lion": "Now I range in circular/ Pursuit of my own power . . ."[49] The twins became increasingly obsessed with their uselessness, their lack of anything of value to give to the world out of themselves. They were "searching for some solution," a friend wrote, "that should justify their immunities, their money, and the grace of luxury to which they had been born."[50] Life seemed to have in store some ultimate, momentous test, a day of reckoning, when they would have to prove that their pale devotion to divine love and beauty had some value in a world of hard reality.

When America entered the European war in 1917, they soon discovered their opportunity. At first they were drawn into volunteer Red Cross work and donated generous sums of money, like many rich New York society women. But the war had intruded disturbingly on the complacent way of life they depended on even as they fretted against it, as Gladys wrote in "Extra" (a newspaper headline shouted in the street):[51]

> Sheltered and safe we sit.
> Our chairs are opposite . . .
>
> But a voice in the street draws near;
> A wordless blur of sound
> Breaks like a flood around:
> "Trust not your hopes, for all are vain . . .
> War is the one reality."
>
> Are we awake or dreaming? . . .
> Listen, dear:
> The clock ticks on in the quiet room,
> It's all a joke, a poor one, too,
> Or else I'm mad! This can't be true?
> I light the lamp to lift the gloom.
> My world's too good for such a doom.
> One fact, if nothing else, I know,
> I'll die sooner than have it so!

The war challenged their idealism and the patrician foundations on which it rested, symbolized by the safety and comfort of their home. But this disruption also opened up an exhilarating prospect of the kind of noble, daring action that had always lain outside the perimeters of what was possible in their lives. On their golden island, they could only yearn for the "real," but in war they could face it firsthand. In 1917, perhaps encouraged by the legendary example of Florence Nightingale, they enrolled as Red Cross canteen workers to be sent to the front in France and spent the summer learning to drive a vehicle, to work in a hospital, to dispense food and drink.

"I was from the beginning discouraging about their going," Mary Colum wrote, "knowing how unprepared they were to face what they would have to experience. . . They were rather nervous of men and had no notion at all of what war conditions or soldiers were like; they had lived such a sheltered life that they had never been in a subway or a public conveyance of any kind until just before they left for France. When they came to bid us good-by they told us with excited interest they had come on the subway, having got rid of their car."[52] They were still euphoric on the Red Cross ship that zigzagged across the Atlantic in February 1919 to evade German submarines, quite different from the leisurely voyages of bygone years. "There is the usual slamming, sliding, and swinging," Gladys wrote to Padraic Colum, "but otherwise this trip seems unlike others. When they shut us in at night we feel as though we *were* the submarine. . . . There are Red Cross meetings every afternoon but we are busy enough listening to stories such as:— the boat is loaded with lead and will sink to the bottom; the boat is loaded with iron so the compass isn't right—! It is great fun—and I wish you and Mrs. Colum were here!"[53]

The "great fun" soon gave way to dismal shock, however, when they were stationed at Châlons-sur-Marne, handing out hot drinks and bread to weary French soldiers under the brutal German bombardment of March 1918. They did their duty faithfully for months, earning a reputation as "twin angels." In September they admitted that their resolve was becoming shaky and asked to be transferred to an American evacuation hospital behind the lines to work as nurses. In October they were beginning to show signs of mental instability. But when the Armistice came a few weeks later they seemed cheered, like everyone else, and anxious to return home.

They arranged for a maid to reopen their apartment, and boarded *La Lorraine* at Bordeaux on January 19, 1919 with a party of Red Cross personnel.

The twins' extreme nervousness and odd behavior disturbed a Red Cross officer, who suggested that they be watched; deep depression and a sense of letdown were common following the elation at the end of the war. Gladys called for Dr. C. L. Purnell (a woman), asking for "something that would allay the pains in their heads and put them to sleep." Dr. Purnell later described them as "tired, nervous and hysterical." Dorothea had been observed agitatedly, and with an apparent attempt at secrecy, tearing a sheet of paper to bits.

The next day, as the ship sailed, Dorothea sat in the reading room again filling sheets of paper with writing but tearing them up as if she could not satisfactorily say what she wished. The day passed uneventfully. At seven that evening, in heavy darkness, as the *Lorraine* made its way down the long channel of the Gironde toward the sea, the sisters strolled on the deck, their long cloaks blowing out in the winter wind, passing a sentry who paid little attention to them. Then he was astonished to see one of them—probably Gladys, who always took the lead—place her foot on the rail and leap into the water. Her sister followed almost immediately. As the newspaper account reported, "Neither of them screamed or made any noise, and the splash when they struck the water was drowned by the noise of the tide rushing along the ship's side in the shallow river." A YMCA worker said "he heard a faint cry on the port side and on looking over the rail saw the two women whirled away by the seething tideway." Unaccountably, it was twenty minutes and five miles later before the captain knew of the event; too late then to stop, and impossible to turn around in the narrow channel.

The sisters left notes addressed to their brother, Seymour L. Cromwell, a banker and stockbroker, who, in closemouthed family fashion, did not release the contents but said only that "both physically and mentally they had broken down."[54] Their action had been carefully planned, for they had recently made out new wills whose identical wording began: "If my sister and myself die in or as the result of any common disaster or catastrophe, whether simultaneously or otherwise, . . ."[55]

The horror that drove the Cromwell sisters to suicide has been attributed to their exposure to dirt, savagery, and ugliness on a scale they could never have conceived in their inexperience and idealistic innocence. While this is undoubtedly true, it does not account for the particular mechanism of their breakdown. Gladys provided this in a poem, apparently hastily written under stress and published posthumously, "The Actor-Soldier," which reveals the bankruptcy of their bold attempt to immerse themselves finally in a reality which had always been defined for them in idealized masculine terms. It ended as only a male masquerade, still cut off from authenticity as all their life had been:[56]

> On the grass I'm lying,
> My blanket is the sky;
> This feeling is called dying . . .
>
> The wonder of it is,
> I'm by myself at last
> With plain realities.
>
> No one is here to cast
> A part for me to play;
> My term of life is past . . .
>
> The Soldier and the Son
> Were my seductive parts . . .
> The Soldier part was my best,—
> 'Twas my last and favourite.
> Every gift that I possessed
> I displayed for their benefit.
> Who are They? . . .
>
> But now on the grass I turn
> To ease a little the pain;
> It is not too late to learn.
>
> Last night I lay in the rain
> Until my body was numb,
> Hearing like a refrain:

"O Masquerader, come!"—
And even like a drum
It beat into my brain:
"O Masquerader, come!"

THREE

Opening
Doors

* **T** * HE CROMWELL SISTERS had lived in such isolation that, once released, they leaped fatally to the opposite extreme—from a peaceful nest of female affection to an open field of male violence and chaos. Armed only by their innocence, the innocence patriarchy instills in women, they were forced to confront the reality of power in its most naked form and were quickly overwhelmed by their own powerlessness and inability to sustain one another. Yet their story is only an exaggerated version of the problem facing all women who chose to reject domestic confinement.

Creative women of the era were ambivalently attracted to the male model of power, yet repelled by its inappropriateness; Gladys Cromwell discovered too late that she had falsely idealized "the Soldier and the Son." But there seemed to be no clear-cut alternative. The need for a distinctively feminine image of power grew intense as women entered the competitive world intending to establish their work on a basis of equality with men's. Women were continually alert for others like themselves, in a kind of unspoken readiness to find confirmation of their capability for self-determination.

A friendship based on such an attraction is featured importantly in Babette Deutsch's youthful autobiographical novel *A Brittle Heaven* (1926). The novel's heroine, Bianca Ernesti, as a teenager awakens to the stirrings of creativity; like Joyce's Stephen Dedalus, she discovers the mystery and beauty of the language of poetry. Bianca's awakening, however, is associated with her friendship with another girl named Trudy, linking her aroused imagination with the love for someone who embodies feminine power. Trudy is slim, firm-bodied, and boyish, the Diana type who recognizably possesses the kind of self-reliant freedom that is unshaped by male expectations.

In contrast, Bianca at home is suffocated by a mother and two aunts whose only interests are food, the dressmaker, and the weather, and who worry about how the neighbors will judge the clothing hung on their clothesline. "Mammy believed the whole duty of her sex lay in the feeding and flattery of the other."[1] These women are trapped, providing only the example of "a wife, a mother, a domestic drudge, part of the old, tedious, ugly pattern."[2] The wisdom of her stepfather, a middle-class nonentity who gets caught in shady business practices, is limited to lecturing her to "follow the right path" and be "true to the best ideals of womanhood,"[3] presumably represented by her mother and aunts.

Bianca's greatest need is to reject the identity she has inherited from the confined women of the past, as she searches for confirmation of her emerging self. Her first glimpse of new possibilities is with Trudy—the breath of adventure, of athletic competence, of intimate sharing which stirs the imagination and sense of growth. Deutsch's poem "Anna," from her first volume, *Banners* (1919), celebrates such an awakening of feminine power:

> Is there a more fit altar for worship?
> Limbs of a young Aphrodite . . .[4]

Bianca and Trudy come excitingly close to a sexual encounter, for Eros is involved in any awakening of creativity. Deutsch, however, does not pursue further the implications of their relationship, but views it as a phase of adolescence, a sort of rehearsal for the men they will eventually meet, rather than the ritual of empowerment it seems potentially to be. Here Deutsch yields to conventional heterosexual standards that require a woman to limit significant emotional relationships to a male mate, and reveals a commitment to finding compromise and accommodation with men rather than revolutionary change in male-female relationships.

Like Babette Deutsch, many poets went first to other women as sources of artistic stimulation and self-discovery before accepting marriage as unavoidable, or yielding to men as arbiters of their professional lives. This primary reaching out to one another was vitally necessary: women's efforts to redefine themselves were resisted in every conceivable way, for reasons Lillian Rubin has pointed out: "There is no greater power, nor a more heinous abuse of it, than the ability of those who are powerful in a society to define selfhood for those who are not. This is why the powerful so jealously guard this particular aspect of their dominion."[5] It is not surprising that power-seeking attachments between women, which escaped conventional definition, were surrounded by self-protective privacy and were regarded by men as mysterious, threatening, or abnormal.

"To me, as to all men," W. H. Auden confessed, "the nature of friendship between women remains a mystery, which is probably a wise provision of nature. If we ever discovered what women say to each other when we are not there, our male vanity might receive such a shock that the human race would die out."[6] Auden's facetious remark reveals the extent to which men have arranged for women to support male self-esteem, and how little men perceive that women might wish to do the same for each other. Lillian Faderman has documented the almost invisible history of women's friendships in her book *Surpassing the Love of Men: Romantic Friendship and Love between Women from the Renaissance to the Present*, where she quotes the Irish novelist Edith Somerville: "The outstanding fact, as it seems to me, among women who live by their brains, is friendship. A profound friendship that extends through every phase and aspect of life."[7]

Through such friendships talented women could realize a just valuation of their capabilities and escape the confinement to "junior status" that relationships with men usually imposed on them. Such friendships flourished more readily, however, in the sexually segregated female subculture of the nineteenth century, when they were not perceived as threatening to men. But as women broke free from institutionalized segregation and began to aim at total equality with men, their mutually supportive friendships rapidly underwent redefinition. Male-fashioned psychologies of the twentieth century classified as "perversion" any intense emotional attachment other than the male-dominated, conventionally heterosexual. The result was that defensiveness and shame were introduced into the kind of deeply sustaining relationships that were now needed more acutely than ever.

Some women—Sara Teasdale is a conspicuous example—were confused and uncertain about how to deal with the emotional needs they felt in relation to other women. Teasdale's extreme commitment to the patriarchal ideal, with its posture of subservience, stimulated a counterreaction—a hunger for the powerful feminine identity she was denied. Suffering from continual lassitude, colds, and sore throats, and advised by male doctors to rest and be even more inactive in order to subdue her inner disquiet, she was drawn to lively, energetic women who could excite her sense of feminine worth. Her idealization of Sappho and Greek goddesses reveals her need for a powerful feminine image that would release her own trapped energy. Here is Sara Teasdale's diary speaking about a visit to the Louvre in 1905, at age twenty-one, to drink in a vision of the Venus de Milo: [8]

We went down-stairs next, and when we got to the door, I looked to the end of a long, long corridor and way at the end of it, against a dark red curtain, beautifully lighted, stood the most beautiful thing in the world—the Venus de Milo. Oh, I could hardly contain myself, her beauty made me so happy. She is far, far more lovely than any reproduction that I ever saw. The nearer I came to her, the more I loved her. Yes, I really love her—almost as one loves a real person. . . . I cannot express the pleasure one has in being near this glorious woman. You are glad, as was Theophile

Gautier, that her arms are gone, because they might hide her body. I have never seen so noble and pure and unconscious a woman as this Venus. The marble is so magnificently carved that it looks like flesh.

During one winter in her mid-twenties, Teasdale set up a little altar to Aphrodite in her room and recited poems before it. "I can confess to you," she wrote a friend, "—tho' I'd be afraid to tell most people—that she is more real to me than the Virgin."[9] Some of her earliest poems were sonnets dedicated to the tragic actress Eleonora Duse and dramatic monologues on legendary great women like Helen of Troy, Sappho, and Guenevere. But Teasdale was never able to visualize these women, in spite of their disruptive power, as free. Their energies invariably ended frozen in suffering, bowed like the chaste women with downcast eyes in art-nouveau stained glass. Nathalia Crane, a youthful prodigy-poet of the 1920s, caught the same image in her poem "Venus Invisible":

> But we are sworn as artists
> To postures dutiful,
> And Venus bending forward
> Becomes invisible.[10]

Sara Teasdale grew up in the segregated atmosphere of a private girls' school, where friends recalled her crush on a girl "tall and slim with finely chiseled features"[11] named Bessie Brey, to whom she wrote some of her first lyrics. After graduation, she joined with seven other young women in a loosely knit arts club they called The Potters, following the model of older St. Louis women of the prestigious Wednesday Club. It has been debated whether women's clubs merely reinforced the separation of "women's sphere" or provided upward mobility for professional women. They probably did both; for while they kept women safely outside the male sphere, they often provided young women like Sara Teasdale the only organizational means of gathering strength through association with other women.

The Potters were dominated by their most forceful personality, Williamina Parrish, called "Will." Like Edna St. Vincent Millay and her college friends ("Vincent," "Harry"), groups of young women often used male nicknames for each other. Power, after all, was defined in male terms. Some performed male roles in the plays they staged (Millay played Marchbanks in *Candida* at Vassar), some like "Ned" (Edna) Wahlert and others of the Potters dressed as males for costume parties. Sara Teasdale, however, always chose for her image the stereotype of the "lady," and looked for a mentor she could hold in admiration, shying away from any leadership role for herself. She let Will Parrish take charge of preparing her first collection of poems for publication.

Teasdale's first deeply transformative relationship, however, did not occur among the Potters, but with a young philosophy professor at the University of Arizona, Marion Cummings Stanley. Mrs. Stanley had read Teasdale's poetry, and finding one of her students to be a mutual acquaintance, launched a correspondence that excited them both with the idea of meeting another woman so like-minded. Teasdale traveled to Tucson for a ten-week visit in the winter of 1908–09. In their intensely charged, long hours together, Teasdale opened up her deepest feelings, discussed for the first time her most intimate concerns and asked the questions about men, women, and sexuality that had always been clouded for her in secrecy. Marion Stanley urged Teasdale to stop being dependent on doctors and parents, to quit viewing herself as fragile and inadequate. Instead of continual rest and fluttering concern, she needed work, self-assertion, self-determination. Marion Stanley, eight years older, was a gentle, sentimental person who could empathize with Teasdale maternally while speaking from her profeminist views and her own history of self-reliance. Her parents had divorced and Marion had grown up, close to her mother, in near-poverty and a struggle for survival. Her background resembled Millay's in its feminine self-dependence and its escape from patriarchal domination in the household. Marion was never able to accept conventional marriage. She was soon to divorce Bruce Stanley; later she married a Columbia University philosophy professor in a kind of professional companionship.

Sara Teasdale eagerly placed herself in the hands of this woman who electrified her with talk that exposed the mystery of herself.

Teasdale, who habitually put in ironic, polite distance between her guarded inner self and others, was prone to sudden, effusive infatuations for other women, and occasionally men, who brought life to some huddled, thirsting part of herself. The passionate love she then poured out upon the sometimes startled recipient had a large measure of gratitude in it for such deliverance. She wrote to Marion Stanley,

> You bound strong sandals on my feet,
>   You gave me bread and wine,
> And sent me under moon and stars,
>   For all the world was mine.[12]

When Teasdale returned to St. Louis profoundly unsettled by this encounter, she was overstimulated, restless, and begging for letters from Marion almost daily. "Oh my dearest," she wrote, "I wonder—I honestly, I really wonder—how I'd live without you. . . . Dearest, on the whole, I've been a very sensible lover since I've been back—but oh sometimes I'm so hungry for you, and sometimes . . . I almost wonder if it *can* be true, if I really am so dear to you, and if you will love me always. Oh tell me so again."[13] All her physical symptoms and severe depression returned in force. "My stomach is acting like a fiend,"[14] she wrote Marion; she was soon at the mercy of doctors and worried parents again. Her problem had always been diagnosed as overexcitability, wrought-up nerves, and so she was sent off to a sanatorium in Cromwell, Connecticut, as she had been the previous year, for a rest-cure—exactly the kind of treatment Marion Stanley had advised was more harmful than beneficial. Strenuous, purposeful work did not hurt women, she held, but gave their lives meaning; idleness was their enemy.

Cromwell Hall was a classic incarnation of Victorian medical views about middle-class women. Although patronized by both men and women, it was a notable gathering place for genteel, well-mannered women suffering from debilitating personality conflicts caused by the repressive forces inherent in family life. The official program aimed to quiet their nerves through a regimen of arts and crafts, soothing physical therapy, and isolated life in small cabins scattered about the grounds. Social life included occasional parties and picnic excursions, although guests who became too excitable were severely restricted until they calmed down. Teasdale was once confined to her cabin, the size of a jail cell, for several weeks and forbidden to write either poetry or letters. Any probing of the actual problems of the patients might question the validity of marriage and family life, and so they struggled against amorphous, undefined fears and depressions. The object was to return these women to a state of cheerful, passive acceptance. All her life Teasdale had been conditioned to adopt such an attitude, and fell into it almost by habit. She expressed it succinctly once in a kind of indirect lecture to the unruly Zoë Akins: "I am trying to see all things more clearly and kindly than I used to—trying to be content even tho' other people's ideas are so terribly at variance with mine, and to realize that nothing is all bad. . . ."[15]

In Cromwell Hall's artificially calm atmosphere of repressed and carefully supervised emotion, friendships, jealousies, and antagonisms flourished. Sara Teasdale met here a young woman named Harriet Gardner, who kept a journal of her stay at Cromwell Hall, and wrote, "Sara has been completely spoiled and overexcited by a Mrs. Stanley whom she came to know through her poetry and whom she has just been visiting in Arizona. Sara had to come here to recuperate from that experience!"[16] Gardner, like Teasdale, had an antagonistic relationship with her mother and found Cromwell a happy escape. She suffered from migraine headaches and "sinking spells" and worried a great deal about overextending her energy, as indeed all these quiet, nervous women were taught to do. Like Teasdale, she believed herself indefinably ill, filled with "dark fears and dreads and thoughts of death."[17]

The friendship that developed between Gardner and Teasdale—they met at Cromwell again in subsequent years and saw each other occasionally outside—was a curious foil to Teasdale's attraction to Marion Stanley, for Teasdale and Gardner shared the same kind of oppressive family situation, and in a sense reinforced one another's tendency to passive acceptance of female suffering that Marion Stanley had tried to combat. It is significant that the Teasdale-Gardner friendship never grew, but seemed to subsist on reminders of pleasant times they had together in the dubious peace of Cromwell Hall.

The intensity of Teasdale's love for Marion Stanley began to wane rather quickly, perhaps because Marion pressed for changes that Teasdale could not manage; for example, Marion insisted on the value of formal education and persuaded Sara to take some college courses, which Teasdale found tedious and inconvenient, with a tiresome streetcar ride across town. A year after the grand excitement of the visit to Arizona, Teasdale wrote to a friend that Marion "is a very dear person, but she does not loom as large as she did in the beginning."[18] Yet, half a dozen years after they had lost touch with one another, Teasdale wrote in "Day's Ending (Tucson)" about those memorable weeks together: "It was not long I lived there,/ But I became a woman/ Under those vehement stars."[19] If Marion Stanley had not been able to effect any fundamental change in Teasdale's regressive emotional pattern, she had at least given her bracing encouragement to see herself as a "real poet-writer"[20] and not merely an amateur female dabbler fearful of taking her ambition seriously.

Marion Stanley had also stirred Teasdale from the unconsciousness of the segregated female life, with its immersion in sympathetic feminine affection. After her initiation into the new analytical approach to emotion, Teasdale experienced a fall from innocence: Although she continued to respond impulsively to women whom she needed for a kind of affirmation of herself, she found such relationships tinged with the fear and suspicion of abnormality. She began to read unsystematically in whatever works on sexual psychology came her way—Freud was not among them, though Krafft-Ebing and Havelock Ellis were—dwelling with increasing fascination on "perversions" and the male psychologists' destructive critique of emotional ties between women. Teasdale was aware of sexual liaisons among women. In a letter to Marion Stanley she described Will Parrish's obsession with another of the Potters, a possessive mania that drove Will to try to break up the young woman's engagement. Teasdale was also perfectly aware of Sappho's reputation, but insisted on viewing her as the inspirational head of a girls' club not unlike the Potters or the women's groups she was familiar with.

The increasing conflict and confusion Teasdale felt regarding women were precipitated when she met Eunice Tietjens, a hopeful poet about to become an assistant to Harriet Monroe at *Poetry* in the summer of 1913. "Eunice was as tall and dark as Alice [Corbin Henderson] was blond and little," Monroe wrote in her autobiography, "and her olive skin and midnight eyes were emphasized by a heavy mass of dark brown hair. . . She was less ruthless than Alice, more tender toward the hapless aspirants whose touching letters might move us to tears of sorrow or mirth."[21] Teasdale was dazzled by Tietjens' warmth and kindness, her capacity for instant sympathy, and, above all, her seeming freedom from emotional inhibition. It was a similar promise of liberation that had drawn her earlier to Marion Stanley. Teasdale later recorded the impact of their meeting in a sonnet dedicated "To E.":

> The door was opened and I saw you there
>   And for the first time heard you speak my name;
>   Then like to sun your sweetness overcame
> My shy and shadowy mood. I was aware
> That joy was hidden in your happy hair
>   And that for you love held no hint of shame;
>   My eyes caught light from yours, within whose flame
> Humor and passion have an equal share.
> How many times since then have I not seen
>   Your great eyes widen when you talk of love,
>   And deepen slowly with a far desire;
> How many times since then your soul has been
>   Clear to my gaze as curving skies above,
>   Wearing them like a raiment made of fire.[22]

But the very praise of Tietjens' emotional freedom was turned painfully back against Teasdale when the poem was published in the *Little Review* in April 1914. Tietjens' mother, a sophisticated artist who had lived many years in Europe, was angry and offended, calling it an obvious lesbian confession and an embarrassment. Teasdale never again allowed herself an unguarded public expression of affection for women, and either kept silent or couched her feeling in indirect, restrained language.

Eunice Tietjens moved among a bohemian and theater crowd in Chicago, and, like other people inspired to take Sara in hand and educate her, introduced her to Floyd and Marjorie Dell and friends who defied convention and lived and slept with whomever they pleased. Teasdale recoiled violently from this Midwestern "Swinburnian hell." When she attached herself to Eunice Tietjens' carefree openness, she had seen it in rather idealistic terms, not bargaining for people who believed in "going as far as possible . . . It seems to me to be an ugly thing—just ugly,"[23] she wrote to Jean Untermeyer. Struggling to harmonize her admiration with this shockingly unsuspected side of Tietjens' tolerance, she wrote a poem satirizing her own romantic innocence, "The Star":[24]

> A white star born in the evening glow
> Looked to the round green world below,
> And saw a pool in a wooded place
> That held like a jewel her mirrored face.
> The star was romantic and young and good,
> And thought she had never been understood.
> She said to the pool: "Oh wondrous deep,
> I love you, I give you my light to keep!
> Oh more profound than the moving sea
> That never has shown myself to me!
> Oh fathomless as the sky is far,
> Hold forever your tremulous star!"
>
> But out of the woods as night grew cool
> A brown pig came to the little pool;
> It grunted and splashed and waded in,
> And the deepest place but reached its chin.
> The water gurgled with tender glee
> And the mud churned up in it turbidly.
> The star grew pale and hid her face
> In a bit of floating cloud like lace.

One can assume that Eunice Tietjens is the pool that reflects the innocent star—which is Teasdale herself—and the pig is the offensive sexuality that blunders in to reveal the illusory depth of the pool and the pool's own delight in piggish sensuality. But Teasdale is also making fun of her own inexperience, and one feels that the star is peering through the lacelike cloud to see what she can. The imagery of the "moving sea," in contrast to the pool, is sometimes associated in Teasdale's poetry with the heterosexual love of men and forms a rich and complex body of symbolism ranging from yearning to violent, invasive power and drowning, generally threatening the loss of her identity. The isolated pool, on the other hand, even with its unexciting calm, is safe and has a boundary. Here, the contrast of the pool and the ocean "that never has shown myself to me" succinctly reveals Teasdale's preference for a feminine relationship because of its capacity to help her define herself.

The two remained lifelong friends. It was Tietjens who brought together Teasdale and Ernst Filsinger and virtually engineered their marriage. It was again to Tietjens that Teasdale turned in her last years when the marriage failed; Tietjens was one of only two or three people in whom she confided the emotional problems that had plagued her all her life.

*

Teasdale's hovering between self-assertion and shrinking back, even to the point of cancelling herself, that impelled her to seek support from other women, can be observed, too, in Adelaide Crapsey, a poet who found her métier in the female academic world. Adelaide Crapsey, born in 1878, was the third of nine children of a liberal Episcopal minister in Rochester, New York who was tried for heresy. (He rejected the Virgin Birth and other supernatural aspects of Christian belief, as well as becoming involved, perhaps more disturbingly, in radical social reform.) Adelaide shared something of his skepticism, his mental independence and rebelliousness. She is the only one of his children mentioned by name in his autobiography *The Last of the Heretics;* and according to a relative, "discussions at the Crapsey dinner table were chiefly between Dr. Crapsey and Adelaide."[25] Her mother's individuality seems lost in the welter of childbearing and housekeeping, neither of which had any appeal for Adelaide.

Adelaide Crapsey's death at the age of thirty-six from tuberculosis, and the delicate diminutiveness of the haikulike poems she called "cinquains," for which she is largely known, have left an inappropriate impression of a pathetic, ladylike poet in the nineteenth century mode. Like Sara Teasdale's, her small-scale work and concern for detail assert an intense force which rigorously enclosed itself rather than spreading outward like, for instance, the work of Lola Ridge or Babette Deutsch.

The sense of enclosure which both protects and gives strength reflects the academic world of the girls' boarding school she attended, and Vassar College, from which she graduated in 1901. Everything about her seemed to be an extension of a paradoxical play of opposites. Adelaide was short, small, childlike in appearance, but with a full mouth and strong chin, and a robust interest in athletics. She managed several class basketball teams while at Vassar. She traveled alone in Europe for extended periods when it was considered improper and unsafe for a single young woman to do so. One side of her was mischievous and fun-loving, rebellious; the other, dutiful and self-sacrificial, as befitted a minister's daughter. She was liked for her unfailing sense of humor, whose chief target was pomposity, and she directed it also upon herself with wry irony. A friend from girls' school, Elsie Draper, remembered her "as a very adventurous person; almost a rebel, who was also, strangely enough, a person of such diffidence as nearly to counteract the vigor of her personality." Draper attributed to her a "violence of emotion" and a "rebellion against things as she found them."[26]

Although she wrote a few early student poems expressing conventional sentiments about love as the high point and salvation in a woman's life, Crapsey's undergraduate short stories poke fun at young men. Her sardonic, deflating attitude toward male vanity is epitomized in a letter to her mother from Rome in 1909, in which she describes watching a young man in a window across the street meticulously parting his hair and tying his cravat before a mirror, spending more time than she does completely dressing herself. She appears to have had no romantic interest whatever in any particular men, and, like many creative women, plenty of reasons observable in her own family household to avoid relationships that threatened her autonomy. That her rebellious attitude was directed essentially toward men is suggested by her poem "The Witch":

> And have you heard (and I have heard)
> Of puzzled men with decorous mien,
> Who judged—the wench knows far too much—
> And burnt her on the Salem green? [27]

The expansive side of her spirit is best represented in her quatrain, "Adventure":

> Sun and wind and beat of sea,
> Great lands stretching endlessly . . .
> Where be the bonds to bind the free?
> All the world was made for me! [28]

Illness and the threat of early death put her capacity for irony to the utmost test. Yet all her life already had been held in suspense between self-assertive freedom and self-effacing surrender, of which death was the ultimate requirement. She taught literature at girls' schools, in the environment where she was most at home, but made two prolonged stays alone in Europe—1904–1905 and 1909–1911— studying art and archaeology and poetic metrics. It is further characteristic that she did not take her own poetic talent very seriously and instead devoted her waning strength to an almost obsessive analysis of English metrics, hoping to produce a definitive work— a deflection of her originality into a rather sterile academicism.

When Crapsey returned from England in 1911 to take a professorship of poetics at Smith College, she was already ill, though the cause of her spells of weakness and depleted energy was yet undiagnosed. Her kinship with Emily Dickinson and Sara Teasdale, who both dressed in monotones, is revealed in her adopting the color grey, not only in dress but in all accessories, even to the use of grey pencils—a sameness that aims at obliterating conflict. Louise Townsend Nicholl, a student then at Smith, described her impression of Adelaide Crapsey:

. . . a small figure in grey—grey shoes, grey capes, grey dresses, nothing but grey she wore—walking very softly and quickly. Her arms would be full of books; her smooth head, often hatless, always a little bent; her brown hair heavy on her neck; and her little soft grey shoes moving so quietly, so quickly, so lightly! I have never seen any feet but hers which were really like those mouselike ones about which Sir John Suckling wrote.[29]

Her poems, throughout, make little reference to color, except for grey, black, and silver. Blue and gold appear as possible influences of Italian religious painting. In harmony with her monochromatic appearance, she spoke in a low, quiet voice.

When finally she had to be hospitalized for tuberculosis at Saranac Lake, New York, in 1913, Adelaide Crapsey did not find it easy to give up. By macabre circumstance, a cemetery lay adjacent to the sanitarium, stimulating her to her last rebellious impulse, a poem she titled "To the Dead in the Grave-Yard under My Window: Written in a Moment of Exasperation."

Oh, have you no rebellion in your bones? She asked."[30]

The phrase she appended to the title—"Written in a Moment of Exasperation"—is a characteristic apology that undercuts her protest, and returns her to the role of selfless daughter who wishes not to inconvenience others with her personal problem. She maintained her self-deprecating humor to the last, describing an unsuccessful, exhausting attempt to collapse one lung as "not what one would choose for a diversion."[31] She wrote to a friend a few months before her death, "But really I'm going to move as soon as some suitable tomb or other can be found."[32]

Adelaide Crapsey had no malicious critics or enemies, evidence perhaps that her rebellious spirit made little impact externally. She inspired warm and dedicated friendship among the women who knew her. Perhaps her closest friend was Jean Webster, a classmate at Vassar, a grandniece of Mark Twain and later a popular author of juvenile fiction who used Adelaide as a model in some of her stories. Jean Webster stood by Adelaide through her long illness, leaving New York and her play *Daddy Long-Legs,* just opening on

Broadway, to be with her in Rochester when she died. Another intimate friend was Esther Lowenthal, an instructor of economics at Smith College, who had Crapsey's manuscript on metrics typed and who arranged for its publication after her death. Lowenthal also had Crapsey's poems typed so she could arrange them for publication while bedridden.

The emotional quality of these friendships is difficult to assess, marked as it is by Crapsey's stoic courage and self-mocking humor, by her lifelong determination to display self-restraint, to yield to no opportunity for pity or dependence on others. In all this, she seemed to be avoiding a traditional definition of femininity, just as in her devotion to the study of metrics she was overturning the previous century's view of women as intellectually incompetent, given to emotional effusiveness rather than disciplined technique. Her rebellion, while not external and disruptive, was nevertheless profoundly centered inwardly; and in groping for self-definition against the threat of annihilation—though a minister's daughter, she did not believe in survival after death—Adelaide Crapsey found friends among other competent, trained, and productive women who could affirm the validity of her own chosen course.

*

Adelaide Crapsey's poems were published posthumously by Claude Bragdon in Rochester. But it was women who had helped prepare her manuscripts, women who afterward kept alive her reputation, who recorded her life and who responded to the vibration of her personality. She had moved about in her short life so inconspicuously that she inspired women who had never heard of her to assist in rescuing her from oblivion. Lola Ridge wrote of how "the thought of you/ hovers at my heart . . ."

> It is, almost, as though you had not spoke,
> but existed merely
> as some certain
> function of the spring,
> and shall return with primroses.[33]

With little in the way of formal organization to channel their support for one another, women spontaneously formed nucleuses of sympathy and encouragement that were tremendously important in the rapid flowering of poetry by women between 1915 and the early 1930s. Harriet Monroe, for example, served as the pivotal center and clearing house for uncounted dozens of women, many of whom, like Sara Teasdale and Eunice Tietjens, came to know each other through her. Monroe traveled widely, staying at the homes of women friends when carrying the proselytizing message about the new poetry to the women's clubs she addressed. Her magazine, *Poetry,* provided a forum for women's voices and even a political rationale for women's work, in her passionate democratic belief in social equality and nondiscrimination against women or ethnic minorities. *Poetry* was staffed largely by women during Monroe's editorship.

Monroe, in fact, had to defend herself against the charge that she was an unwholesome influence in feminizing American poetry. An editorial in the Philadelphia *Record* in 1920 complained, "The vigorous male note [is] now seldom heard in the land, and almost never at all in the pages of *Poetry. . . . Poetry* is edited by a woman; its policy is largely dominated by another woman with radical and perverse notions of the high art of singing, and most of its contributors are feminine by accident of birth, while the majority of the male minority are but thin tenors."[34] It is interesting that the writer's discomfort with modernist, experimental work is projected in sexual terms, so that the threat to the status quo is perceived as a feminine attack on masculinity. Ironically, Alice Corbin Henderson, the person referred to as dominating *Poetry*'s policy, actually preferred male poets, and claimed that "more rotten verse comes from women than from men." Monroe patiently pointed out that by actual count, *Poetry* in the previous year had published twice as much poetry by men as by women, and that the male poets included businessmen, lawyers, and war veterans. The advances women had made were still quite modest: "The modern woman has yet to prove her equality as an artist." But women, she wrote proudly, "recognize that . . . the feminine note is quite as authentic, and should be, in its own way, quite as vigorous and beautiful, as the masculine. Perhaps women," she concluded prophetically, "are just beginning their work in the arts, and the twentieth century may witness an extraordinary development."[35]

The hysterical male reaction that greeted women's venture into any male sphere was a source of considerable stress for women, who had to face ridicule or patronizing belittlement. Carrol Smith-Rosenberg has documented, in her essay "The New Woman as Androgyne: Social Disorder and Gender Crisis, 1870–1936,"[36] how the first women students at newly coeducationalized colleges like Cornell had to thread their way through large clusters of contemptuous male students deliberately gathered on lecture-hall steps to embarrass them with stares and their massed presence. Ezra Pound, in a review of work by Marianne Moore and Mina Loy, utilized most of his space to ramble and pontificate, and then awarded a head-pat to the poets: "These girls have written a distinctly national product."[37] (Moore was over thirty.) Such small examples can be multiplied endlessly to indicate the climate of gender polarization and male hostility in which women were obliged to work.

The national network of women's clubs provided the most extensive means through which the poets could organize sympathetic feminine support for women's creative work. To a far greater extent than men, women perceived the arts in the context of community, of education, uplift, and personal fulfillment. Harriet Monroe blamed the "waning of the Puritan ideal," the loss of early American spirituality, along with the legacy of Puritan strictures against sensual pleasure, for "the dryness, the drabness, the thinness of life in this land where generous nature invites to richness and beauty." She urged women's clubs to rise to the occasion and stir up a new appreciation of art and beauty, a birth of inner spiritual richness, whose thwarting leads to social problems and crime. Girls, she remonstrated, put all their love of beauty into clothes instead of the arts. "Every woman's club should be an agency through which its members, their children and their community in general, can advance to more complete self-expression in beauty."[38]

Eunice Tietjens praised the General Federation of Women's Clubs as a vital movement for spreading the love of poetry. America was stirring "with an ever growing and deepening love of beauty,"[39] she wrote; creativity was penetrating the schools, where the future hope of the poetic culture lay in teaching children to write poetry. Tietjens herself provides a valuable glimpse into the convergence of women's groups, creativity, and personal awakenings that rose from friendships forged there. With her second husband, Cloyd Head, a theatrical producer and director, she settled in Miami, Florida in the 1930s and became active in women's clubs, lecturing and teaching. Her inspirational warmth stimulated other women to inner growth and belief in themselves. Ethel ("Sheelah") Murrell, a woman who participated in one of her classes and became a personal friend, expressed her tribute to Tietjens in moving language that reveals once again how the mother-daughter link—whether literally or by analogy—underlies self-recognition and the freeing of women's imaginations:[40]

The Lord and I alone know (or care) how many doors you have unlocked, and cracked, and swung wide open for me. They have been important doors. I didn't find a poet, or a sculptor, or a statesman behind any of them . . . but I did find an integrated personality. This person thinks her own thoughts, has formulated values, and is hot in quest of understanding. Thank you for the key.

It's only fair to warn you that in my next incarnation I shall seek admittance to this confused globe via your womb, or sperm sack. I want the running start that you'll give me. Looking around at what we're shaping for our future incarnations I am damned sure I shall need a running start. There won't be any place for "them as sits thru thirty years" making up their minds to what they are and want. It's pretty tough on you, but unless you swear you to a life of celibacy (and I'm not afraid of that) some sunny morning you'll wake up and there will be ME in your bassinette. All of which is simply to say . . . You are a great guy and I'm glad to know you.

Mrs. Murrell became an outspoken advocate of equality for women and confronted hostile audiences, sometimes even being refused permission to speak. "The opposition," she wrote on one occasion, "consisted of wild waving of arms, announcements that I represented a dangerous minority, callings upon God, and provings by Genesis, but no mention of the Florida law!"[41] She noted the tendency of reactionary opinion to brand any threat to the status quo as communist-inspired. When a poll of National Federation of Women's Clubs membership in 1944 showed them six to one in favor of an Equal Rights Amendment, Murrell exulted: "We want equality and we're going to get a Constitutional Amendment which declares we have it. Then we can get back to biological amenities untroubled by political rivalries."[42] Murrell wrote unpolished poetry for her own pleasure, with strong, raw force of feeling, expressing her sensuality, her love of the colorful, the tropical, and her sense of the fundamental experiences of birth and death; not sonnets, she said self-deprecatingly of some of her poems, "just fourteen-liners."[43]

Club women have long been the target of male ridicule, on the assumption that most of their members are trivial-minded, affluent, and in search of harmless ways to fill vacant lives, as satirized in *New Yorker* cartoons. But in that supposed wasteland there was a genuine hunger for the example of dynamic, achieving women, and leaders like Eunice Tietjens, Amy Lowell, Jessie Rittenhouse, and Harriet Monroe were in continual demand. They worked indefatigably to encourage the writing and appreciation of poetry both in the schools and among the public generally. Far from reinforcing cultural conservatism, they were instruments of change, often acerbically critical, bringing to these democratic masses guidance in a more modern taste than they had been educated in. "Creativity" as a forceful concept in American education was furthered by the support and publicity rising from women in the community.

Poets whose work was publicized among the women's clubs became themselves the object of fascinated curiosity and were popular speakers on the women's club circuit. Sara Teasdale, who was too shy to make such appearances herself, met her idol W. B. Yeats when he addressed a women's club meeting in Santa Barbara in 1921. In 1926 Teasdale visited her friend Jessie Rittenhouse, who had settled in Winter Park, Florida and had organized a State Poetry Society, speaking also before local arts groups. Teasdale wrote with gentle amusement of Rittenhouse's labors to educate her followers:

"She does the job grandly, with touches of inimitable tact in asking this diamonded lady or that shabby college professor (there is a college here, too) what she or he thinks on this cloudy point."[44] There is no way to estimate how many copies of books of poetry were sold because of women's aroused interest, or how many doors were opened as they were for Ethel Murrell. But it was all in the vision of the leading women of that era to fulfill Whitman's admonition, adopted by Harriet Monroe as the motto of *Poetry:* "To have great poets there must be great audiences too."

The importance these women attached to building and educating an audience reflected their awareness that they had little share in the serious audience dominated by men. Perhaps nothing reveals the advance toward assuming power for their own creative lives better than the rise of forceful women publicists. Even though they advertised the new poetry written by men and women alike, the important fact is that women writers were included on an even footing, and that the promulgators themselves were women. Every new woman poet arriving on the scene was acutely aware that her success would depend, to some degree, on her capacity to manipulate or command favorable public interest. The painful knowledge of Emily Dickinson's shy, discouraging effort to draw attention to herself, with the attendant weight of silence enjoined on women, lay heavily on any woman wishing to be noticed. Carol Schoen, in her critical study *Sara Teasdale,* points out that a major conflict in Teasdale's earliest work centers on whether she ought to be "singing" at all, or keep silent as women were supposed to do. Yet even the reticent Teasdale was soon learning the art of self-promotion, the diplomatic skills of charming editors, the arranging of favorable reviews by friends, of publicity in libraries and bookstores; the endorsement by prominent poets, the careful creation of an image her public admired. Vachel Lindsay, who, in his campaign for regional poetry, begged Teasdale to stay home in the Middle West, finally caught on to her reason for centering herself in New York: "You get more fish lines into your hand, you rascal."[45]

While many women, like Teasdale, Rittenhouse, and Tietjens, tried to keep a conciliatory low profile in the male-dominated professional world, a few, most notably Harriet Monroe and Amy Lowell, accepted the consequences of taking bold, assertive positions. We have already seen how Monroe was feared in some quarters as an Amazon leading women to take over American poetry. Amy Lowell was subjected to such extreme personal abuse that her real achievements still remain hidden by a cloud of dismissive comic anecdotes. There can be little doubt that the hostility to Lowell is largely male-inspired and centers on her formidable powers of making herself felt, and on her overweight figure; Ezra Pound, stung by her apostasy, called her the "hippopoetess." Women in the main, however, saw nothing comic in either her size or her self-assurance. Glenn Ruihley, in the *The Thorn of the Rose: Amy Lowell Reconsidered,* one of the few wholly sympathetic studies of Lowell, cites a symbolic incident on one of Lowell's lecture tours: "Miss Lowell inquired about the effect of her lamp on the eyes of a lady seated in the front-row. She answered, 'I see another light.' "[46]

Amy Lowell arrived at the integration of her character and her abilities only on the verge of middle life, after a tortured period of preparation. Her immense wealth, her zestful exercise of privilege, her distinguished Boston family background are familiar in the Lowell legend and need not be recounted here. She suffered excruciatingly as an adolescent from a glandular condition that made her feel physically awkward and unattractive, as well as from a sense of her own originality and difference from others. Lowell's unhappiness can be traced, in great part, to the oppressive patriarchal values that conflicted with her strong, assertive individuality. This is evidenced in her youthful striving to live up to conventional expectations of femininity, even though the harder she tried the more a failure she felt. As a student at fourteen, answering a questionnaire that asked, "What character (female) in all history do you most dislike?" she replied, "Joan of Arc." Why? "Joan of Arc was too masculin [sic]." The quality she liked most in a woman was "Modesty"; the most disliked, "imodesty." She admired "manliness" in men, and her idea of greatest happiness was "To be loved."[47] Amy felt herself to be hopelessly unlovable in a romantic sense and sat out many dances in forlorn misery.

Yet, glimmers of the future woman of forthrightness and energy in combat shine through. The trait of moral character she most disliked was "deceat" and her "idea of misery" was "not to be allowed to tobbogan."[48] Although she became a public figure with a flair for politics and the dramatic, her achievements were never reached at the cost of deluding herself or deceiving others; her failures were usually a matter of faulty but honest judgment, of willingness to throw herself into any challenge that attracted her. Lacking the arts of beguiling men and ruefully conscious that her personality was a drawback in conventional society, she felt lonely and craved sympathetic companionship. Lowell began to keep an impressively honest diary at fifteen and wrote:

I feel very much in need of a *very* intimate friend, a friend whom I should love better than any other girl in the world, & who would feel so toward me. To whom I could tell all that is in my heart & who would do so to me.

We should love to be alone together, both of us.[49]

This yearning for a deep feminine friendship sprang from the same need we have seen repeatedly in other creative women—for an image of feminine power, a reflection of one's capabilities. But Lowell continued to live for many years in frustration, with a tormenting belief that everything about her, her force, her talents, her cravings, were miscast in the world she was condemned to live in, as first an ungainly debutante and then, after the death of her mother, the mistress of the ancestral home. She suffered what has been called a prolonged nervous breakdown that lasted from 1898 to 1905.

The turning point toward recovery came in 1902, when Lowell attended a performance of Eleonora Duse in Boston. The great actress, who had also inspired Sara Teasdale with the liberating vision of a woman of expressive power, filled Lowell "with infinite agitation." On returning home from the performance, she sat down to write her first poem, a seventy-one-line blank verse tribute. "The effect on me was something tremendous," she wrote later. "What really happened was that it revealed me to myself, but I hardly knew that at the time. I just knew that I had got to express the sensations that Duse's acting gave me, somehow." The poem she wrote had, she said, "every cliché and every technical error which a poem can have, but it loosed a bolt in my brain and I found out where my true function lay."[50]

Lowell, who had been filled with a desperate longing to find some meaningful purpose in life, threw herself into the discipline of learning to write poetry, hoping to make a name for herself. Yet in 1913, at age thirty-nine, after her first self-published volume *A Dome of Many-Coloured Glass* had been judged a failure, her talents still seemed unused, and she had failed to find the kind of empowering love relationship that could liberate her energies. In that year she wrote "Miscast," a poem that juxtaposes the related needs of giving free play to both mind and emotion. "I have whetted my brain until it is like a/ Damascus blade," she wrote; but it was an instrument that had no use. Similarly, her richness of feeling had no means of expression: "My heart gapes because it is ripe and over-full . . ./ But how is this other than a torment to me!"[51]

The integration of mind and emotion was a troublesome question for women because of the long history of assigning the realm of the intellect to men; emotion and the body to women. The Italian-American poet Emanuel Carnevali summed up his attitude toward women in a typically male mixture of consolation and disgust: "I had in my soul the image of a hen that was hatching eggs: something sweetly familiar and quiet and fecund and fertile, but something dirty, too, because all that is familiar and quiet and fecund is, in the end, dirty."[52] Arthur Davison Ficke expressed it more comprehensively in a letter to Eunice Tietjens, commenting on a poem of hers:[53]

The animalism of the second stanza rather repels me: but I don't suggest that you change it, for it is quite possibly an authentic and valuable expression of just that animality which is so much profounder in woman than in man. Man isn't an animal at all: he's an angel whom woman has imprisoned in flesh for specific ultimate ends of hers: and all man's animality is confined to the region of this one function. But woman is an animal through and through: the real wonder is that spirit emerges at all from so close-woven a cage—just as it would be a wonder if poetry came out of a boiler factory.

The venture into use of their minds cast women in the allegedly unnatural role of the male, and this in turn warred against the body and feelings. Sara Teasdale had capsulized the problem in an early poem, "Vox Corporis" (1910), in which emotion that draws people together is of the body, preyed on by the mind, which is characterized as masculine:

> The beast to the beast is calling,
>   They rush through the twilight sweet—
> But the mind is a wary hunter;
>   He will not let them meet.[54]

Lowell's poem above, "Miscast," implies an androgynous ideal, for she feels "miscast" in both masculine and feminine roles. There is no outlet for either her mind or her emotions, and the answer for one is bound up in the answer for the other.

A possible resolution had been pointed to by Edith Somerville, quoted here earlier: "The outstanding fact . . . among women who live by their brains, is friendship. A profound friendship that extends through every phase and aspect of life." Although sexual love is sometimes involved in such relationships, the point here is the empowerment and self-definition that result. Amy Lowell finally found such a friend in Ada Dwyer Russell, an actress whom she met in 1912. Mrs. Russell, a widow, moved into Amy Lowell's home in 1914, and the two women formed an inseparable companionship that evenly balanced their personalities. In an interesting turnabout, Ada Russell became the silent manager behind the scenes, seeing that the complex logistics of Lowell's life ran smoothly, while she coached Lowell in the stage techniques that turned her into a successful lecturer and allowed the long-submerged force of her personality to come forth in full play. The result was, at last, a happy torrent of public action and poetic creativity that lasted until Lowell's untimely death by a stroke at the age of fifty-one (1925). Lowell left her estate in trust to Russell, as her poem "Penumbra" anticipated: "My love will go on speaking to you/ Through the chairs, and the tables, and the pictures,/ As it does now through my voice . . ."[55] The intimate details of their relationship have been speculated about, but Ada Russell effectively checked public curiosity by destroying their correspondence after Lowell's death and declining to discuss their relationship personally.

Amy Lowell's liberating influence on other women poets is not easily measured. Some poets, not surprisingly, felt embarrassed and apologetic at the effrontery of a woman who would clash with men and smoke cigars in public. She seemed too noisy against the background of traditional feminine silence. But when Lowell could once be perceived apart from the male reaction, she emerged as an authentic, often inspiring presence. Sara Teasdale had met her a number of times, always under some social pressure, and had taken the usual amused view of the Lowell phenomenon. But after a careful reading of Lowell's new book in 1919, *Pictures from the Floating World,* a new insight unfolded, and she wrote her: "It seemed to me that I realized for the first time what you are. . . Suddenly I knew you—the violence and the delicacy—I found you something that I can love in my own way."[56]

In her championship of free verse and experimentation, Lowell seized the initiative from the male poets (for which she has been excoriated) and by her example helped to free women from the tight, small-scale lyrics that were considered women's special provenance. Amy Lowell could be exhilarating to a woman who was herself in search of freedom. The poet Grace Hazard Conkling, now better known, perhaps, as the mother of the child-poet Hilda Conkling, found in Lowell an artistic model and source of guidance. Conkling had turned her back on an unhappy marriage and come to Smith College in 1913 to teach English and start life afresh; she had begun to publish some of her own work before meeting Lowell through the recently formed New England Poetry Society. Lowell enjoyed making forays into the academic world to shake up the "old fogeys" and visited the Smith campus to lend support to Grace Conkling's effort to establish a course in modern poetry, a proposal adamantly opposed by her conservative department head. Lowell met and thrilled a half dozen young women poets among the students Conkling was grooming. Following one of her weekend visits at Sevenels, the Lowell estate in Brookline, Conkling wrote, "I am still blessing you for the criticism which I needed so much, which nobody else could give me, and I didn't think you would! . . . Your splendid hospitality and your friendship and your poetry have filled my imagination."[57] Conkling and Lowell came to share discussions of intimate aspects of their lives and to support one another in trouble.

From a glance at Conkling's halting earlier poems through the more self-assured work she produced after falling under Lowell's influence, one feels that Lowell indeed helped her find herself. Conkling was an inveterate traveler abroad, and found in themes of travel the kind of liberating spirit that women sought—"To feel the wind that sets you free."[58] (Compare Crapsey's "Sun and wind and beat of sea," and Teasdale's "I love my hour of wind and light.") Conkling applied the lessons that Lowell had taught her in giving full play to her rich, exotic sense of color and the vivid evocation of particular moments of tactile experience.

The Lowell-Conkling friendship provides a glimpse, too, of the ways in which women promoted each other's work, as well as of the jealousies and competition that evolved along with women's successes. Conkling asked Lowell to write an introduction to the first collection of her nine-year-old daughter Hilda's poems in 1920; Lowell cheerfully did so, and her considerable reputation doubtless enhanced the book's reception. Lowell had urged Conkling to write a review of her own *Pictures of the Floating World* for *Poetry* in 1919, feeling that Harriet Monroe disliked her and had not given her fair treatment in the past. Since Monroe, who looked kindly on Grace Conkling, did not know that Conkling and Lowell were close friends, it was a good opportunity to smuggle some favorable publicity into the enemy camp. Lowell believed, with some justification, that Monroe and "the Chicago crowd" were hostile toward the East, with both Monroe and Lowell jockeying for leadership in the poetry renaissance. Monroe, however, rejected Conkling's review, saying, "This is not criticism, it's a blurb."[59] After a series of delays and misunderstandings, a review by Conkling never got published, and Lowell relieved her anger by directly blasting Monroe in a letter that, she said, "should take her head completely off . . . I hope all of Harriet's hair will drop off when she gets my letter, although of course there is not much to drop."[60] One recalls Lowell's likening her mind to a "Damascus blade."

Amy Lowell's great function, though nowhere explicitly acknowledged, was to have sought escape from the prison of self-rejection in which creative women were trapped, into the freedom of making the most of herself as she found herself. The image in a prose-poem Lowell created spontaneously in a letter to Grace Conkling stands as a haunting self-portrait:

> A cloud wreath. A dryad. Wind through beeches.
> Little waves over glittering sand. An unhappy woman
> tinged by time, grievous with memories, impatient at
> the world's dust, seeking a home for those thoughts
> which will in no wise be contented if caged.[61]

Written in 1922, three years before her death, this fragment reveals the persistence of the old division within herself, though now softened into acceptance and made to serve her imagination: on one side, the free nature spirit, with her untroubled kinship with wind and cloud, the direct clarity of mind like water over sand; on the other, the woman burdened with the memory of confinement and therefore compelled perpetually to seek the freedom the dryad possesses by birthright; a feminine ideal that generates transformation of the real.

FOUR
Men and
Marriage

* **F** * OR A WOMAN bent on self-determination, marriage
was a hazard, either to be avoided or to be redefined by her
desire for freedom and equality. The most satisfying and
enduring companionships seem to have been those of women friends
like Amy Lowell and Ada Russell, H.D. and Bryher; or Marianne
Moore and her mother. In such relationships women not only fed
one another's need for empowerment but escape the conflict generated by the privileges of male power in conventional marriage.
Yet the majority of the women poets of 1915–1945 did marry and
tried to fashion the marital relationship to accommodate the primary importance of their creative talents and careers.

The taboo against women taking authority and initiative in
male/female relationships, however, usually led to strain in gifted
women's marriages. The right to sexual self-determination was an
implicit issue lying everywhere just below the surface of these wom-
en's lives. Even the staid, conservative Sara Teasdale expressed envy
of prostitutes who have the freedom to "ask for love" in "Union

Square" (1911).[1] Edna St. Vincent Millay's notorious faithlessness to
her lovers—"I loved you Wednesday,—yes—but what/ Is that to
me?"[2]—is an assertion of a woman's right to take love when and
where she pleases. Elinor Wylie's three marriages trace her quest
for a relationship that would satisfactorily balance love and power,
and the rough handling she received from the press and her social
circle tell how unready the public was to see the balance of power
altered by a woman daring to leave behind relationships she had
outgrown.

Elinor Wylie fled first from a schizophrenic young husband
obsessed with a fear of inadequate masculinity and expressing it in
aggression against her. She eloped with an older man, a sensitive
mentor who could nourish her talents and self-confidence. "It was
Horace who made a poet and scholar of me,"[3] she is reported to
have said. Elinor and Horace Wylie lived together unmarried in
rural England as "Mr. and Mrs. Waring" from 1911 to 1915, when
the Aliens Restriction Order, brought about by the war, forced
them either to disclose their true identities or leave the country.
They returned to America, where they continued to live incognito
in various places from Maine to North Carolina, without close friends
or enough money and in constant fear of exposure and reprisal.
Elinor on occasion would venture out only with her face covered
by a veil.

In July 1916 Wylie's legal wife Katherine filed for divorce, freeing
Horace and Elinor to be married shortly thereafter in Boston.
Although they could now appear openly in public, only a few former acquaintances would still accept them; Elinor's own brother
Henry campaigned against her in the family. The idyllic, peaceful
isolation in which her relationship with Horace Wylie had flourished in England was never to be recovered. Ironically, as soon as
they were married they began to drift apart.

The reason for their separation after all the pain they had shared
has been attributed to the stress under which they lived, to Horace's demoralizing decline into shabbiness, and (according to a male
biographer) to Elinor's readiness to discard men when she could
no longer use them. But the likely explanation is less simplistic.

Elinor Wylie discovered that no matter what part men played in a marital scandal, it was always the woman who bore the heaviest share of condemnation.

Although she was continually assailed by malicious gossip and insult, Elinor worked steadily on her poetry. Some of her best known lyrics were written during this period when she gathered strength to stand against the world:

> Avoid the reeking herd,
> Shun the polluted flock,
> Live like that stoic bird,
> The eagle of the rock.[4]

Her creativity developed as an expression of pride, a positive response to indignity and rejection. She no longer relied on Horace Wylie to shield her, but found a way to assert her own sense of self-value through her work. Like Sara Teasdale in search of beauty, who wrote, "Buy it and never count the cost,"[5] Wylie made her poetry the central, redeeming factor in her life, worth the price paid:

> Better to see your cheek grown hollow,
> Better to see your temple worn,
> Than to forget to follow, follow,
> After the sound of a silver horn.[6]

The emergence of Elinor Wylie as an accomplished poet coincided with the breakup of her marriage to Horace. Her maturity was hardly compatible any longer with the position of an inferior, dependent on an older guide and patron who could hide her from the world while she received the education she had missed. In the fire of exposure, she became a poet through adversity rather than reclusiveness.

It was probably not the fault of either Horace or Elinor that their relationship failed to grow and adapt to the radical changes they faced, both inner and outer. It has been noted that Elinor was deeply disappointed in not being able to bear a surviving child during her years with Horace, and spoke frequently of her failure. She underwent three pregnancies. The first child was born dead; the second died shortly after birth. The third pregnancy ended in miscarriage. Elinor Wylie's anxiety to produce a child suggests a compulsion to prove herself, to be seen as playing the nurturing role that socially defined her as a woman, since she had flouted the public sense of decency in her route to success as a poet. Perhaps, too, as a poet who continually translated her life into metaphor and symbol, she might have said with Adrienne Rich, "I had been trying to give birth to myself,"[7] a self whole and triumphant. There is a discrepancy between her conventional desire to be a mother and her actual view of marriage as a partnership that supported her creativity, with little room for children. One of the attractions of William Rose Benet, the man who succeeded Horace Wylie in her life, may have been that in contrast to the paternalistic Wylie, Benet was the kind of person she could mother.

Elinor Wylie met Bill Benet in Washington, DC through her brother Henry; the two men had been close friends since their student days at Yale. She and Horace had moved to Washington in order to occupy a house owned by her mother while Horace looked for a job. Benet, at the same time, had come there to work on *The Nation's Business,* a publication of the U.S. Chamber of Commerce. Benet, already a published poet with useful connections, was dazzled by both Elinor's poems and her person, and began energetically to help her market her work. A widower who wanted a woman to fill the accustomed place of caretaker, he must have sensed immediately that Elinor hungered for someone to take care of. He returned to New York in the spring of 1920 to work with Henry Seidel Canby on the *Literary Review,* where he was in an even better position to help serve Elinor Wylie's career.

The moment when Elinor Wylie and Bill Benet realized they were in love with each other cannot be pinpointed, but by December 1920 she was finding excuses for a visit to New York—not only to see Benet, but to meet other writers through the Poetry Society of America. She felt isolated in Washington, where she was still a social outcast. Within a month she had made up her mind to separate from Horace Wylie and move to New York on her own, and was bargaining with her mother for help in financial arrangements.

"We may have to wait two or three years," she wrote to Benet concerning the prospect of marrying him after divorcing Horace, "for the sake of other people and because of our own comparative poverty."[8] She was not able to leave Washington until late summer of 1921, but spent the intervening months traveling often to New York and carrying on a heavy correspondence with her new love.

"Dearest boy," she wrote Benet, "poor adorable infant fish," "I loved you and wanted to take care of you."[9] After sitting next to a ten-year-old boy in the theater, she exclaimed, "O, I do love small boys—I always pretend that I like little girls better, but it's a lie! Funny that these lovable, elfin peterpanish creatures should grow up into the noted sex! (But you haven't grown up too much; enough to wash dishes, not too much to be my darling boy.)"[10] She called him "son," "poor child," "Billy"—"You look so innocent and drooping"—and in spite of her severe headaches, dangerously high blood pressure, bouts of depression, tensions over her abandoned marriage, disagreements with her mother and her sister Nancy, and the shock and grief over the suicide of her brother Henry the previous summer, Elinor tried to spare Bill Benet her troubles and show him only the clever and entertaining side of her that would make him feel good. "Do you think I ever for one instant forget, when I am so selfish as to show you my moments of depression, how doubly wicked I am to do so?"[11] "You shall not be moaned to,"[12] she swore.

But Elinor Wylie was an impulsive, excitable, forceful human being, not a maternal saint, and the question of power was not long in bursting on their delicately balanced relationship with upsetting intensity. Sometime in the early summer of 1921, when they were together at a social function in New York, Elinor unwittingly made remarks that injured Benet's fragile self-esteem. He said nothing to her at the time, but after she had returned to Washington he followed up with a chillingly accusatory letter. "This is an impossible situation," she cried. "I cannot come to New York to find myself completely at the mercy of your prides and moods." No man could endure the suffering her headaches inflicted on her, she said, explaining why she may have behaved oddly; "O my god to think that you could turn on me and be angry and bear grudges and mull it over and over in your mind. . . . What then is always behind that face? a sort of cold withdrawal which I cannot understand. . . . I am afraid of you, now that I know you are cruel."[13]

After several days of impassioned letter writing and telegrams between them, Wylie's fear and anger subsided and she was begging for his love: "I will try to change myself and try to please you always."[14] Benet apparently pressed his advantage, and objected to one of her letters, for which she further apologized. The only course seemed to be to adapt herself to the despotic aspect of his emotional childishness, though it disturbed her deeply to discover that while he accepted her generous outpourings of love and sympathy, he seemed to feel little compassion for her own suffering when it threatened to intrude on his peace of mind. "You hate complaints," she said; "you would shoot nightingales. Only, of course they are clever about hiding."[15] In that bit of spontaneous poetry she symbolically expressed the danger to herself as a poet, and indicated her self-defense, in a relationship that forced a greater person to trim herself to a lesser.

This was only the first crisis in the two years before they were able to marry. The issue of power between them rose repeatedly to the surface and was never fully resolved. Wylie was curiously oblivious to the fact that while Benet might privately welcome her maternal nurturing, he also had a traditional male's resentment against "domination" by a woman, a problem Horace Wylie did not have in his secure and self-confident paternalism. The contradiction puzzled and sometimes amused her, as when Benet objected to a poem she wrote about taking his cold hands and warming them at her breast; he felt the poem belittled his masculinity. "Well, Bill," she said, "you will have to find some woman in China who has never known you to believe that you have the mind of a stoic and the physique of Mr. Dempsey. If you don't like my wanting to take care of you and comfort you why are you always longing to have me do that very thing? You want it both ways, you crazy kid; don't you see that?" So both ways it would have to be: "I shall try to be the mother of consolation and the friend and adoring pupil and child."[16]

Wylie was baffled that her great outpouring of love, which to her was humbling and selfless, could be taken as a desire to control him. "I am not really proud, I am not really proud enough; that's where you're wrong; I never want to be top-dog, never, never, I only want you to love me; I SWEAR BY ALL THAT I HOLD SACRED THAT NEVER IN MY LIFE HAVE I TRIED TO MAKE ANOTHER MORTAL DO A THING TO PROVE THAT I HAD POWER."[17] But no matter how absolutely she renounced power and offered unconditional love, he, instead of reciprocating, seemed ready to interpret her impulsive actions as aggression. Wylie admitted she had a "diamond tongue" and tended to be forceful, even wild, in her emotional intensity at times, but these traits did not constitute a deliberate attack on his masculine self-esteem. She appealed to him to understand and excuse her, for such behavior rose naturally from her intense, prolonged suffering as a woman, a suffering that she should not have to point out to him, that was very painful even to talk about. Of her lost children, for example, a topic that arose during one of their disagreements over the disposition of his children: "When the demand was made upon me to disinter the infinitely precious bones of my own children, those innocents who had so many Herods crowding to knife them at the very instant of their birth, I bowed my head under a visitation unlooked for even by my fears, which you know are often unreasonable."[18] Her strength as a woman and a poet was woven from the pain she had been required to endure. In looking to Benet to accept the centrality of suffering in her life, she was, in effect, hoping to find in a man's unconditional love a reversal of what male-dominated society had done to her; perhaps even a kind of absolution, as her poem "Epitaph" suggests:

> For this she starred her eyes with salt
> And scooped her temples thin,
> Until her face shone pure of fault
> From the forehead to the chin.

In coldest crucibles of pain
Her shrinking flesh was fired
And smoothed into a finer grain
To make it more desired.[19]

Although the basis of their relationship was flawed for both of
them, they settled into an accommodation that seemed satisfactory
and that gave Wylie the new freedom of action she desired. She
separated quietly from Horace Wylie in the summer of 1921 and
moved to New York, rooming with a woman friend, trying to avoid
the kind of sensationalism that usually followed her movements.
Elinor and Bill, however, made no secret of their attachment and
were seen everywhere together. As she was "discovered" and rose
to fame with astonishing swiftness over the next few years, she again
became the object of derisive gossip and fascinated interest. Like
Amy Lowell, she accumulated a train of anecdotes which were passed
about with amusement and meanness. Her startling beauty was
caught by Benet in words that others thought wonderfully apt: "Her
bronze hair seemed to have wings, and her head on its beautiful
throat to bear the face of one flying."[20] Yet her beauty seems to
have been resented as much as admired, and tales of her childlike
vanity and emotional scene-throwing were repeated with relish.

Elinor filed for divorce from Horace Wylie in the fall of 1922
and married Benet a year later, to the disapproval of both her own
and Benet's family, none of whom attended the wedding. The
newspapers derided her many marriages—"Elinor Hoyt Hichborn
Wylie Benet"—much as Hollywood actresses have been ridiculed in
a later time. Amy Lowell congratulated Elinor, but was overheard
warning her, "But if you marry again, I shall cut you dead—and I
warn you all Society will do the same. You will be nobody."[21]

By the time of their marriage in 1923, the relationship of Bill
Benet and Elinor Wylie had found its permanent pattern. Benet
may have flared again on occasion, but he impressed their friends
as docile, passive, adoring, protective, and willing to put up with
almost anything. Benet was genial and widely liked, a generous man
described as incapable of making enemies. Louis Untermeyer was
perhaps typical of male friends in his growing resentment of Wylie,

who seemed to him "petulant, full of childish whims, unreasoning demands. She sent Bill on silly errands, gave way to groundless fears, even to phobias of persecution. Because Bill showed no displeasure, his friends resented it all the more. She seemed not only to dominate him, but to absorb him; she almost put out his light." The depth of Untermeyer's malice toward a supposedly domineering woman is revealed in his anecdote of swimming with her on a summer outing while at the MacDowell Colony in New Hampshire. On their swim back from the raft in a lake, Wylie felt tired and asked to rest with a hand on his shoulder. "Then I felt burdened; frail though she seemed on land, I was conscious of her weight in the water. . . . Now I thought of Shelley. I thought of him in the harbor of Leghorn—drowned. And, for a moment, I wished that Elinor was with her beloved idol."[22] One recalls Rebecca West's perception of her: "She always wanted people she could not count on."[23] Such people, one gathers, were usually men.

Edmund Wilson saw the Wylie-Benet relationship more disinterestedly: "It seemed to me that from a literary point of view he was so inferior to her that it made her marrying him inappropriate. . . . When I expressed my doubts about their union, she had said with her harsh and rather callous laugh: 'Yes, it would be a pity that a first-rate poet should be turned into a second-rate poet by marrying a third-rate poet.'"[24]

Elinor Wylie's dilemma was to utilize the power she felt within herself—her great strength, her verbal brilliance, her ambition, her nobility of mind—while at the same time bending to pressures from all sides to assume the posture of humility and repentance. Her overpowering behavior seems probably to have been an expression of her anxiety at finding her power continually undermined. Wylie's marriage with Benet must have seemed to offer the possibility of resolution. Probably, given her background, she believed that marriage legitimized a woman and was therefore essential. It also allowed her to comfort and nurture herself through the mothering that flowed from her so copiously to Benet, a kind of healing love and approval without reservation that she needed far more than he did.

Wylie's deeply wounded sense of self-worth persisted, however, as she began to fear that her personal beauty was not admired enough, or her talents appreciated, or that people were trying to block her achievements. Eunice Tietjens spent some weeks of a summer at the MacDowell Colony when Wylie was there. One evening Wylie was asked to read one of her poems, and did so reluctantly. She had been "sitting in a peculiarly rigid manner, tense and white." Afterward, with Tietjens and Herbert Gorman, she "broke out in a desperate burst of rage and terror."[25]

"Did you see how they hate me, how they all hate me?" she cried. "They are all trying to drown me, to injure me, to keep me from working. But I won't be drowned! I have a typewriter and a better brain than any of them, and they won't succeed. I'll beat them all yet! Did you see how they asked me to recite so they could laugh at me?". . . She was quite out of control, shivering, half screaming, and literally clawing the air . . . "And did you see how they left the door open on purpose so that the mosquitoes would get in and bite me tomorrow when I am trying to write? The mosquitoes! I tell you they will stop at nothing!"

Although the social pressures under which Wylie had lived for so long drove her to hallucinations of persecution, to a pathetic craving for approval and praise, she remained generous and unenvious toward others' achievements, something that could not always be said of their attitude toward her. Her view of herself as essentially giving and noble-minded has some demonstrable validity. Sara Teasdale said, "She seemed heroic if you liked her, hysterical if you didn't."[26]

Elinor Wylie's smothered, beleaguered quest for empowerment gradually assumed a most remarkable form. From the age of seven she had intensely admired Shelley, and over the years had familiarized herself not only with his work but with all available biographical details, dwelling with increasing absorption on his personality and mannerisms. He became an actual presence, a sort of guiding spirit who always accompanied her like the cloud of his poem. She imitated his tastes, ate the food he liked, even cultivated the shrill voice and laugh he was said to have had. Her cry, "They are all trying to drown me," is a spontaneous reference to him, and a curious confirmation of Untermeyer's secret thoughts. Some said that near the end of her life she believed herself to be a reincarnation of Shelley.

In 1926 Wylie published a novel about Shelley, *The Orphan Angel,* that surely ranks as one of the more astonishing tours de force in American literature, and that provides a key to Wylie herself as a woman coming to terms with the question of male power in relation to her own. The novel's disconcerting lack of distance between author and admired chief character reveals it to be the enactment of a fantasy in which Wylie can play an idealized male role. *The Orphan Angel* opens ingeniously as an American captain fishes the nearly drowned Shelley out of the sea at Leghorn and transports him back to America, calling him "Shiloh," not having caught his name correctly. (Shiloh was also Byron's nickname for Shelley.) Shiloh-Shelley appears as the luminous angelic double of an evil-spirited sailor, Jasper, who has just been killed accidentally by a fellow sailor in anger. The resurrection of Shelley from the sea in exchange for the death of Jasper is Wylie's way of eliminating the violent, antifeminine side of male nature for a kind of purified androgeny. "All who beheld him marvelled at his beauty and the singular triumph plain upon his brow"[27]—female beauty and male triumph, the two attributes which to Wylie signified power.

The problem for Wylie was to unite her actual female identity with her imaginative projection of a male self who possessed the power to accomplish all that she felt frustrated in doing. Shiloh-Shelley logically needed a female counterpart as a goal for such a union. The evil dead Jasper, it seems, had a good twin sister named Sylvie, who, somewhere in the West, must be located, told of his death, and set free from an oppressive guardian. The novel then becomes a quest across the continent for Sylvie by Shiloh and a male companion. It has been observed that "Sylvie" suggests "silver," the color Wylie herself felt struck the note of her personality; and that Benet, in his long autobiographical poem *The Dust Which Is God,* gives Wylie the fictional name "Sylvia." In other words, Wylie as a woman is the object of the quest by Wylie the creative, power-possessing male spirit.

Sylvie is always under the care and control of men, as indeed are almost all the female characters in the novel, in contrast to Shiloh, who announces, "Any infringement of my personal liberty makes me sick with revolt."[28] Shiloh's adventures across America are chiefly a series of encounters with women, some of whom threaten to deflect him from his goal by falling in love (he is immune to that), others who must be rescued from abusive males. He is compared to the prince seeking his Cinderella, a high-minded idealist who must save women from suffering and degradation. The novel is like an extended dream in which the dreamer plays all the key roles that dramatize her troubled thoughts about gender. Wylie cannot imagine a woman liberated by her own power: she must be "saved" by a man, since the society in which she lives has convinced her that for a woman, self-determining behavior is destructive. Yet the dreamer can play the role of the man and thus become her own deliverer.

After the urgent quest to unite these dislocated selves, the ending of the novel falls curiously flat. Shiloh cannot marry Sylvie because he is already married (a specious excuse, since no one knows his identity, he is believed dead, and plans never to return to his wife); and he is too high-minded to accept her as a mistress. Actually, he is very little interested in women except to rescue them from suffering and cannot bear any kind of restraint on his personal freedom, including marriage. Having fulfilled his promise to find Sylvie and arrange for her return, he loses interest in her, and the novel ends as he stands on a rise looking yearningly out over the infinite ocean, a new poem forming in his mind. The freedom-loving, creative power of the male, with which Wylie identifies herself, is not able to unite with the victimized female. Sylvie's somewhat sinister guardian, Don Narciso, has pressed Shiloh to take her on any terms, telling Shiloh, "You have rejected yourself; you have rejected your desires, and your luminous dreaming mind; you have rejected your own soul. It is yourself that you reject in Sylvie, because you love her."[29] This is the only moment at which the union of male and female is explicitly stated as essential to creativity. But the split between the powerful and the powerless, male and female, created a gap that Wylie could not bridge in either imagination or life. By placing her hero, Shelley, in frontier America, she integrated him—

and herself—in the context of expanding American imperial power. Shiloh's adventures naively embody many cliches about white America's conquest of other ethnic groups; there are "vermin Indians" and "greasy," "dirty Mexicans." Wylie was, after all, a daughter of the ruling class, and in spite of her struggle to free herself from its crippling grip on women, she could not escape its assumptions about power as triumph of the aggressive male spirit.

After only three years of marriage with Benet, and spectacular popular success, Elinor Wylie began in 1926 to travel alone to England for long periods, where she associated brilliantly with literary people and members of the aristocracy. She was largely admired, but struck a few as mentally unbalanced because of her self-obsession. Aldous Huxley took her to dine with Leonard and Virginia Woolf, where she made a bad impression, bringing out Virginia Woolf's capacity for snobbish meanness: "I expected a ravishing and diaphanous dragonfly," Woolf wrote to Vita Sackville-West, ". . . a siren, a green and sweetvoiced nymph—that was what I expected, and came a tiptoe into the room to find—a solid hunk; a hatchet-minded, cadaverous, acid voiced, bareboned, spavined, patriotic nasal, thick legged American. All evening she proclaimed unimpeachable truths; and discussed our sales: hers are 3 times better than mine, naturally."[30] Although Woolf creates an imaginary person few would recognize as Elinor Wylie—Wylie was proud of slim, well-shaped legs, for example—her description penetrates to the imperial American within, who wrote *The Orphan Angel*.

It became open knowledge that Wylie's third marriage was falling apart as the previous ones had, though she apparently assured Benet she would remain a friend and not formally separate. One suspects that the marriage with Benet had required too much bending and prostration of herself, even though so many friends and acquaintances saw her as the powerful one and Benet as the servant of her whims. Before their marriage, she had written to him, "You were a funny old rabbit-kitten . . . even to think I wasn't a domestic woman . . . I would scrap every bit of doggone poetry that I ever did or ever will write to make you and your children well and happy."[31] There seems to be little doubt that she saw her relationship with Benet as requiring not only maternal nurturing but self-renunciation in order to protect his masculine pride. Her fantasy of self-identification with Shelley rose in compensation from her unconscious like a powerful assertion of her own value that would not be denied.

As Wylie again set out on her own, she again seemed to be looking for some kind of male companionship that would strike the balance she had so much trouble finding. She associated England with the peaceful years with Horace Wylie, and it allowed her some relief from the poisoned atmosphere of America. Angered by gossip, she wrote to her mother, "But the damfool silly letters I get from New York! Scared, mysterious, afraid of their rotten little lives—what *are* they afraid of? . . . Swine is the only word for it. . ."[32] She even wrote an astonishing letter to Horace Wylie in May 1927, offering to return to him if he wished: [33]

A strange thing is going to happen to you, for that thing is going to come true which undoubtedly you once desired, & for which you will now not care a straw. I am going to admit to you that I wish with all my heart I had never left you . . . I love you, Horace, with an unchanged love which is far more than friendship, & which will persist until my death . . . Well, my dear, do not think I am divorcing Bill or something like that. He is the best boy imaginable . . . But I loved you first, I loved you more, I loved him afterwards, but now, that I love you both, I love you best . . . If you ever want me, I will come back openly.

But Horace Wylie had no interest in trying to revive the past.

In her drift back to the idea of a male mentor as a more suitable kind of husband after all, Elinor Wylie was falling in love with a married Englishman, Henry de Clifford Woodhouse, who possessed the qualities of quiet strength and literary discernment that reminded her of Horace. She was a frequent guest at the Woodhouse home in Henley-on-Thames and a friend of Woodhouse's wife Rebecca. He became the subject of many of her last poems, but to her disappointment refused to let their relationship develop into a love affair.

Elinor suffered a stroke while at the Woodhouse home in May

1928 and fell on the stairs, injuring her back. Recuperating in London, she had still another stroke, in October 1928, that paralyzed one side of her face. She was only forty-three. She bitterly accepted the truth that a liaison with Woodhouse was impossible, like her attempt to revive Horace's love. Exhausted and unwell, she returned to New York and Bill Benet at the end of November. On December 16, 1928, a Sunday, just after completing work on her last book of poems, *Angels and Earthly Creatures,* according to Edmund Wilson's account, she "had gone to the kitchen to get them some supper. In a moment, her husband heard her call, and went in and found her fainting. She asked for a glass of water and when he gave it to her said . . . 'Is that all it is?' He carried her to her bedroom, where she died."[34]

Lola Ridge, who had admired and felt a deep affection for her, recounted seeing an apparition of Elinor Wylie in her apartment, "beautiful and great poet . . . . She stood with crimson roses in her hands—in my high room in Thirteenth Street—three days after she died. Thank you, lovely. She stood in that chill different half light—dusk around us."[35]

*

The difficulty of thinking of their own power in other than male terms baffled not only Elinor Wylie but other prominent, successful women poets whose marriages also reflected their struggle with contradiction. Sara Teasdale, perhaps more than any other, was inwardly divided into warring halves she could not reconcile. On the one hand, she was a passionate, ambitious woman bent on achieving artistic mastery and popular success. She found her poetic voice and the release of her creative energies through youthful friendships with other women who could support and validate her chosen path. On the other hand, this major thrust of her life directly contradicted the patriarchal idea of love and marriage which she also accepted: the obligation to exchange her submissive devotion for a man's protective care.

Through the decade of her twenties, Teasdale produced a voluminous body of poetry—probably half the output of her entire life—

from the emotional tensions that pulled her in these opposite directions. As a poet, a "singer," she portrayed herself as isolated and lonely—the ostracism she felt as a woman choosing a creative professional life—yearning for a man's love that would restore her to life's mainstream. The constantly reiterated desire for love in her early poems has a certain desperation, an air of overstatement, that makes it suspect. And indeed one catches glimpses of an underlying revulsion against the very thing she appears to want so badly. The immense popularity of her youthful poetry no doubt rests on the ambivalence felt by many women toward the love that is supposed to be the center of their lives but robs them of their autonomy. Sara Teasdale therefore faced a choice of two alternatives, neither of which was satisfactory: being an "old maid," a failure as a woman (in patriarchal terms); or marrying and giving up too much of the self-determination she prized. The choice could not be held in suspense indefinitely. At thirty she made up her mind to marry.

In spite of her pose as a woman dying for love, Sara Teasdale had in reality shied away from men, and aside from a shipboard romance (at age twenty-eight) with a charming but irresponsible Englishman on her way home from Europe, she had no firsthand experience in dealing with love between men and women. Ironically, the poet who celebrated love as a transcendent force that intervened in women's lives set about in a deliberate way to secure a husband. Her realism is not surprising, considering the subversive undertone in her work and her impatience at the taboos prohibiting women from taking the lead in love.

Teasdale settled on John Hall Wheelock, a genteel love poet and male counterpart of herself with whom she enjoyed an affectionate intellectual companionship; she spent most of the fall and winter of 1913–1914 in New York trying to capture his interest. Wheelock unfortunately (and unknown to her) was deeply in love with another woman whom he was not able to marry, and became alarmed when he realized Teasdale had fixed her sights on him. The revelation came one evening after one of their long, meditative walks in Central Park, when he returned her to the Martha Washington Hotel, the very proper woman's hotel she called her "nunnery." She "took my hand," Wheelock recalled, "and then she sort of muttered under her breath, but quite clearly, 'You love me and I love you,' and then turned away quickly and went upstairs."[36] After that, he was careful to avoid any appearance of responding romantically, though she did not give up.

Teasdale's matchmaking friends Harriet Monroe and Eunice Tietjens could see that her hapless quest for Wheelock would end in failure, and decided to help by providing alternative candidates. Monroe pushed Vachel Lindsay—whom Teasdale had come to know, and who was indeed falling in love with her—envisioning a romantic union of two great poetic talents. Tietjens, however, knew that the quixotic Lindsay would make a disastrous husband, and came up with her own aspirant, a St. Louis businessman-friend named Ernst Filsinger. Unknown to Teasdale, Filsinger had taken a kind of obsessive interest in her from a distance, noting her comings and goings in the news, memorizing her poems, and building her up in his mind as the woman he would ideally like to be in love with. Eunice Tietjens arranged a meeting between them. Teasdale was favorably impressed—he reminded her somewhat of Wheelock—but Filsinger seems to have been overwhelmed at the actual prospect of getting this paragon to take him seriously as a suitor. In his own mind, he greatly exaggerated her interest in Lindsay, his rival, and fretted about his own shortcomings to the point of appearing uninterested. Sensing that he might botch it, Tietjens secretly supplied tips and encouragement.

In this feverish and rather demeaning exercise in husband-getting, Teasdale visited Monroe and Tietjens in Chicago, sitting on the floor in the office of *Poetry* as they weighed the merits of the two men. "I can't get Wheelock out of my head,"[37] Teasdale protested; so she returned to New York in a last-ditch attempt to discover whether Wheelock was, or might ever be, in love with her. To test his interest, she told him how besieged and confused she was by Lindsay and Filsinger, both of whom now wanted to marry her. To her intense chagrin, Wheelock did not react jealously, but promptly advised her to marry. With that, she tried angrily to put him out of her mind—a precious year of youth had been wasted and her pride injured in offering herself to a man who did not respond—and summoned first Lindsay and then Filsinger to New York to meet her friends and undergo, as it were, a trial of their opinion as well as of her affections.

Ernst Filsinger was the predictable winner. Teasdale could not really dismay her affluent parents by marrying a penniless bohemian poet whom they might have to support. In any case, Lindsay at the last moment became frightened at the role of bourgeois, money-making husband he was about to assume, and begged her to wait a year while he thrashed out the problem with himself and his "Franciscan-Buddhist" ideals. Teasdale knew what she really wanted: a marriage that appeared to fulfill all the patriarchal criteria while leaving her free to pursue her own growth and development as a poet.

But since love was supposed to be the dynamo propelling men and women into marriage, Teasdale could not decently accept Filsinger without prolonging the courtship for at least a month so that she could try to develop some feeling for him, and the love she celebrated so famously in her poetry could appear to be taking its course. Interestingly, it was Filsinger who appeared to believe in the love myth more than she, when reality put them to the test. Although he scarcely knew her, he was rapt with devotion, obedient to every small request, sighing sympathetically over her headaches and colds and trembling with fear that she might decide to write him off. She rather coldly told him that while she didn't love him yet, she might come to do so. Teasdale invited him to her parents' summer home in Charlevoix, Michigan that August in 1914 for them to inspect him, and for the final act in the drama she was staging, the moment when she could bring herself to say she loved him. Emotionally drained by what had become an ordeal rather than the consummation of her youthful dreams, she consented to marry him. Afterward she stood alone in the garden, thinking dismally, "Why am I marrying this stuffed shirt?"[38]

Filsinger could hardly believe his good luck. "She told me this morning it had all gone more quickly than she had any idea," he wrote gratefully to Tietjens. "I think I have really swept her off her feet."[39] To his parents, he wrote that she was a "glorious, *womanly* woman—no 'female rights' sort of person. . . . Ever since I have known her she has put the duties of true womanhood (motherhood and wifehood) above *any* art and would I believe rather be the fond mother of a child than the author of the most glorious poem in the language."[40] To Harriet Monroe, Teasdale wrote, "I can see that I am pretty likely to love him. . . . You must not blame me, oh you *must* not. . . . I am doing what seems right to me. I may be all wrong, but I can't help it."[41]

Ernst Filsinger's unconscious acceptance of the highly conventional roles they were playing must have made it doubly difficult for Sara Teasdale to negotiate her way through the complex truth that came with her own keen consciousness of what she was doing. Out of practicality, she had chosen a life of intimacy without love, because no other alternative seemed acceptable; this, after having probed the profoundly liberating idea that a woman must be free to determine the course of her own loving. Once married, she at first recoiled and felt trapped. She insisted on separate bedrooms from the start, complaining that it was impossible for her to sleep in the same room with another person. She was ill, even hospitalized twice, during much of their first year of marriage with severe bladder inflammation and pain that would have precluded sexual relations. Countless other women also married, and suffered, simply because the patriarchal social order required it, probably including Teasdale's own mother. No doubt Teasdale believed that in acquiescing she could manage a balancing act, keeping her creative life separate and untouched. This would be in harmony with her assumption that women's poetry was not in competition with men's, but supplemented it, occupying its own smaller territory. However, that idea also expressed deference toward male superiority. It was not possible to sidestep the direct impact of patriarchal power in marriage, or the depressive effect this would eventually have on her creativity.

Like many women, Sara Teasdale took on herself the responsibility of fashioning her relationship with her husband into something acceptable to them both. But Filsinger never knew where he stood in relation to her unpredictable moods, her shifting from severity to melting affection, from indifference to playful companionship. Every day, he said, was a challenge. He seems to have been afraid of her, and offered inarticulate adoration in the hope of placating her. At times his clinging devotion irritated her, as when he insisted on reading aloud to visiting friends new poems she had written, and broke into uncontrollable sobs. In the first months of marriage they even attempted joint composition of poems, some of which were published under her name, though the results were notably flat. In spite of, or perhaps because of, his distressing impulse to collapse the emotional boundaries between them, she was careful not to awaken his consciousness of her real self, for that would mean relinquishing the precariously maintained identity that marriage threatened to swallow up. Women without pride give away too much of themselves, she told her young sister-in-law.

I mean that they give too much of their *souls* away. No highly developed, thoroughly self-conscious modern woman can really give her soul and be proud of it. I used to always think that I wanted to lose myself in the man I loved. I see now that I can never do that, and that I was foolish to wish that I could. The man who wants a woman's brain, soul and body wants really only a slave. And a woman who wants to give *all* of herself, spirit and intellect and flesh, really doesn't want a lover but a master. . . . I am saying all this for myself, just to put on paper some random thoughts that have come to me as a sort of shock since my marriage.[42]

Like Elinor Wylie, Teasdale felt suffocated at times by a husband so well-meaning, so emotionally dependent on her, that friends and acquaintances would charge her with selfishness and lack of appreciation. When Filsinger was considered for a foreign trade post in Buenos Aires in their early years together, Teasdale panicked, seeing the end of either their marriage or her career. Harriet Monroe (herself unmarried), hearing her complaint, did not sympathize, but told her it was her duty to follow her husband wherever his work led. Luckily, he took a position in New York instead.

Teasdale lived in her marriage defensively. She was not prepared to challenge the nature of the patriarchal marriage relation itself, but looked instead within herself for some inadequacy that rendered her unable to meet its demands. She read avidly in works of abnormal psychology, trying to perceive her problem in sexual terms. This only worsened the conflict, since it shifted the issue away from power in the institution of marriage to a matter of personal maladjustment. Teasdale concluded that her "problem" was excessive sexual inhibition and restraint, imposed by her Victorian upbringing. In this, she accepted the self-diagnosis of the age in which she lived. The vigor of the revolution in the arts was fueled by sexual liberation, a connection she did not fail to notice with curious interest. Teasdale developed a sophisticated candor about sexuality in the context of dinner parties and talks with friends, even composing witty off-color limericks. The only one to survive, as remembered by Louis Untermeyer, is this:

> Elinor Wylie, Elinor Wylie,
> What do I hear you say?
> "I wish it were Shelley
> Astride my belly
> Instead of poor Bill Benet."[43]

Teasdale, however, did not go beyond this superficial kind of sexual liberalism. Her inner resistance was much too strong, and so she felt trapped in a deadly conflict between "Spartan and Sybarite," the puritanical and the sensual; "With my slow blood dripping wet/ They fight from sunrise to sunset."[44]

Terms that lead only to a stasis of suffering indicate that something is wrong with the diagnosis itself. The revolt against Victorian inhibition was led by men in their own interest, and may even have reduced the scope of women's liberation by stressing their sexual service to men. Male poets and artists could shake off the legal restraints of marriage and enjoy women as mistresses, providers, earth mothers, without feeling guilty or incurring responsibility. While sexual freedom on such terms eased the tension for men, it reinforced the body/mind conflict for women and made intellectual and creative activity even more anxiety-ridden. Sara Teasdale, in perceiving her own conflict in sexual terms, could only see herself as a failure, doomed to a fatal inner struggle: "Whichever it is, when the end has come,/ I shall be the defeated one."[45] She recognized the body/mind problem in her 1924 poem "The Hawk," where she is

> Driven always two ways
> By the two quarrelling shepherds
> The Flesh and the Mind . . .[46]

In effect, Teasdale recognized the need for rebellion, but did not identify the real oppressor. Even if she had been able to "liberate" her sexuality as she believed she should, it would only have been under conditions pleasing to men, an exchange of an old kind of oppression for a new. While she wrestled futilely with the question of sexuality, Teasdale was moving away from the patriarchal marriage relationship on a deep, instinctive level, in the interest of psychic self-preservation. Little by little she established financial self-sufficiency, supplementing her limited inheritance with the proceeds of her own work; financial dependence was one of the reasons she acknowledged for having to marry. According to Wheelock, she confided in him (probably in 1917, in the third year of marriage) that she was pregnant and planned to get an abortion, feeling that she could not handle both motherhood and a demanding career. Her reasons for aborting the pregnancy doubtless were more complex than that, and involved a skepticism toward the entire patriarchal marital arrangement, the "motherhood and wifehood" her husband had extolled. Then Filsinger's work began to take him abroad for long periods, as she settled into her own separate existence, not entirely unwelcome. Although she complained about his frequent absences, she stiffened at his exuberant homecomings, the knocking of hats askew with embraces and kisses, and often left immediately for a week or two of "rest" in some country inn alone. "Oh why must I lose myself to love you,/ My dear?" she wrote.[47]

At its best, their relationship became that of loyal and understanding friends. Teasdale valued her husband's moral integrity; and they had done much to help further each other's successful careers, and felt proud. Still, the underlying malaise was beyond their control, and the relationship slowly eroded away in hurt feelings, flare-ups of indignation, peevish complaints and bitter accusations centering on small things. Teasdale recorded her downhill slide into emotional paralysis obliquely in her poems through the 1920s. The massive effort to free herself seemed impossible, and she tried to resign herself stoically to self-denial, passive acceptance, the "good girl" pattern of her childhood.

In 1926 Teasdale—then forty-two—through a fan letter met a college student named Margaret Conklin, who electrified her by reflecting back the image of the vital, expansive young woman she herself had once been. Teasdale virtually adopted Conklin as a daughter, and the alliance began to foster a confidence that she could recover the sense of will and personhood she had lost in marriage. In 1928 Teasdale developed a plan for extricating herself, privately consulting a lawyer about a divorce and sounding out Filsinger for his probable reaction. Realizing that he would oppose the idea vehemently, she waited until spring 1929 when he sailed on a business trip to England and South Africa that would keep him abroad for at least six months. At the end of May she traveled to Reno with a female companion (a nurse whom Margaret Conklin knew), covering her movements with such elaborate secrecy that none of her friends, except Wheelock, realized she had gone. No doubt she recalled painfully the notoriety surrounding Elinor Wylie's divorces. From Reno in June she wrote to Filsinger at Johannesburg, demanding his consent to the divorce and flatly refusing to negotiate a reconciliation. "You will realize that complete freedom for both of us is the happiest, in fact is the only solution of our lives," she wrote. "I beg you to spare me emotional letters or cables. . . . Let us take life as it is, and act like the disciplined and mature people we are."[48] She did not wish alimony, but preferred to live on her own earnings.

Stunned, Filsinger reacted wildly, as she expected; but, always willing to do what she wanted, he soon acquiesced meekly and followed instructions. After obtaining the decree early in September, she returned to New York filled with mingled remorse, shame, and hope that she might begin life again as a free woman. Teasdale's friends, offended at being excluded from her action, tended to sympathize with her wounded husband, feeling that she had been selfish and unfair. Virtually no one saw it as a desperate and courageous act of freeing herself from the patriarchal trap. It is probably not coincidental that she had begun to read and admire Virginia Woolf at this time, and that she seemed to be consciously reaching out to Margaret Conklin in order to heal her damaged sense of identity.

*

Both Teasdale and Wylie had married sensitive, appreciative men who respected their talents and were willing to honor a high degree of independence. The fact that even such marriages failed indicates that the basic patriarchal pattern had only been liberalized, not eliminated; that the emotional dependence of a "nice" husband could be only another mask of male domination.

The wives of male writers have had a much harder time of it than these husbands of female ones, though until recently they have received less sympathy, sacrifice for male genius being considered fitting. Scott Fitzgerald's ruthless exploitation of his wife's literary talent and experience to support his own success is now well known, and it cost Zelda her own possible career. Vachel Lindsay married Elizabeth Conner, a young school teacher, in 1926, and nearly destroyed her with his alternations of violent love and hate, culminating in paranoid hallucinations that she and her father were trying to poison him, until his suicide—by taking poison—in 1931. Elizabeth Conner Lindsay not only faithfully stood by him, but concealed his mental deterioration from friends and the public in order to protect his reputation. Intellectually, she was her husband's equal, if not superior: knowledgeable, more adventurous, and without his narrow moralism in exploring contemporary writers like Proust and Woolf.

Floyd Dell, a bohemian and feminist who extolled women's achievements, was typical of the liberated males of his generation, who saw no contradiction between their advocacy of women's freedom and their continued patriarchal attitudes. The different roads traveled by talented women and men are vividly illustrated by Dell and his first wife, Margery Currey. Their avant-garde open marriage in Chicago seems to have been chiefly beneficial for Dell, and turned out to be, in actuality, a transitional phase toward complete separation. Dell went on to New York, publishing voluminously and building a name for himself.

Although Margery Currey hoped for a career in journalism or promotional writing, she was continually pulled by financial necessity into low-paid work demanding service and selflessness, and lacked both the driving self-interest and the opportunities that led men to success. She felt keenly the death of a young painter, Martha Baker, in 1912, of peritonitis just before an appendectomy could be performed; the waste of a woman's talent haunted her, one imagines, like a premonition of her own life. She enjoyed a brief burst of exhilaration working for the suffragist cause and the short-lived Progressive Party. In contrast to Floyd Dell's, her life was a wandering around the country in search of a possible place, a work, in which she could fulfill the dreams and yearnings for a valuable use of herself. For a while she taught in a one-room school in Napa, California, living on a chicken ranch with a woman friend. Still hoping to write, to work in some meaningful way, she signed over her interest in the ranch and went to her two sisters in Vancouver, British Columbia for a period of reassessment. Then she landed a job as advertising and publicity director for a building company in Seattle: "It is a dandy," she wrote Eunice Tietjens, "but no one thinks of salaries, especially for women, in terms of the cost of living. I am supposed to have one of the finest jobs of its kind in the West—and it does not pay enough to keep me going properly." Her boss liked her, they had splendid rapport, the "the only thing the dear will *not* do is pay real money to a woman."[49] She begged friends to help her find a job in Chicago writing publicity, and pressed the Chicago Art Institute with the then-novel idea of a publicity director; they liked the proposal, but hired a man. She managed to return to Chicago to work for the American Art Bureau writing pamphlets "For the Promotion of Art in the Home," a suitably domestic focus for a woman. Floyd Dell, even as a rebel and iconoclast, acted in the theater of power. Margery Currey drifted in the powerless society of women, where social idealism did not mean making a name for oneself, but humbly serving the needs of others.

Dell found in Edna St. Vincent Millay, in her Greenwich Village period just after the First World War, a woman who seemed to support the kind of sexual emancipation he believed in. The bohemian attack on the bourgeoisie centered on the institution of marriage, which men believed deprived them of the freedom essential to their creativity. Dell, like Edmund Wilson and other men who fell in love with Millay, assumed that what she needed was to dissociate herself from her youthful attachments to other women and develop "mature" relationships with men. The heterosexual standard as the ultimate test of maturity, reinforced by the wave of popular interest in the theories of Freud and other psychologists, not only upheld patriarchal assumptions about women but served to cut them off from the possibility of finding confirmation of themselves through other women. Loosened standards of sexual morality, which permitted divorce, sleeping around, or living together without marrying, did not much change the basically patriarchal structure of male/female relationships and were far more advantageous to men then to women. Floyd Dell, in any case, was putting himself through psychoanalysis and was growing more and more interested in finding a successful long-term relationship along conventional lines. Millay apparently sensed a trap, and declined to marry him.

However, Floyd Dell turned out to be the link connecting Millay with the man she did marry: Eugen Boissevain. At the time of his love affair with Millay, Dell was rooming with Max Eastman, editor of *The Masses* and active in the Provincetown Players, a group with which Millay was also associated. Boissevain, a friend of Eastman's, was thus drawn into the circle of friends that included Millay. Boissevain, who was running an importing business in New York, came from a family of Dutch-East Indian merchants. He had been married to the feminist-activist Inez Mulholland; she had died suddenly from pernicious anemia in 1916. Twelve years older than

Millay, he was a large, athletic, comfortably pagan man, who had been through analysis with Jung and who had what many of those who knew him called a "feminine" side. Edmund Wilson observed that this urge to nurture expressed itself in "assisting the careers of gifted women."[50] Like Wylie and Teasdale, Millay responded to a man who appeared to respect her autonomy and was not resentful of her achievements, who indeed willingly submerged his interests in hers.

They married in 1923, and Boissevain quickly took charge, cutting off friends and acquaintances who sapped her concentration and energy. The bohemian days were over. They purchased a run-down berry farm, which they called Steepletop, at Austerlitz, New York, in the Berkshires, and there they withdrew for a life devoted to Millay's work, under Boissevain's watchful supervision. While there has been a tendency to emphasize the very real harmony and deep affection between them, and to dwell on how much Boissevain did for her, their relationship, as it recedes in time, seems to take on something of the character of an ambitious stage mother and her daughter. Boissevain gradually assumed management of virtually every aspect of her life in order to free her to write, traveling with her on her reading tours, negotiating publication of poems, answering her mail, fending off admirers and intruders (he once threw out Millay's own sister Norma to put a stop to the sisters' frequent quarrels), even doing the cooking and housekeeping when hired help wasn't available and handling the entire management of the farm. Millay could rise and retire as she pleased, could eat or drink or smoke, or play the piano, could live in isolated concentration on her emotions and the generation of poems. When she grew restless and slipped away alone to New York for a rumored fling with other lovers, Boissevain allowed her the freedom of a long tether, knowing she would return to dependence and the control he exerted over her through his devoted service.

The paradox of the quest for freedom that ends in captivity is even more pronounced in Edna St. Vincent Millay than in Sara Teasdale or Elinor Wylie. Recently Millay's critics have begun to discover the hidden tensions in her work. Jane Stanbrogh writes that the "image of liberation and self-assurance," of Millay's bold, unconventional, promiscuous behavior, "is the public image Millay deliberately cultivated, the self-projection that stole the show, demanded applause or attention, suited a loud and raucous jazz-age temper. For half a century she has captivated readers and critics and minimized or veiled entirely a private anxiety-ridden image of profound self-doubt and personal anguish with which Millay contended all her life."[51] The deeper theme of her poetry, Stanbrogh holds, is feminine vulnerability rather than boldness, "submission and constriction" rather than carefree abandon.

Edmund Wilson adopted the fashionable mode of explaining Millay's troubled psyche by attributing it to childhood experience, for which women were to blame. He believed that Millay was driven by a desire to escape from a claustrophobia associated with her girlhood, where she lived in isolation with her sisters, wrapped in their studies of music and poetry, while their mother was away for weeks at a time on a nursing case. But at the same time, she learned to require such isolation and solitude for her creativity. The result, Wilson thought, was an irresolvable tension. "She was always . . . extremely shy of meeting people," he wrote; "and she was terrified of New York, of which I do not think she saw much, for she would not cross a street alone."[52] While Wilson associated Millay's "claustrophobia" with the society of women—he admittedly viewed her family with some distaste, feeling excluded—implying that relationships with men and the urban environment held out a promise of freedom she couldn't bring herself to accept, the truth may be exactly the opposite. Millay's "submission and constriction" may rather be her reaction to men, to the threat of losing the freedom she enjoyed in the company of her all-female family. To love men was to open herself, as Teasdale also found, to losing herself, to the treachery of the emotions that rendered painful both union and the subsequent necessary separation.

Eugen Boissevain seems to have been unique in sensing that the only man who could hold Millay would be one who identified himself with the nurturing roles of her mother and sisters, allowing her complete freedom from conventional domesticity. The evidence indicates, however, that their relationship provided only the illusion of freedom—freedom to be the person Boissevain conceived her to be—and may have severely inhibited her mature growth. Millay suffered spells of prolonged depression, telling Edmund Wilson once "not long after her marriage, when she had apparently spent weeks in bed, that she had done nothing but weep all the time." On another occasion—after five years of marriage—she had burst out, "I'm *not* a pathetic character!"[53] The drama of her personality that always involved those around her in intoxicating excitement seemed turned in on herself, without the interaction she had always thrived on. At times she drank too much; in 1944, at the age of fifty-two, she was hospitalized in New York for a nervous breakdown. It was commonly observed by those who had known her over the years that she did not age the way most people do, but seemed to wither while remaining undeveloped, like an apple drying.

Edmund Wilson, after visiting Millay and Boissevain in 1948 after an absence of many years, left a chilling account of what their relationship had come to:[54]

"I'll go and get my child," [Eugen] said. I did not realize at first that this meant Edna. . . . She was terribly nervous; her hands shook; there was a look of fright in her bright green eyes. Eugen brought us martinis. Very quietly, he watched her and managed her. At moments he would baby her in a way I had not seen him use before but that had evidently become habitual, when she showed signs of bursting into tears over not being able to find a poem or something of the kind. My wife said afterwards that Gene gave the impression of shaking me at her as if I had been a new toy with which he hoped to divert her.

Millay's "profound self-doubt and personal anguish" are feelings common to women struggling to assert themselves. Wilson describes a woman shorn of power and self-confidence, virtually reduced to infanthood. Eugen Boissevain's life mission, "assisting the careers of gifted women," apparently did not include supporting their own power, but rather appropriating it to himself as one who knew better. He seems not to have thought of her dependence as unhealthy for her. Millay could not rebel against someone playing the role of her mother, protecting her gift, who lovingly gave her exactly what she believed she wanted. Ironically, the one thing in men she feared—the tendency to control women's lives to satisfy their own needs—was what, in the guise of protection, she received. Although much younger, she survived his death by only one year.

It would be a mistake, however, to assume that Millay really wanted a perpetual childhood, or that she and Teasdale and Wylie deliberately chose suffering. If they made an error, it was in their respect for men's power, in accepting the belief that their own empowerment was inseparable from it. In the end all three were broken by that misjudgment, and were forced to settle for less than they had aimed for, leaving them with "Broken words left half unsaid." Teasdale tried to make the most of her losses:

> Broken things, broken things,
>   How quietly they comfort me,
> Riven cliffs, where I can watch
>   The broken beauty of the sea.[55]

This was not the case with the male poets who were their contemporaries. The modernist masters Joyce, Pound, and Eliot did not hesitate to use women as the supportive base for their own creative power, and owe an unacknowledged degree of their success to women, just as the women poets, conversely, lost to men something of the stature they might have had. When H.D. evaded too deep an involvement with Pound, and chose to spend much of her life with a woman companion, she knew that her survival as an artist was at stake: "Ezra would have destroyed me and the center they call 'Air and Crystal' of my poetry."[56]

*

Women afflicted with "profound self-doubt and personal anguish" could not avoid the impact of the new psychological sciences, which classified their condition as an illness and promised relief through treatment. Sara Teasdale's avid reading in search of self-understanding only led her further into self-destructive thoughts. Edna St. Vincent Millay sensed the danger, and resisted Floyd Dell's advice to get herself analyzed. She viewed Freud's ideas, Dell said, as "a Teutonic attempt to lock women up in the home and restrict them to cooking and baby-tending."[57] H.D. had gone to the source, Freud himself, for sessions of analysis in 1933 and 1934, to find out why she felt drifting and purposeless, a chronic condition that she had already explored with Havelock Ellis and Hanns Sachs. The title of her memoir, *Tribute to Freud,* suggests both the conscientiousness of her effort to idolize him and the subdued ironies that threaten continually to surface.

Freud's method demanded that he play the role of an absolutely authoritative parent, and it is painful to read H.D.'s meek, fearful concern at displeasing him, "of impinging, disturbing his detachment, draining his vitality,"[58] of failing to find the right kind of gift for his birthday. There is a touch of megalomania in Freud's obsession with the historic importance of his work, his readiness to make a torchbearer out of her. Although he considered her mystical, religious tendencies unhealthy, he appears not to have minded her canonizing him. When transference did not seem to be occurring, Freud angrily pounded the headpiece of the couch, bursting out, "The trouble is—I am an old man—*you do not think it worth while to love me.*" H.D. felt "exactly . . . as if the Supreme Being had hammered with his fist on the back of the couch where I had been lying."[59] His cigar smoke was sacred incense, he was the possesser of sacred objects; she was awed and submissive at his most ordinary gestures, which she invested with profound significance. After all, he was "the greatest mind of this and perhaps many succeeding generations."[60] When she began to feel like a caged bird, she blamed herself: "It was I myself, by my own subconscious volition," who trapped her. From Freud she picked up the idea of the unconscious censor always on duty, playing games, ready to trick her, so that she was continually troubled by an insidious doubt as to what might really lie behind her actions or thoughts, for like God he knew her in ways she could not know herself. The more time she spent with him, the more powerful his image grew, the more weak and insignificant she became in her own eyes.

Freud's opposition to the idea of female power is revealed in his interpretation of a vision H.D. had in 1920, which she described to him. She had been with Bryher on the Greek island of Corfu; to her astonishment prophetic images began to form and shift on a blank bedroom wall. Bryher joined her to encourage her in the intense concentration needed to keep the vision flowing. It culminated in the figure of the goddess Nike, symbolizing victory. Freud did not see this vision as a woman artist's desire for empowerment, as something significantly shared by two women: he told her, instead, that it was "a dangerous symptom."[61] "The Professor had said in the very beginning that I had come to Vienna hoping to find my mother [now dead]";[62] the vision proved to him her "desire for union with my mother."[63] The implication that the need for a shared identity between mother and daughter is a "complex," an evidence of sickness and immaturity, and the vision a disturbing hallucination, strikes at the heart of female power.

By the 1930s the psychiatric profession was well established in the United States, and other women poets—like Louise Bogan, Babette Deutsch, and Marjorie Seiffert—sought medical help from male physicians for overwhelming depression. Bogan twice hospitalized herself for psychiatric treatment, once undergoing electric shock treatments, as H.D. later did, when her conflicts, essentially over gender, incapacitated her. Deutsch in her sixties also elected to have a series of electric shock treatments to dispel profound depression. Marjorie Seiffert's life followed much the same pattern as others: youthful ebullience, an expanding sense of power and hope, gradually declining into feelings of nothingness and immobility. At forty-seven, after several years of being "threatened by demons but demons too impalpable to materialize before the analytical eye,"[64] Seiffert underwent psychoanalysis with a professor at the University of Iowa.

Like many of the women poets of her generation, Seiffert perceived her creative work as arising from the dislocation of herself, from the incongruity of being a woman aspiring to the status of artist and finding no way to integrate that powerful possibility into her life. She had been trained in music at Smith College. One day when she performed some songs, her own compositions, for her friend Arthur Davison Ficke, the poet-lawyer of Davenport, Iowa, Ficke suggested that she channel her talent into writing poetry, since she had given up a career as a concert pianist and composer for marriage and children. That decision opened up realms of hope, floods of excitement and energy: "I am a huge EGO, a capital I," she wrote Harriet Monroe, "a howling dervish whirling about the axis of my own being."[65] Marjorie Seiffert had a streak of audacity, ironic self-awareness, and honest realism that gave her work a refreshing bite, when she allowed it to play. "I think any adventuring which risks something and costs something is the way to achieve the pang necessary to write,"[66] she wrote to Ficke. She conceived risk, in its happiest sense, in terms of the socially defiant behavior of the jazz-age generation—mocking the complacent morality of the middle class, drinking and partying all night, posing as worldly-wise, saying shocking things such as "It must be Hell to be a Practicing Christian!"[67] She admired Edna St. Vincent Millay, partly, it seems, for her "bad girl" image and for the insubordinate idea that women could claim the same freedom as men to spend their energy in a violent rush.

Marjorie Seiffert divided herself between serious poetry and lighter verse that cast a mordant eye on marriage and the women of her class; "Mrs. X," "Too well fed for rebellion,/ Too lazy for self-respect, too timid for murder," but living happily ever after; "Mrs. Andsoforth," in her forties, "frenzied, helpless . . . a fly, drowning in a cocktail."[68] She felt most free-spirited when doing this kind of work under pseudonyms. When she was exposed as a participant in the Spectra hoax, she wrote fellow-conspirator Witter Bynner, "What am I to do with all my riotous fancies now—such as are not all that a young girl should fance."[69] Seiffert's early serious poetry, however, tended to be quite conventional, centering on the themes of love-yearning, separation, and beauty common to women's magazine verse. Only occasionally did she apply her subversive insights to women's problems on a deeper level, like "Maura," with its haunting depiction of self-loss in love and marriage. "The

Old Woman (A Morality Play)," while mockingly satirical, is too grim for light verse, and shows how her talent could edge into black humor. An old woman is unceremoniously dragged from her bed, apparently not yet dead (no one cares), by a doctor and a deacon, and bundled "Out in the lot/ Where ash-cans die." A young woman comes to rent the same room, and everyone is satisfied, for the ritual tragedy will eventually repeat itself—"Same old lady/ With a pretty new face."[70] The horror underlying Seiffert's busy, affluent life was the threat of losing her personhood; for while her honesty allowed her to see through the sham, it also revealed a depth of emptiness and her need of creative expression to fill her with a sense of having an existence.

The title of Seiffert's first volume of poems, *A Woman of Thirty*, was borrowed from Balzac's novel, *La Femme de Trente Ans*, with its implication of lost innocence and worldly knowledge of the truth about marriage. Her father paid for printing the book, though "I didn't want him to,"[71] after a skirmish over the impropriety of some of her attitudes. Like Amy Lowell, Seiffert realized that money could help ease the way into the literary world. Penniless artists and little-magazine editors were flies to her honeypot, although she seems to have been too wary to give much, for it was a matter of self-respect to be recognized on her own merits. She did contribute at various times to funds to help Emanuel Carnevali and Lola Ridge, to Harriet Monroe's *Poetry*, and occasionally other ventures. But she spent money freely only for dinner parties and having a good time with literary people in Chicago and New York. Of the late teens and early twenties, she said,[72]

It was a wonderful time to write—the "new verse" was a challenge and many an evening in New York I would collect a group for dinner at my 3d. rate hotel and afterward take them up to my room where we would sit on the floor and read our poems to each other, and everyone was a keen but loving critic, and we would argue, praise, criticize and come away from it excited, refreshed, envious, pitying, loving and dedicated to the success of each other.

I was not the only party giver, but perhaps the most popular as I could afford a couple of quarts of whiskey.

Seiffert gathered whoever was available—sometimes Bill Benet and Elinor Wylie, William Carlos Williams, Lola Ridge, Alfred Kreymborg. Williams referred to Seiffert's New York trips as "a sabbatical two weeks from her husband and children."[73]

The literary world was never a way of life for Marjorie Seiffert, but a temporary escape from domesticity, to save her from the lurking threat of extinction: "Somehow through thick and thin, children, housekeeping, husband and all," she wrote Harriet Monroe in 1925, "I do keep going, don't I, though not making much headway. Anyway not dumb and buried yet."[74] If she dreamed of leaving her family for a life wholly her own, she suppressed the idea as impossible. The conflict is dramatized in an unpublished short story she wrote, probably in the 1920s, titled "Rebellion." The central character, a farmer named Joe Haynes, is under the managerial thumb of his wife Annie, who, in her tart, commanding way, works him ceaselessly "like a slave." He feels that his manhood has been defeated and yearns to escape Annie's control. One day while splitting rails he encounters a woman idling through the countryside in a covered wagon like a gypsy, with her pet mastiff Tolstoi. Olive, dark-haired in contrast to the blonde Annie, is a free spirit who takes jobs only sporadically for enough money to survive, and spends the rest of her time roaming, camping, and selling books to farmers. She foreshadows the self-liberated generation of the 1960s. Joe Haynes is powerfully attracted to her, and after long hours of talk into the evening, is so infused with her philosophy that he begs her to let him join her when she moves on the next morning. Olive agrees, but only on condition that he face Annie and have it out with her. Joe returns late to the house to find that Annie has retired, but has left a plate of homemade bread and jam for him, a gesture revealing her complacent assurance that he will always return. He spends the night lying outdoors on the grass in wakeful anguish, trying to master his fear of facing Annie with his rebellion. At dawn Olive's wagon passes by; she never looks his way but keeps her eyes serenely in the rising sun. Joe is left behind, a failure, deeper in his misery than ever.[75]

If Olive is Seiffert's stifled feminine ideal, a more developed version of Maura, a Maura who has not only heard the "silver horn" but has awakened from sleep to follow it, then Joe and Annie are the reality, the two personalities at odds within herself. Like Wylie and most of the women poets of her generation, Seiffert conceived of her creative life in terms of gender conflict: the role of the creator is male, but it is kept in slavery, as Joe Haynes is, by the grip of domesticity. Joe's defeat is Seiffert's expression of hopelessness that she herself can ever escape by uniting herself with the liberated woman of her imagination.

Marjorie Seiffert claimed to outsiders that her marriage was happy enough, and was careful never to criticize her husband to her literary friends; he was "on the whole as satisfactory as any husband could be, in a world obviously not designed for marriage or monogamy, and for a poet, who in all certainty belongs to one of the groups for whom marriage should be legally prohibited."[76] Nevertheless, her feeling of an impending crack-up intensified through the 1920s. "I've been on the verge of a nervous breakdown," she told Harriet Monroe in 1926, "but have managed to pull back into quite good health again. Life gets so damned hopeless and dumb."[77] Although she tried consciously to accept without regret the devouring demands of family and social life, she felt "as though I were sitting on the ultimate edge of nothingness, with nowhere to jump to. . . . I do not understand my state of mind, my misery and tension. . . . I do not know whether I need to make friends or shun human beings. If I let go I will surely have a nervous breakdown, and if I hang on I will probably crack."[78] At 3:30 A.M. on December 17, 1929, one of many insomniac nights, she wrote "The Mouse," a baleful self-portrait:[79]

> This is the nest
>   Of a stupid mouse,
> Upon this shelf
>   She made her house . . .
>
> The Powers found her,
>   Now they start

To tear her flimsy
   Nest apart.

Hurrah, hurrah,
   What splendid fun!
Hear her squeak,
   See her run!

"I have no courage,
   I have no breath,
Strike me down,
   Beat me to death!

"I only lived
   From day to day,
I always feared
   It would end this way.

"How can I struggle?
   I was not made
For combat. I
   Was born afraid.

"I send my squeak
   In bleak despair
To Higher Justice . . .
   Is anyone there?"

At almost the same time she wrote "The Mouse," Seiffert touched on the buried dream of female power that she felt all women knew in their secret thoughts. Almost her favorite poetic subject, she wrote Ficke,[80] was Queen Hatshepsut, a figure who appealed to every woman who went about her

large important affairs (it just might as well be housecleaning, or running a subcommittee on the women's club), having her daughter with her, and a nice romantic experience to dream about who doesn't want any buttons sewn on his B.V.D.'s, dismissing her legal lord with a snap of the fingers, bustling about beautifully in Egypt, sending expeditions to Punt and ending up with a regular Freudian, phallic-symbol-filled daydream which simply whangs the bull's eye with a resounding clang in all ladies' most unsuspecting souls!!!!! And being the great handsome He-woman most of us want to be in our heart of hearts.

"The Mouse" suggests, however, that Seiffert feared the destruction of her family life as much as she feared that the family might extinguish her. By 1930 she felt frozen, and had virtually stopped writing poetry: "My life has become so purely domestic that I wonder whether I will know how to behave when, and if, I emerge into a different world again."[81] In February 1932 she began psychoanalytic sessions twice a week with the University of Iowa professor to "find out whether he can do anything to restore my damaged ego . . . or whatever it is that needs restoration . . . so that I can write again."[82] After six sessions she felt like "a new woman. I am gay, nay, merry as a cricket, I enjoy sex, I digest my food and I hope to live as long as the Lord will let me! . . . . Everything is Different!"[83]

The euphoria began to fade, however, when she realized that though she felt "really quite made over, . . . it rather smashes the poetry side of it." The psychiatrist had convinced her that "all I have ever written about was poor, POOR me, and I cannot seem to be much perturbed about the poor, dear, handsome, complicated crazy world."[84] Her psychiatrist added the weight of medical authority to the male literary critics' perennial complaint that women write from personal emotion rather than objectifying. More insidiously, Marjorie Seiffert's legitimate, honest attempt to explore the sources of her psychic misery through her art was dismissed as self-pity, perhaps because it questioned the patriarchal marital arrangement to which the psychiatrist was trying to make her adjust. Her poems had been a statement of refusal to be swallowed up, her one claim to an identity that would otherwise be submerged in others, "my particular method of keeping a hold on sanity and reality."[85] After psychoanalysis she found it harder than ever to write, and grew touchy and sensitive to criticism. To her old friend Witter Bynner, she complained,

I've been psyched, and am no better than before. I know why I am so funny, but I am still just as funny, only sort of danker and sadder. I have not written a line since the last complex was dug up by the roots, and I DO give a damn, (as I shouldn't), because it was a grand compensation for being a silly ass at heart, and now I feel as though all my vital organs had been removed and a lot of wet sponges substituted. It was sort of exciting while it lasted, but now the last big raisin in the pie turns out to be a dead cockroach and I've lost my appetite.[86]

By 1934 she complained, "I am not writing at all, . . . and am in a very low state of mind . . . complete depression and all that . . . sometimes I wonder what I am *for*. Perhaps only a housekeeper, but it does not suffice . . . I feel as though I had been lying in a garbage can for a long, long time, and the collector had simply forgotten to dispose of me."[87]

When Seiffert managed to write poetry again in 1935, she said, "I feel in touch with my world again. . . . I would love to wrap myself in layers and layers of poetry . . . but everything seems so simple and practical."[88] The days of exciting literary dinner parties and sitting on the floor discussing each other's work were long gone. She loved action; an escapade in Chicago in 1929 exhilarated her, though it terrified her family: she and George Dillon, after leaving a late evening party, were stopped by a gunman, but sped away as the man shot a bullet through their car. "Just to see a poet would do me good," she told Harriet Monroe, "if he were a poet with pep, not like a wet baby, needing all sorts of attention and howling bitterly."[89]

By 1937 Seiffert had gathered enough new work for another volume. But the climate had changed radically since the 1920s, when she had published three books in ten years and women poets enjoyed a vogue. John Hall Wheelock, her editor at Scribner's, remarked that the public's interest in poetry had fallen off, sales were down, reviews were shorter and harder to come by. "I feel fairly desperate," Seiffert wrote him, "and very much at sea, and yet I feel if I am ever to amount to anything as a person, not just the maternal head of a family, I must state my case by getting a book out." The negative effects of psychoanalysis, which had taught her that her writing was only a compensation for her inadequacy as a woman, still lingered as she went on to apologize, "Maybe this is just a feminine need for admiration or support, but there it is . . . despite general belief to the contrary, I was never anything but weakly feminine at base. The hard-boiled aspect is merely a very thin armor of defense."[90] And again later, "If I hadn't been psyched, I would probably have a ream or two of tragic stanzas for you."[91] Scribner's eventually published her last volume, *The Name of Life,* in 1938. The title poem defines life as a "wild, wounded flight,"

> For flight is the name of life,
> And we have tasted death
> Like the deer before the hunter's knife
> Is plunged in the heart of it.[92]

Even as the book went to press, she wrote Wheelock, "You'd never be able to believe I ever wrote poetry, either to see me or to examine the contents of my brain. It's as though I had decided ten years ago to be a hausfrau, and poetry has been fighting a losing battle ever since. By now there's hardly a sniper left on the poetry side."[93] Ironically, after years of holding her marriage together as a matter of principle, and at the cost of creative freedom, she felt it had "broken up for good in every respect that matters. However at my age [fifty-five in 1940] a divorce is silly and rather undignified and not too convenient. I shall try not to grow old preserved in vinegar of my own discouragement. Even a lively interest in religion doesn't help much."[94] Marjorie Seiffert's relationship with her husband, so carefully concealed under protective silence, may be better understood when additional letters and papers come to light. One does not know, for example, how much of her personal trouble she shared with her "most beloved friend" Grace Evans, a sculptor and writer who lived in Woodstock, New York and had friends among New York literary people, including Elinor Wylie. "I adore Grace more than most people alive,"[95] Seiffert said.

There was an element of defiance, perhaps, in Seiffert's marrying a man her parents did not entirely approve of. She might have been attracted to his stylishness, even his air of dominance. A Harvard graduate, Otto Seiffert was very successful in business, was an impeccable dresser who wore handmade silk underwear and handmade shoes, and sometimes revealed a harsh authoritarian side. He had little appreciation of his wife's efforts as a poet, and apparently was annoyed by her literary friends when they intruded on his homelife. He detested Harriet Monroe (the feeling seems to have been mutual). He was known to lapse into spells of riotous indulgence, and it was rumored in the family that he kept a mistress in Chicago. Marjorie Seiffert understandably tried to build a separate compartment for her creative work.

After the publication of *The Name of Life,* Seiffert lived on for thirty-two years, dying in San Clemente, California in 1970 at the age of eighty-five. Although she once said that "it gives me a feeling of existence just to put myself on paper,"[96] she made no further effort to write poetry, but turned to painting, carrying her artist's materials on her travels as far afield as Easter Island and Indonesia, filling her house, even the bathroom walls, with her canvases, which, according to her artist-granddaughter, showed considerably less talent than her poetry. She continued to glitter at cocktail parties and social events, where she was in demand as a palm reader, for she had a gift of psychic insight that was sometimes startling. The young woman who had mocked Christianity became, in the end, a devout and very conservative Episcopalian. At seventy-three, she wrote to Witter Bynner, refusing his request to help resurrect the Spectra hoax as a matter of historical interest; she preferred the past to remain interred. "I suppose . . . I have . . . acted like an old crabby, tight-laced Republican bitch," she said, "all of which I admit except the tight-laced."[97]

FIVE
Poets as
Mothers

* **B** *
EARING CHILDREN, as the supreme patriarchal
definition of what it means to be a woman, is inherently
full of subtle but wrenching conflict for creative women.
Motherhood, for the women poets of 1915–1945, was virtually com-
pulsory, in that a childless woman was made to feel essentially a
failure, "unfulfilled," incomplete, no matter what else she might
accomplish. Furthermore, her creative power was held to be either
a substitute for motherhood or opposed to it, so that she was forced
to confront a painful choice of priorities. This pervasive assumption
is revealed glaringly in Ernst Filsinger's praise of Sara Teasdale:
"She has put the duties of true womanhood (motherhood and wifehood) above any art, and would I believe rather be the fond mother
of a child than the author of the most glorious poem in the language."

The majority of woman poets who rose to prominence between
the World Wars did not, however, have children, indicating the
choice of an artistic identity as opposed to the threat of anonymity

that motherhood represented. And those who did have children tended to be stricken with ambivalence and conflict, or highly unconventional, in their resistance to the patriarchal precept. Children posed a greater hindrance to a woman's initiative and independence than did a husband. It was easier to work out an accommodation with a husband for a career, or even to divorce him. Children were inescapably entwined with one's own identity, one's guilt and aspirations, and often were plainly in the way. Being a good poet always raised the specter of necessarily being a "bad" mother.

Only recently have women begun to question publicly the patriarchal assumption that their chief natural function is to nurture children and husbands, or that they have an innately greater capacity for nurturance than men. Nurturance, supposed to be natural to women, is in reality often an exhausting, even frightening, burden. Adrienne Rich confesses in *Of Woman Born* that the role of madonna is suffocating, that women may unavoidably feel anger and indifference toward their own children. The full humanness of women's lives could not be explored by the poets of the 1920s because of the straitjacketing pieties that defined motherhood.

Elinor Wylie's life reveals the compulsive behavior and anguish that resulted from trying to fulfill the "duties of true womanhood"—to bear children, to nurture a husband. Her passionate self-identification with Shelley, however, suggests a deeper level of authenticity, beyond the role of mother and even opposed to it. She talked too much about her many unsuccessful pregnancies, startling people whom she hardly knew with intimate confessions, often exaggerating. She told Eunice Tietjens she had been pregnant eight times. The melodrama with which she presented herself as a tragically denied mother was well known and wearisome in the circle of her friends and acquaintances and contributed to the characterization of her as "hysterical." William Rose Benét's mother and sister did not believe that her interest in mothering his children was sincere, in spite of effusive demonstrations of concern and affection, and they engaged in a family tug-of-war to keep the children from her.

Witnesses to Wylie's obsessive clamor for motherhood might have wondered what had happened to the only surviving child she actually did have, Philip, born in 1907, the son of her first husband. She had been publicly excoriated for having abandoned him in order to elope to England with Horace Wylie. Although she at first expressed grief at being separated from Philip, she soon adopted a policy of silence that she adhered to the rest of her life, resolutely shutting the door on his existence, as if she had divorced herself from the son along with the mad father. It is possible that this was the only way she could steel herself to cope with the guilt she incurred in giving him up in exchange for her own survival and the development of her intellectual and creative gifts. The most intense force of social condemnation bore down on that point: Elinor Wylie was a brilliant poet at the cost of being a wicked mother. It is no wonder that she tried pathetically to show everyone how profoundly maternal she was, even as she buried the existence of her one living child and built fantasies of a male life free of marriage and motherhood.

At her funeral, Elinor Wylie's friends observed a stranger, a shy and awkward young man who had come to look at the famously beautiful face of his mother in death. Philip Hichborn was twenty-one. Eight years later, in 1936, he, like his father, committed suicide.

*

Sara Teasdale, more wary and self-protective than Wylie, was nevertheless caught in the same trap. Teasdale consciously accepted the conventional veneration of motherhood and sometimes expressed her belief that mothering, rather than loving a man or a woman, was the culmination of a woman's emotional life. Like Wylie, she liked to envision her husband as a boy, even though his boyish emotionalism distressed her. When invited in 1914 to contribute to a suffrage edition of the St. Louis *Times,* she produced a rather inappropriate poem entitled "The Old Maid" about a woman who, after death, is found to have kept in a locked drawer a scrapbook filled with pictures of children, inscribed "The children that might have come to me"[1]—the theme that a woman's life is pathetically unfulfilled without children of her own. Teasdale published a pair of poems on the mothers of Jesus and the poet John Hall Wheelock, suggesting that she was fascinated with the idea of the mothering of male, rather than female, genius as the fitting role for a woman.

Steeped as she was in the patriarchal mystique of motherhood, Teasdale, like Wylie, was unprepared for the collision between motherhood and her career that occurred when she became pregnant. John Hall Wheelock, the only direct source of information about this episode, said that she felt forced to choose between her poetry and having a child, that she believed she didn't have the strength or the capacity for both. Indirect evidence points to August 1917 as the time she had an abortion, crying out, "The wrong is done/ . . . The evil stands,"[2] and suffering a violent physical and emotional recoil from which she never recovered. Like Wylie, she carried a secret burden of intolerable guilt for having placed her creative power as an artist above the sacredness of maternity, an act that for a woman was equivalent to Prometheus' theft of fire from the gods.

*

Another way of responding to the conflict between the self-sacrifice expected of mothering and the self-concentration of writing poetry was to draw the child into a sharing of creativity, so that a daughter or a son became an extension of one's aspirations rather than a receptacle of one's guilt (though it is not easy to separate one from the other). It was a mixed blessing to be an offspring of artist-parents, for that usually meant being precociously implicated in the issues of their agitated emotional world. This is vividly seen in the case of Richard Untermeyer, son of Louis and Jean Untermeyer, both poets. Richard, born in 1907, showed early promise as a poet, though Louis admitted to doctoring his childish verses in order to regularize meter and rhyme. The suspicion of adult tampering always surrounds the production of poetry by children, especially when they are encouraged and pushed as Richard Untermeyer apparently was. Always hovering in the background are parents' fears and hopes that a child may reflect well on themselves, or even blossom into the genius they know they fall short of.

The Untermeyer marriage grew increasingly unstable through the 1920s, affected by the postwar atmosphere of sexual liberty and cynicism toward traditional middle class values. The bohemian male attitude—that women threatened a man's freedom to be himself, but were necessary for inspiring his imagination—appealed to Louis, a dutiful son from a conventional bourgeois family. Judging from a memoir written late in life, he yearned for the freedom to love and leave women as his feelings dictated, as if (one suspects) this would put him in a class with the greater artists of his time. In 1926 he ventured into an affair with the poet Virginia Moore, though the cost was to prove much greater than his fantasies anticipated. The family was torn apart emotionally, for Jean did not cooperate. Jean and Louis sailed to Europe together in an attempt at reconciliation, but returned in October 1926 by separate ships. Louis then hastened to Mexico with Virginia Moore for a quick divorce and remarriage, leaving Jean in suicidal depression. His plans, however, were violently interrupted. Richard, the carrier of his parents' hopes and dreams, tossed back and forth on their turbulence, hanged himself on January 25, 1927 in his room at Yale at the age of nineteen. He left an incoherent note for his mother, accusing her of not giving him a large enough allowance—an echo of the sense of neglect that poets' children so often have felt.

The tragedy brought the Untermeyers back together for a few more years before they separated permanently. They tried to make amends to their son by gathering and privately publishing his poems. In their jointly written introduction to this immature and undistinguished work, they solemnly insisted that they could not find a single reason for his act. But Sara Teasdale, who had known the Untermeyers intimately for fifteen years, told her husband, "The suicide of Dick . . . is directly traceable to Louis's conduct." The boy "had lived all his life . . . in an atmosphere overheated and overstimulating. You remember his horribly nervous manner that August night when he and Jean dined with us."[3] Teasdale saw the horror as the inevitable result of struggle between the parents. "Poor Dick was the sacrifice,"[4] she told Vachel Lindsay.

The questions of power, gender conflict, and creativity were usually less explosive than they were in the Untermeyer family, but children instigated by adults to become precocious child-poets have never fulfilled their promise into adulthood, as Myra Cohn Livingston finds in her study *The Child as Poet: Myth or Reality?* Livingston's examination of adults' promotion of children's poetry-writing concludes that children have often been exploited to satisfy adults' needs for an image of romantic primitivism, the free untutored spirit whose genius upwells in spontaneous creativity, thus defining them in terms that preclude maturing.

The idea of renewal through a return to untroubled innocence, to the naturalness and wisdom of the child and a release from emotional constraint, had a particularly potent appeal at the time of World War I and the years immediately following, when an interest in children's poetry flourished. The child, perhaps, embodied the hope of spiritual rebirth, of a better life rising from the shocking slaughter of the war, redeeming its guilty participants. Harriet Monroe viewed the war in the pages of *Poetry* as a cleansing bloodbath bringing revitalization to a stagnant world. "War is a builder," she editorialized. "Out of the ruins of eras it tumbles together foundation stones for new ones. Dead souls it quickens with its searching and devastating fires. . . . If we have war, devastating war that shall relieve us of surplus billions and drain some of our most precious heart's blood, its huge and irresistible flood may wash away much of the accumulated materialism which clogs our souls."[5] She printed Edgar Lee Masters' even more fervent words: "We are remade. . . . A spiritual unity electrifies us. We seem to be obeying the voice of God. . . . May heaven give us a thorough housecleaning abroad and at home. Let us have a world clean-up economically and spiritually. . . . Let us become real."[6] Marjorie Seiffert wrote to Witter Bynner in 1917, "*We need* to fight to waken us from the materialistic wallow we slept in."[7] Monroe envisioned cultural awakening and renewal as rising democratically from the masses rather than being handed down from an educated elite, as Pound would have it; hence, her attraction to the poets of the common people—Frost, Masters, and Lindsay—to the previously unheard voices of women, to the "primitive" chants of American Indians, to all expressions of an emerging consciousness that was closer to the "real" than was outworn tradition. This included the poetic utterances of children.

In 1915 Monroe considered publishing a special number of *Poetry* featuring poems by children. Grace Hazard Conkling heard of the idea through her friend Louise Driscoll, and forthwith sent Monroe a group of pieces by her small daughters Hilda and Elsa. "At her suggestion I send you the little 'poems' my two baby girls have sung or chanted to themselves, unconscious that I was putting them down."[8] Monroe accepted them for the July 1915 issue, and continued to devote a section of the July number to poetry by children annually through 1920, when Hilda Conkling reached the age of ten, Monroe's cutoff date for accepting a child's work. The lack of enough quality material by other children forced Monroe to discontinue the section, for Hilda Conkling had been the perennial mainstay and in some years the only contributor. (Her older sister Elsa had dropped out of the running early on.)

Harriet Monroe's experience proved that not all children were natural poetic geniuses in their ability to produce skilled and original poems as Hilda Conkling did. As Myra Livingston points out, much of what adults found appealing in children's poems was simply the unselfconscious flash of fresh wording that fed the notion of an unspoiled, true contact with reality, a pure awareness adults believed they had lost; children, by that virtue, were held to be natural poets. Monroe, to her credit, insisted on artistic standards while seeking to capture the child's elusive vision. Nevertheless, many parents and poets were enchanted by the occasional novelty of a child's language and tended to overrate it as an exposure of the true soul of poetry. Carl Sandburg, for example, sent Monroe in 1917 some lines by ten-year-old Carmen Cerulli of New York, "The Elephant":

There stands the elephant,
Bold and strong—
There he stands chewing his food.
We are strengthless against his strength.[9]

But like most adults, Sandburg was doubtless attracted to the poem not just for its ingenuousness, but for what it reflected of himself: in this case, its metaphor of male dominance.

The need of adults for inner renewal found its outward expression in a craving for a renewal of language, and children were only one of many sources of verbal freshness. Sara Teasdale found it in the half-illiterate fan letters she received from a New York bricklayer who, like Ernst Filsinger, had fallen in love with her through her poetry. "Once in a while he says something almost beautiful," she wrote. "This, for instance: 'Last night I walked for a long time through the loving fields thinking about you.' . . . He speaks of enduring 'cruel and colored dreams.' (The phrase is his own and I think it good, don't you?)"[10] Such language—of the uneducated, the primitive, the child—held out the promise that adults could be unsophisticatedly in touch with their emotions, could put off the layers of false or pretended feeling and become "real."

Harriet Monroe talked of publishing an anthology of poems by children in 1917, but the idea was never carried out. She returned to publishing a section of child poems in August 1925, with eight pieces under the heading "Pretty Things" by four-year-old Judith Perlzweig of Baltimore. Monroe published another group of her poems in 1926, but Judith did not turn out to be another prodigy like Hilda Conkling. Babette Deutsch was chagrined not to know in advance that a children's number had been planned in 1925. "Had I known . . . ," she wrote Monroe, "I would have taken care to submit the following verses by my young son, Adam Yarmolinsky." These included

dog says bow-wow
duck says quack-quack
road says
  no things

          aet. 2 years, 1 month

and "On Waking at Night,"

> what makes all the twilights
> come here?
>
>   aet. 2 years, 7 months[11]

These submissions by Deutsch reveal very clearly the assumed link between poetry and spontaneous language, and the interest in pushing back the threshold to the earliest possible age, before adult contamination sets in. Indeed, like Hilda Conkling's first "poems" at age four, these are not compositions but sentences overheard by an adult and written down in a form suggesting poetry. The parallelism of "dog says bow-wow" would seem to be imitated from chants or stories the child had heard read, while "On Waking at Night"—a title obviously supplied by Deutsch—is an example of a child's naive questions about familiar phenomena that adults find so engaging, and which suggest the stance of the poet revisioning the world. The artless omission of capitals and punctuation, while intended to convey childlikeness, is simply one of the mannerisms of modern poetry.

The youngest, and therefore most "natural," child poets were actually created by adults—for the most part, by mothers—who arranged their imaginative and unselfconscious chatter into approximate poetic form and set them on the path. Such children probably came from homes rich in books and reading aloud, where adults were language conscious and highly verbal. A poet-mother could hardly resist seeing the shape of a poem in a child's word-play and identifying it with her own creative process, perhaps even finding in it an echo of her own task of building a self. The child-poet, then, might find his or her identity forced into precocious growth and difficult to separate from that of the gifted parent.

This kind of collaboration is seen in its purest form in the relationship between Grace Hazard Conkling and her daughter Hilda. Conkling was unusually sensitive to the problems and dangers of trying to balance the power of an adult to impose its will with the freedom of the child to develop in its own way. She apparently did not set out to make her daughter into a nationally acclaimed child-poet, but was simply struck by the child's remarkable verbal facility. At four-and-a-half, Hilda was reciting fanciful "songs" addressed to flowers, trees, and the moon, which her mother recorded unobtrusively so as not to make her self-conscious. When these are arranged on the page, they appear as rounded and self-contained statements, rather than incidents in a conversation:

> Sparkle up, little tired flower
> Leaning in the grass!
> Did you find the rain of night
> Too heavy to hold? [12]

The context of the child's flow of talk has been eliminated, so that one is left with the undoubtedly false impression that Hilda spoke in such discrete poetic units. Such "poems" must have emerged less well-defined from a more rambling stream of words, with the kind of impulsive starts and stops that children make, unfinished sentences, and many more bits of imagery that were not sufficiently developed to isolate as a poem. One has no way of knowing whether Grace Conkling pared away straggling phrases surrounding the above poem in order to define it. But even so, the command of sentence structure is impressive, and a phrase like "the rain of night" hints at Hilda's exposure to literature. She told Myra Cohn Livingston that her mother read books to her and her sister "regardless whether we could understand them." [13]

"The little girls do seem artistically inclined," Grace Conkling wrote Harriet Monroe, "and altogether sensitive to beauty. I'm hoping that I shall be able to guide them wisely, as they grow up, leaving them free as far as possible, but *willing* them to reach the goal." [14] Conkling, a strong and disciplined woman who had left her husband to support herself and her two daughters alone, seems to have felt the temptation to shape Hilda in an image she might choose. Yet while she insisted on freedom and self-reliance—unwittingly, the model of herself—she provided a presence so compelling and necessary that it was almost impossible to avoid following her wishes.

Hilda emerged from the unconscious "songs" of early childhood to conscious compositions which her mother continued to write down and edit jointly with her, her poems by then appearing in national magazines like *Good Housekeeping*. The exact nature of that transition is of crucial importance in understanding how Grace Conkling brought more discipline to Hilda's creativity, but it is almost impossible to reconstruct. When other poets speculated whether Grace Conkling was actually writing her daughter's work, the joking (and unkind) answer was that it couldn't be, since Hilda's work was better. Conkling, herself a teacher, believed strongly in keeping hands off a child's originality, letting it develop as much as possible without interference. She feared that school hindered a child's natural growth, and as a professor at Smith College, she struggled against mindless conformity for freer and more unconventional modes of encouraging creativity. She approvingly quoted Hilda at six, advising her older sister, "You have to listen to your thoughts and feel what you want to say. Never mind about the rhyme."[15]

Grace Conkling was determined to keep Hilda unspoiled and unaffected by her becoming a national celebrity. "I've not talked any more about her poetry than I can help," she told Harriet Monroe, "for I'm so afraid to make her self-conscious." When her first book, *Poems by a Little Girl*, was published in 1920, Conkling

allowed Hilda to see no reviews, of course; we talk little of the book, and my friends, and the children at school even, understand that I do not want anyone to ask Hilda about the poems. She has not the grown-up point of view about her book. She wrote to thank Mr. Stokes for making it for *her*. She was surprised I could get more copies. So far, there is no self-consciousness; it's all like breathing. And I want that to continue![16]

Conkling was alarmed at the threat of any outside interference. "Who is Bryher, in England?" she asked Monroe. "She has sent Hilda her book 'Development': also a letter so enthusiastic and personal in some ways that I do not think it best to show it to Hilda now."[17]

Hilda was ten. She has observed that she was kept so detached from the public aspect of her childhood career that in retrospect the poems seem to have been written by someone else. Her poetry

came out of a world of daydreaming and fanciful imagining, a
withdrawn, absorbed love of nature, and it was this that Grace
Conkling did not want to disturb.

Yet, as Livingston notes in her analysis of Hilda's development,
the child did not remain in an arrested state of development, but
progressed normally in her grasp of reality. Poems written around
the age of nine reveal a playful consciousness of metaphor and a
gift of acute, objective observation:

> The hills are going somewhere;
> They have been on the way a long time.
> They are like camels in a line
> but they move more slowly . . .[18]

This maturing inevitably had consequences in the relationship
between Hilda and her mother that was the mainspring of Hilda's
creativity. Grace Conkling may have been too much taken with the
idea of natural self-expression, the blossoming of talent like a flower,
with the virtual elimination of any interaction with an audience.
While this may have seemed appropriate for a four-year-old, the
gradual development of social awareness demands some sense of
the purpose of what one is doing in relation to others and to their
reactions. Hilda, lacking such an audience, apparently located it in
the idea of pleasing her mother. Grace Conkling did not want Hilda's
poetry-writing to be always dependent on her. Yet she was forceful
and demanding, and Hilda was a gentle, peaceable child. "Mother
was very dominating," she remembers, "and she was often high-
handed and adamant in her decisions. It was always Do this, that,
and the other thing. To be fair, she was just as hard on herself as
she was on my sister and me. But she was difficult to get along
with. Being a Libra, I hated scenes, so I'd try to keep the peace,
ever the obedient daughter. As long as I did as I was told, we got
along very well."[19] Grace Conkling seems to have underestimated
how large she loomed in the child's evaluation of the work, and
how much less a self-stimulus Hilda's own creativity was. Conkling's
insistence that Hilda be both self-motivated and without an audience led to an uneasiness about just who was listening. Livingston

documents the extent to which Hilda's poems repeatedly ask for her mother's attention and worry about the loss of her mother's love if she should not be able to continue writing. Even before the age of five, she asked,

> Will you love me to-morrow after next,
> As if I had a bird's way of singing?[20]

As Hilda approached adolescence, Grace Conkling fretted over the problem of how to guide her into a more self-reliant and adult control of her writing, a transition from the childish unselfconscious "dreaming" of poems that required the mother to play the role of secretary, editor, agent, and publicist. Her remark to Louis Untermeyer regarding Hilda's second book, *Shoes of the Wind* (1922), that "I am only incidentally the author of the book in being the author of Hilda," reveals the totality of her involvement and the difficulty of separating herself. She thanked Untermeyer

for the many discriminating things you have said about my queer dreamy downright little girl, as tall as I am now, yet still such a baby, so contradictory, so puzzling, so dear. I don't know what on earth to do with her. One month she can spell and the next month she can't. I am still trying to keep hands off. Hilda is trying to write her own things now, but the mechanical difficulties irritate her. The other night I found a poem, "Mist," hidden under my pillow. She is not stopping, she dreams and sings, but more and more secretly.[21]

Grace Conkling decided simply to withdraw from the role of manager, and quit writing down Hilda's poems for her, hoping to force her on her own as a poet. Livingston believes that this well-meaning attempt to make her daughter self-sufficient actually brought an end to Hilda's poetry-writing. The only audience that mattered seemed to have stopped listening. One wonders whether their relationship might have stimulated Hilda's creativity into adulthood if it had developed along the lines of Marianne Moore's with her mother. Grace Conkling was "a very secretive, complex soul," Hilda says, "more so than most. I admired her greatly and was her companion until her death (in 1958). [sic] If she had lived five more years we might have become even better friends."[22]

Grace Conkling's firm belief in self-reliance suggests her link with an older generation of vigorously independent professional women, who usually did not marry. It seems to be a reaction against female weakness and dependence. However, one would not call Marianne Moore's relationship with her mother "dependence" as much as a valid and fruitful collaboration. It is possible that Grace Conkling's anxiety to avoid dependence and cultivate Hilda's artistic self-reliance was also influenced by male-fashioned psychoanalytic theory, which played up the evil of possessive mother-love; and so she may have forfeited the possibility of joint creativity in trying to follow a male idea of selfhood. "If mother had continued listening to me after the first two books," Hilda said, "I would have produced more. She squashed it by her routine."[23]

*

In contrast to Grace Conkling's way of suffusing her homelife with the spirit of the poetry she wrote and the literature she loved, Marjorie Seiffert kept her creativity and her family in separate compartments. She classified her children as part of the conventional life that imprisoned her. Her poetry-writing, her public sphere with its host of never-seen friends, were therefore an alien side of her nature to her son and daughter, a part of her that seemed not to belong to them, that perhaps did not even love them. This haunting sense of estrangement, rising at times to resentment, particularly plagued Seiffert's daughter Helen, who possessed literary gifts she could never find her way to develop.

Marjorie Seiffert's children—Allen, born in 1913, and Helen, in 1914—did not display a precocious talent for poetry in early childhood, so that when Seiffert encouraged them to write as adolescents, one wonders what need this may have satisfied within herself. (Seiffert had suggested in a letter to Harriet Monroe in 1925 that "living in, by and for the children"[24] was only a substitution for a creative use of her energies.) Allen, it seems, was her favorite child, and it was he whom she tried most diligently to groom as a poet. She reveals her conventional outlook in her anxiety that her son might not fulfill some destiny, while it seemed far less important for her daughter to do so. Allen, who was over six feet tall and weighed 162 pounds at the age of fourteen, was bright enough, although he caused his parents continual worry by his inability to do well in school, or to find any center within himself of interest, ambition, or competence. Marjorie Seiffert seems to have thought of writing poetry as a kind of vehicle he could use in finding himself, probably because it had meant that to her in her own life. She made the effort to stir his creativity at the same time she was floundering in depression and heading into a psychoanalysis she hoped would restore her own ability to write again.

Allen was unfortunately little better at writing poetry than he was at other skills, though for a while he seemed to catch her enthusiasm. Seiffert even persuaded Monroe to publish one of his more passable pieces in *Poetry* in 1933. But as she gradually found herself being effaced by the psychiatrist, and Allen making no headway as the anointed one, failing in one school after another, she seems to have given up on both him and herself as poets. "I don't care a hoot about poetry now," she told Morton Dawen Zabel; "Since I finished with the kindly fiend who has uprooted all my miseries, I simply cannot think of anything to say, not even hallelujah."[25] Allen did go on to try his hand at writing radio plays, one or two of which were produced in 1939 on a Moline radio station. Their outlandish, naive plots and overwritten dialogue are evidence of his failure to inherit his mother's literary skills. In one of them, a young couple traveling in Guatemala stumbles upon a white-haired mad scientist conducting experiments with poisonous snakes in the ruins of a temple. The evil old man cages the girl, whom he intends to feed to his pythons, but is shoved into the snake pit where he is devoured by his own reptiles. Maddened by the horror, she is found in a trance, wishing to join the old man whom she now reveres as her master. The Poesque tale might be read as a parable of Allen's own desire for revenge upon the patriarchal power that placed too great a burden of expectation on him, that wrapped the innocent in its coils and mesmerized women to follow its dictates.[26]

His sister, Helen, on the other hand, had voluntarily shown an interest in writing poetry at the age of fifteen. Marjorie recognized a possible talent but did not attempt to offer guidance, feeling that her daughter would reject it. She sent some samples of Helen's poems to Witter Bynner,

just because I think she has an interesting mind. As she has no idea of being a child prodigy or anything like that, I have not "helped" her. They are her own reactions to life, colored very little by reading, but very much by observing and listening. I would like to hear what you would say about them more as human documents than as poetry, for she is so afraid of being unduly influenced by me, that she does not take me for a teacher.[27]

Seiffert seems to be asking Bynner for a word that will help her understand her daughter, to bridge the gap of resentment between them. More interestingly, she speaks as one professional to another, careful to take no responsibility for the amateurishness of the poems, which is blamed on her own lack of supervision. Behind that, perhaps, lies guilt for excluding her children from her life as a poet, a life that seemed threatened by the demands the children made on her. But Helen's own potential creativity was at stake, and Marjorie could not ignore it. (If Bynner replied, there is no record.)

   Helen Seiffert, as she indicated later, actually wanted nothing more than to be included in her mother's large importance, the power Marjorie possessed as a creator of poems, a figure known and publicized. In her silence, Helen's love and envy grew resentful and directed in upon herself as a victim of that power. Marjorie prevailed upon *Poetry* to take two of her daughter's poems in 1936 while Helen was a student at Smith College, and then pressured the editors to get the pieces in print before her daughter's graduation in June so friends at school could see and be impressed by them. Marjorie wrote about Helen to John Hall Wheelock, "She is a nice gal, not bad looking, and has had two poems accepted by 'Poetry.' However I think she is going to get married in a couple of years . . . she is the type, and then good-bye poetry!"[28]

   Helen Seiffert did marry, and to all appearances fulfilled her mother's prophecy. But after years of fearfulness and debilitatingly low self-esteem, she turned to a psychiatrist in 1954, hoping to find the key to release, as Marjorie had done a generation earlier. Helen

Pryor's therapist was somewhat more enlightened than her mother's had been: he apparently recognized her subtlety, her wry irony, her swiftness of mind, her imagination and creative talent, and so suggested that she write poems and sketches as a way to search the truth within herself. She set about exploring her accumulated pain with unflinching directness, revealing a strength and self-honesty reminiscent of her mother's. Her life had been devoted to hiding— from both herself and others—in order to protect herself, but at great spiritual loss:

> The mole is digging in the ground
> Through many ages he has found
> The darkness best.
>
> His ancestors with eyes shut fast
> Burrowed downward till at last
> They all grew blind.
>
> O small brown mole in quiet curled
> Lie sleeping in your sunless world
> A heavy rest.
>
> Scurry below and never dare
> To go above, a sky is there
> You cannot find.[29]

Her poems show striking parallels with the private obsessions and unpublished self-analytical work of Sara Teasdale—for example, Teasdale's belief that her body lacked a normal epidermis, so that she was more sensitive and exposed to shock than other people. Helen Pryor's poem "No Armor" figuratively finds the same deficiency:

> A person who lacks the first layer
> Of skin that fits so closely
> And so completely over
> Other people's blood and bones
> Must learn to move carefully
> And not run into things.

She too prefers silence:

In the mind, never heard
Never uttered is the word.
Never try to tell the story,
Never make it auditory.

Helen, or "Peg" as she was nicknamed, was sensitively aware of how mixed and complex was the cloud of feeling obscuring the image of her mother. Her psychiatrist, predictably, seems to have aimed at uncovering anger toward her mother, this, rather than love, being the focus of male psychoanalytic interest in mothers. She drew a series of stick-figure cartoons for him, many of them reflecting her interaction with him as well as her own self-perception. In an early one, the doctor requests, "Please just report any feelings of anger." In the thought-balloon over the figure of herself is an image of her and the doctor with drawn rapiers, fencing. In another, she depicts herself falling off his couch with a look of astonishment as he asks, "It surprises you that you don't love your mother?" But as she follows his lead, the cartoons increasingly show resentment at the mother's apparent preference for her poetry to her own children. "I couldn't *live* without my poetry," she announces, while brother and sister slink away dejected. Or the doctor says, "I like your mother's poetry," while she covers her ears. In another, the little girl, slumped and crestfallen, has offered her mother a bouquet of flowers: "Not right now, dear. You can see Mama's reading." A prose sketch titled "The Play" dutifully tries to recall the kind of negative material the psychiatrist is searching for, but she is not sure it is true:

She can remember that she was put in her room by The Person when she should have been allowed to go with Cook to the beach. She twists her hands, beats the wall, but very quietly . . . She can hear her brother (The Person approves of her brother) playing with the dog on the terrace. . . .

Somewhere in her body she must have wanted to kill The Person, but this is so entirely unknown to her that she is already planning to be so quiet, so sweet, so rested the next day that there will be no question of the Ritual Nap. She does not even know that somewhere in her body is the clear understanding that The Person will never say, "Yes, you are so quiet, so sweet, so rested that you may go to the beach today . . ."

Babette Deutsch, c. 1909, evincing, at an early age, the unswerving ambition to become a poet and a scholar. *(Babette Deutsch Papers, Mss. and Archives Division, New York Public Library, Astor, Lenox and Tilden Foundations)*

Angelina Weld Grimke, c. 1900. The uncertain identity of a motherless, mixed-race child. (*Moorland-Spingarn Research Center, Howard University*)

Anne Spencer and Edward A. Spencer with their grand-daughters in her Lynchburg, Virginia garden, 1928. "This small garden is half my world." (*Chauncey Spencer*)

Their friendship flourished during the 1950s.

Right: May Sarton, 1960. "It would be wonderful indeed to feel that I had an ally." *(Lotte Jacobi, by permission of May Sarton)*
Below: Louise Bogan, 1951. *(Rollie McKenna, by permission of Ruth Limmer, Trustee, Estate of Louise Bogan)*

The photograph of Margaret Conklin that Sara Teasdale kept on her mantel: "She told me that I was the daughter she would have wanted."

A photograph of Sara Teasdale taken by Harriet Monroe in Teasdale's St. Louis home, 1914. "Am I not the dissipated old thing? But the kimono is pretty." *(Newberry Library, Chicago)*

Marianne Moore and her mother, Mary Warner Moore, c. 1938. "I seem to need very humane handling, mothering by everyone—the case all my life, I think." (*Arthur Steiner, by permission of the Rosenbach Library and Museum, Philadelphia*)

The patriarchal family was the setting for a clash between motherhood and artistic creativity.

Left: Marjorie Seiffert and her granddaughter, Allyn Pryor, c. 1950. *(Allyn Asti-Rose) Right:* Seiffert's daughter, Helen Seiffert Pryor, 1952. *(Allyn Asti-Rose) Below:* One of Helen Seiffert Pryor's drawings for her psychiatrist. *(Allyn Asti-Rose)*

Exotic costume and adventure symbolized the quest for identity.

Above: Eunice Tietjens, c. 1912. *(Matzene, Chicago, by permission of the Newberry Library) Right:* Elinor Wylie, c. 1927. *(Cecil Beaton photograph courtesy of Sotheby's London)*

Women defending the victims of entrenched power: Edna St. Vincent Millay (*left*) and Lola Ridge arrested for picketing the State House on behalf of Sacco and Vanzetti, Boston, Massachusetts, c. 1927. *(UPI/ Bettman Newsphotos)*

She does not know that she finally gave in. Really, she does not know this. The Person won, finally, absolutely.

At eight or nine, after giving in, she stopped "crying, vomiting, being afraid at night, having tantrums." Then her life became a play of being a good girl, the "darling daughter," fearing what otherwise might be taken away from her. "After thirty years she stopped the play and she is terribly frightened. Frightened because she does not entirely believe or remember the fear and the not-loving. She thinks sometimes that the fear and the not-loving, that *they* must be the play." In a cartoon, the child is shown trying one technique after another to capture her mother's attention. But "Tantrums won't help," "Tears won't help," "Being good won't help." "What *will* help, Mummy?" "Nothing. I don't like children."

There is no violence in any of Helen Pryor's fantasies on the psychiatrist's couch—only a wistful yearning for love and attention from a mother who shut her out of the world of her power and would not share it.

> "This creature is not mine,"
> Echoes in the mother's head, not spoken,
> But the child can hear.

As a child, even at four, like Hilda Conkling, Helen made up jingles and poems which her grandmother wrote down and preserved. They reveal a natural facility for imaginative word-play, though they are not as accomplished as Hilda's. Perhaps with the kind of encouragement and editorial guidance Hilda received from her mother, Helen Seiffert might also have blossomed early, or at least found a basis for later development. The poems of her childhood and youth were "love poems" to her mother, she said; but her mother, on seeing them, never gave her the response she expected, and so her gift went underground, like the mole.

The results of three years of psychoanalysis left Helen Pryor, she felt, no better than before. Like her mother, she felt deprived of the vitality and color of pain. When everything is explained, the quest is over. She weighs "The Price of Peace":

Nothing ever again will be worth as much
Since nothing ever again will be costly—
I have spent it all,
Flung away reticence, remorse, despair,
And the grayness comes creeping in . . .

Such words as I have used
For telling fear
Are foolish now.
What new words can ever
Say so much, and who will care to hear?

"The search, the hunting-out are all," she says in "The Search." "The figure of a weeping woman/ Is more alive than she who rests/ Holding solutions in her one hand,/ And in the other, death."

Helen Pryor's poems and sketches suggest that while she repeatedly approached her own emotional history from an angle that might have yielded liberating insights, even bridged the forlorn gulf between herself and her mother, her psychiatrist drew her back toward his own biases, naming the pain without supplying a remedy. "The doctor asked me the other day," she wrote in 1956, "if I had read Simone de Beauvoir's book 'The Second Sex,' and I said no, because why should I read one more account of some woman's rage at being a woman? I'd rather try to figure out *why* for myself. Why we're all so mad, I mean." Her psychiatrist had given her Freud to read, and she had dutifully accepted the theory of penis envy. But she had her own ideas about how Freudian theory might apply to herself. The fantasy she spun for the therapist "was that what I should have had was cut off on the OB table by a mutual agreement between my mother and the doctor. If I could put it into words, it is much as if they said to each other, 'This one's no good anyway, we'll make her a girl.' " But she had to explain why not all woman felt this way. The lucky ones, content to be themselves, were those whose mothers welcomed the child as an extension of themselves "during the pre-Oedipal stage. . . . If the mother, upon birth of the girl child, can, with no shrinking and no misgivings, fondle, caress, love this small reproduction of her own femininity, all will be well. If she takes pride in being a woman, she will communicate this pride to the child. Then and then only will the little girl forget her loss and cherish her individuality."

Helen Pryor had ventured into territory that would not be explored by women for another generation, and she was understandably not equipped to follow through the implications for herself and her mother. One can suppose that Marjorie Seiffert, fundamentally conservative in her views on gender, could not comfortably accept the role of poet-creator she tried to play so jauntily, for in her mind it must have had an essentially male identification. That assumption hovered in the background thoughts of most of the women poets of that era, distorting their view of themselves. By keeping her professional career apart from the female sphere of her life, Seiffert could not help resenting femininity as a negative force, inimical to her creative freedom, even as she dutifully lived out its demands. If a mother despises her own femaleness as a weakness, it is inevitable that a girl-child will feel an antagonism directed against herself, for being a woman is the most important thing they share. And so Marjorie Seiffert futilely tried to make a poet of her son, while feeling baffled at how to do the same for her daughter. Inevitably, she could only see in Helen the potentiality of her own divided self; and so Helen inherited the conflict as her own. "My two selves struggle, breast to breast," she wrote.

When both mother and daughter sought help from a male technician of the soul, they were taught to accept a mutilated status as natural to women, to stop resisting. Helen, at least, saw the glimmering of a new possibility: a loving union of mother with daughter that would reinforce their pride and individuality. Therein lay the answer to the agonized question she posed in "Cain":

> Cain must have cried to the empty sky,
> "Why is it I who am not loved?"
> He must have questioned what was in him
> So unlovely and unlovable. . . .
> Abel could have lived if there had not been

In Cain this anguished knowledge that,
Of the two children, Cain alone was chosen for
not-love.

Abel can be seen as the creator, the poet who might have been, murdered by lovelessness. Although Helen Pryor did not write the polished poetry she had dreamed of doing, she did produce a body of poems and prose sketches that impress one with their impromptu force and searching honesty, with the light they throw on the hazards faced by creative women.

*

The crippling isolation of a daughter from her creative mother seems not to be inevitable, if there is the essential sharing. For Helen Seiffert, the enclosure and rigidity, the assigned emotions, of conventional middle-class family life only intensified her excruciating sense of isolation. For Perdita, H.D.'s daughter, shuffled erratically about Europe, cared for by others, sometimes only half noticed by a dreamy, offhand mother whose writing consumed all her interest, there was nevertheless the indispensable life-giving connection. The name "Perdita" itself, after the infant in Shakespeare's *The Winter's Tale* who was forcibly taken from her mother and cruelly abandoned, but restored years later, touches on the tragedy of women separated from one another by male power. The gods allowed no peace until the two were rejoined. H.D. was not sure she wanted the child, fathered by Cecil Gray while her husband Richard Aldington was away at war, and while she herself was drifting into the lesbian relationship with Bryher that would dominate much of her life. "H.D. was hardly an archetypal mother," Perdita wrote, with considerable understatement. Yet their experience proves that a "successful" mother can just as well be an erratic bohemian as a middle-class matron. In fact, the unconventional union between H.D. and Bryher provided Perdita with two mothers, and a completeness beyond what one woman alone could supply. Bryher was the dynamo of practicality, the arranger, dauntless and reliable; H.D. was the elusive spirit, the dreamer.

"We lived in Switzerland with her friend Bryher," Perdita (now Perdita Schaffner) wrote,

isolated from the world. Visitors came by from time to time; mostly writers, adults only. I never consorted with other children, other families, other mothers. So, for all I knew, everybody's mother was a poet; a tall figure of striking beauty, with fine bone structure and haunting grey eyes; and frequently overwrought, off in the clouds, or sequestered in a room, not to be disturbed on any account.

She was intensely maternal—on an esoteric plane. She venerated the concept of motherhood, but was unprepared for its disruptions. She flinched at sudden noise, and fled from chaos. Mercifully for her, she was well buffered. We had a staff, almost a bodyguard. I could always be removed. *"Madame est nerveuse; viens ma petite!"* Or Bryher would step in and marshal me off. "Your mother's very nervous today." Every day, it seemed. So, fair enough, that's the way it was. A mother was someone who wrote poetry and was very nervous. And who walked alone and sat alone. And was capable of overwhelming affection, but on her own time and terms, preferably out of doors. I accompanied her on her daily walk, clasping a bag of crusts and crumbs. Always the same time: ten o'clock, when her morning's work was done and put away. . . . Then she reclaimed her solitude. . . . She spent the afternoons in her room, reading, writing letters, and thinking—concentrating on everything and nothing, in an intense trance-like meditation. . . . When she left the door ajar, I sidled in and joined her. She never objected; she quietly made room for me in the armchair. And I never wriggled, chattered, or wished I were anywhere else. Those were privileged interludes, all the more so for being surreptitious. I dreaded an outsider barging in, breaking up our rapport, our shared secret.

H.D. would talk with her child as she did with other adults, in her sometimes mystic and mystifying way; but "I could always follow. I just had to grow up first, and find my own bearings." And as Perdita did grow up, H.D. "became a much better mother. We respected each other as individuals. We were adults together, and friends."[30]

SIX
Love and Politics

C ONTRARY TO male theory that women's creativity was primarily biological, the women poets did not derive creative satisfaction from bearing children. Producing a child and producing a poem were two different orders of experience; the analogy between them was false. Carrying a human embryo in her womb, assuming responsibility for a child's nurturing, were uses of herself that a woman, in the patriarchal scheme, could not freely choose. Childbearing was a destiny to be passively accepted, a drowning of personal identity in the ocean of life. Artistic creativity, on the other hand, brought an intensification of active will, a directed sense of purpose, an ambitious, well-defined individuality. A poem was an object fashioned by one's mind and hands; a child was many things, but not that.

The exhilaration women experienced on discovering that they, as well as men, possessed authentic creative powers can hardly be overstated. Elizabeth Barrett Browning's trembling exultation and fear at using the "royal name" of poet (in *Aurora Leigh*) typified the emerging women of the Victorian era. The women of the 1920s took the inevitable next step, and confidently, joyously, asserted, "I am a poet."

To claim the name of poet, however, was to encroach on the mystique of artistic greatness men had assigned to themselves alone, and to flout the mystique of motherhood that served to keep women in their supporting role. Artistic creativity was therefore a profoundly political act for both men and women, in that it affirmed or challenged patriarchal power at the most basic level, that of sexual differentiation.

Most of the women poets between 1915 and 1945 did not think of themselves as rebels, however, but simply aimed at achieving the same kind of success as men. This was actually, even if unwittingly, an initial stage of political confrontation, which women hoped to accomplish without disturbing the status quo. Indeed, in a remarkable burst of productivity and publishing successes, women came close to reaching their goal before the momentum subsided and the male establishment rallied to crowd them again to the periphery. Perhaps they were too trusting, too innocent, lacking either a feminist insight into the nature of power or the makings of a solidarity movement among themselves. Only a few particularly bold and adventurous women went further than the quest for personal success to perceive their creativity as an act of defiance against oppression so fundamental as to require a new social vision.

Babette Deutsch is one of the most interesting poets whose starting point was the defiant, visionary radical ferment of the World War I years. She was more excited by the atmosphere of change, of revolutionary new possibilities, than by any of the Marxist or anarchist movements. Such movements, while welcoming participation by women and professing feminist principles, made female liberation subordinate to broader social change, and in practice were often blindly insensitive to their own sexist treatment of women. Deutsch cautiously avoided any commitment that would undercut the value she placed on herself as a woman, even though this deprived her of a recognized intellectual position and required her to redefine herself continually. Her life, a journey through the minefields of male power on both left and right, exposes with particular clarity the gender politics that have shaped literary history.

Babette Deutsch conspicuously avoided the Greenwich Village radicals in their heyday, between 1915 and 1925, a time when a number of other women poets were drawn there by the promise of a new, freer way of life. The radical men considered sexual liberation to be at the core of their revolt, a notion that appealed to women's own need to be free of sexual oppression. But the men gave the idea of liberation their own twist: they embraced Freud's version of women as passive and sexually repressed, the result of "Puritan" inhibition. Women could be cured by psychoanalysis—making them better sexual partners and inspirers of male creativity. This form of liberation, essentially a service to patriarchal males rather than to women themselves, obscured and deflected attention from the issue of male dominance. And it confused a generation of women who believed that their "problem" was lack of the kind of uninhibited sexual appetite avant-garde men had set up as the new feminine ideal. The hidden agenda behind male encouragement of female sexual freedom is disclosed in Otto Rank's remark to Anaïs Nin, "When the neurotic woman gets cured, she becomes a woman. When the neurotic man gets cured, he becomes an artist."[1]

The radicals' underlying program of male dominance is revealed in the sexual imagery and role-playing which they projected into their ideas of the revolutionary and the artist. The class struggle, for example, was a kind of sexual competition: the middle and upper classes were scorned as degenerate, womanish, and ripe for overthrow by the real men of the working class. Michael Gold, communist editor of the *New Masses,* idealized "rough" working-class males like stevedores and lumberjacks and affected a proletarian machismo in his personal life, with carelessness of dress and a tough-guy pose. Gold employed abusive sexual terms to express his hatred of the bourgeoisie, calling Proust the "master-masturbator of bourgeois literature," branding middle-class intellectuals as "pansies" and "fairies," heaping scorn on T. S. Eliot, Thornton Wilder, and the Harvard Humanists for ignoring the suffering of the working class for their own "precious little agonies."[2] Gold's attitude toward women and family was highly conventional, even puritanical—not inconsistent, though, with his womanizing.

Liberal-to-radical male writers throughout the period commonly idealized the virility of the working class; and as intellectuals, they privately dreaded being thought effeminate. Women were "ladies," linked with the supposedly played-out, over-civilized upper classes, too weak to perform the arduous work of creating "great" poetry. To Alfred Kreymborg, the poet's relation to his muse was not "any lofty lady-like pirouetting on her part, any silk-hat doffing on his." A favorite of men who longed for masculine assertiveness was the common man's poet, Carl Sandburg. Kreymborg extolled Sandburg's maleness in his review of *Cornhuskers* in 1918, picturing him as "hiking down some smelly old alley, suddenly smitten with a mood, like a blow between the eyes. I can see him sticking a Pittsburgh stogie in his mouth." Imagery of roughness and violence enhanced the idea of masculinity: Sandburg's struggle with his poetic material is like a "slugging or wrestling match. . . . I advise anybody who is disturbed by this non-pretty theory to attend a prize-fight. That's the game—something more than a boxing contest—a man undertakes with art."[3] Sandburg's "non-pretty" he-man verse inspired a tribute with erotic undertones from Egmont Hegel Arens, later a founder of the *New Masses*. Arens feels that all his "clever defenses . . . go down before the impact of your beefy lunge":

> Your hairy fist,
> Like a ton of rock,
> Smashes me in the face.
> I take the count—
> One, two, three, four—
> To come back bloody,
> Laughing:
> Every time you hit me
> I get a stronger hold on myself.[4]

Even as amiable a freethinker as Max Eastman, who cherished the company of women and considered himself a feminist, who ridiculed Hemingway's "style, you might say, of wearing false hair on the chest,"[5] still saw the social struggle in masculine sexual terms, tough, larger-than-life males overthrowing the corrupt, effete, moneyed classes. As editor of *The Masses,* he was happy to have Sandburg's "outbursts of unwashed reality . . . Too many of our poet-contributors were on the delicate side."[6] Eastman's women had to be beautiful to look at, his male friends bursting with power, like John Reed: it frightened "milk-blooded people with a near-sighted morality, consisting principally of fear and decorum, [to] see a young man so full of power and poetry . . ."[7] Men were desperately anxious to escape the suffocating aura of female pow-erlessness, the castrated creativity of the lady in her parlor; but at the same time they preferred to keep her in the place for which they professed such abhorrence, not wanting to see her "full of power and poetry" like themselves. John Reed himself exemplifies the double standard in his brief friendship with Sara Teasdale in 1913. They walked the sidewalks of New York on spring nights talk-ing "social reform," which Teasdale enjoyed. But Reed apologized for drawing her into a man's world of thought: "Why on earth should people like you bother with injustice and dirty things?" He praised her "delicate lyrics," urging her to "go on and sing. I'll never depress and brow-beat you with 'social reform' again." Teas-dale, always chagrined at the depowering label "delicate," sighed, "It just seemed very interesting talk."[8]

Warriors, like Reed and Eastman, whether on the barricades or in the boardroom of the bank, turned to women essentially for maternal comfort, while fearing the power this gave them. Max Eastman wrote to his first wife, "Your love is around me. I am warm. I am not fearful or distrustful."[9] Yet he suffered as a child from nightmares of something threatening to envelop him, a shape-less "awfulness" that in later years "assumed the form of a woman, still too undelineated to be a hag, but dreadful in a softly implacable way."[10]

This heavy emphasis on masculine power and disdain for the feminine among the radicals indicates that their psychology was not significantly different from that of the men of the elite class they opposed, and so did not provide a functional basis for their feminist ideology, which was limited essentially to enlarging women's economic benefits and political rights. Women inspired by the revolutionary hope of a more equitable society for themselves had to deal with a kind of doctrinaire feminism underlain with an implicit patronizing and sexual exploitation of women, if not with outright hostility.

Radical women poets like Babette Deutsch were understandably reluctant to conform to male intellectual models. They tended to veer off in their own directions, undogmatic, inconsistent if necessary—partly because of the lack of a developed feminist outlook, partly because they had to employ whatever strategies were available to serve the silent side of their own rebellion. This pragmatic and individualistic kind of radicalism is conspicuous in Deutsch, who drew strength from wherever she could find it. Her path was guided at almost every point by her revolt as a woman against the enveloping presence of male power. She was determined not only to survive, but to win; there is none of the attitude of "making the best" of being a woman, the settling for tragedy, that is seen in some earlier poets, like Teasdale. Deutsch's son has remarked that although his mother was "not a feminist," "she did not let men put her down."[11]

Babette Deutsch rejected the central premise of radical men regarding female sexuality: that women's "problem" was Puritan inhibition, and the cure was promiscuous activity with men. Deutsch was not a bohemian. An obvious distaste for sexual libertinism can be sensed throughout her work. It crops up amusingly even in old age, in her reaction to a mention of herself in *The Autobiography of Emanuel Carnevali,* edited and published in 1968 by Kay Boyle. Carnevali, a poverty-stricken Italian poet who lived for a time in the United States shortly after World War I and impressed many, like Boyle and William Carlos Williams, as a charismatic, Rimbaud-like figure, had paid a visit with a friend to the young Babette Deutsch, who was then still living at home with her mother. Deutsch, he said in his sole reference to her, "showed us her leg covered by a stocking full of indecent holes. But her mother was quite aristocratic."[12]

"What false memory can Carnevali have had?" Deutsch cried out to Boyle.

I showed them, I remember, several poems. . . . I did NOT show them my "leg," covered or uncovered, and I never wore a "stocking full of indecent holes." Indeed, in those days, when I was living at home and badly spoiled, if there was a small hole it was promptly and exquisitely darned by my mother. I earnestly beg you to make clear to anyone to whom you present the book that in this instance Carnevali was fantasying. . . . a piece of pure and shameful falsification.[13]

While Deutsch's incensed reaction might be thought somewhat excessive, illustrating a middle-class sexual conservatism—and therefore her failure to be "modern"— it reveals rather her stubborn refusal to be treated as a sexual object. Only a man would have mentioned her legs rather than her poetry. This may have made her a bad sport among the bohemians, but it indicates a deep feminine pride and a recognition that sexual exploitation disguised as modernity was not liberating. Deutsch was no prude. Her work is candid, sensual, and vigorous. When Harriet Monroe winced at the forthrightness of a poem she submitted to *Poetry* in 1918, Deutsch replied, "I must confess I'm surprised at having so shocked you. I can never understand why franknesses lauded in dead poets are unseemly in living ones."[14]

Deutsch, like most women inclined to radical political sympathies, picked up usable ideas from male mentors in her own selective way. Born in New York City in 1895, daughter of an importer of German toys, she had grown up as a pampered only child amidst conservative middle-class attitudes, good food, and well-made fashionable clothes. She was something of a swan among ducks, intellectually gifted, willful, infatuated with books and learning. Although her parents had little in common with her interests, they indulged her in whatever she wanted, and allowed her to go to college, even though they probably expected her to follow the domestic example of her mother and female relatives. At Barnard College of Columbia University, Deutsch studied under Charles Beard, James Harvey Robinson, and others who aroused her to think critically and ironically about her own upper-middle-class background. She absorbed the ideas of Dewey and Veblen, even working as Veblen's secretary in 1919 at the New School for Social Research. She was perhaps most deeply impressed by the charismatic off-campus radical Randolph Bourne, with whose group of friends and followers she was associated for a time.

Bourne's message was a powerful stimulant to the generation maturing in the years of World War I. "The ideas of the young are the living, the potential ideas," he wrote; "those of the old, the dying or already dead."[15] He justified the revolt of youth against the world created by its elders with this figurative death sentence, and glorified the innate radicalism of the young, based on their "constant susceptibility to the new, [their] constant eagerness to try new experiments."[16] Deutsch echoed Bourne's ideas in her Class Day poem on graduating in June 1917:

> Something there is in us to answer the thrill
> Of things untried . . .[17]

Deutsch exulted in the Russian Revolution, using the title of her poem about the red flag, "Banners," for that of her first book of poems in 1919. Yet the revolution Deutsch envisioned could not be defined as Marxist, or by any other recognizable political terminology. Like most of the radically inspired women, Deutsch saw revolution primarily as a symbol of personal liberation. To do otherwise would be to betray women's need by making it subordinate to the power struggles among men.

However, the celebration of youth as the driving force of radicalism was not enough to sustain her development into maturity, for the challenge of personal liberation raised profound questions. As she approached her thirties, Babette Deutsch, now married and a mother, was obliged to pause and evaluate the rather undefined course she had followed, to locate a center that would hold together the outward contradictions of her life. This self-exploration was conducted in an autobiographical first novel, *A Brittle Heaven.*

Deutsch had thought a great deal about history, both her own and that of Western culture, and she could see the undesirability, the impossibility, of wiping clean the slate of the past in order for a pristine future to be born. That could seem reasonable only to the young and inexperienced. Progress depended on the continual introduction of new, liberating ideas; but innovation not only destroyed with its fire the outworn old, it was nourished by the best of the old as well. Beginning as an ardent revolutionist, she realized she could not carry her revolt to the logical conclusion of disavowing all she had known and been. She had never broken the loving ties with her parents or renounced their comfortable way of life, continuing to live at home until marrying at age twenty-six. The conservative side of Deutsch, seen in her desire for reconciliation and continuity, was as strong as her will to shatter old idols.

In *A Brittle Heaven,* Deutsch grappled with the problem of how a woman can break free of the stereotypes that bind her and the women around her—mothers, aunts, friends—while retaining a sense of female identity and a unity with other women. Or to put it another way, how she could repudiate stereotyped femininity without repudiating women. Deutsch's heroine Bianca Ernesti is destined to be a poet and novelist, because of her keen sensory responses and an absorbent mind that builds a colorful and structured world out of the ordinary experience of a rather sheltered middle-class girl. In her teens, an inner movement of the spirit seizes her and she begins writing verses, discovering the thirst for creativity that will become the central drive of her life. This creative awakening occurs at the same time as her passionate, idealizing friendship, verging on the erotic, with another teenage girl, Trudy. There is a power in Trudy, expressed in her athleticism, her difference from others, her unconcern for feminine typecasting. She is, in fact, the antitype to the overwhelming conformity of most females. She provides for Bianca the empowering image of womanhood that releases within herself the power to create.

Although Deutsch catches this prophetic glimpse of a radical feminism, she does not develop its implications, but falls back on the psychological truisms of her time: the Bianca/Trudy relationship is explained as a stage of adolescence that both will outgrow as they approach the "normal" heterosexual world of adulthood—

an indication that Deutsch hopes to work out her rebellion within the existing social pattern. Yet their passionate friendship remains one of the central experiences of the book and is far more convincing than Bianca's later romantic involvements with men.

Deutsch's ambivalence leaves her with the problem of exactly where to locate the unique rebellion of a creative woman. The women of Bianca's class are depicted as vapid, interested chiefly in getting a man and a house to fill with objects, capable only of fatuous, shallow conversation about clothing and food. Exposure to Marxist thought seems to offer an explanation of suffocating bourgeois domesticity and the money culture that produces such castrated women and such fundamentally corrupt men as her stepfather, who is arrested for illegal business practices. Bianca gravitates to a group of radical young men who put her to work on behalf of the garment workers' strike. Although she works to liberate others from the assumed enemy, capitalist oppression, Bianca herself feels no elation or sense of freedom. The young women volunteers often feel aimless, unaware of what is transpiring, while men occupy the leadership positions, issue all the orders, and enjoy all the excitement. Bianca drifts into a state of virtual anomie, troubled by her inability to feel a sense of union with others or any sustained excitement for the cause. The radical commitment has separated her from her own background without providing a unifying new consciousness. The sense of self-alienation becomes most acute when she gathers statistics in a tenement district and is sickened by brutal conditions of filth and suffering. The revolution she is working for will not free her—it will more likely destroy her along with her privileged class, as she tells herself:

And you, you too, . . . will be swamped in the mess of it: dirt and blood, more dirt than blood, piling up in a suffocating wave over you: your neat tailored suit, your crisp little hat, your kind, calmly glowing refuge of books and pens won't save you then. You'll go under, you'll be submerged under the rabble.[18]

Bianca then retreats from radical activism as she had earlier fled the stifling limitations of her family. There still remains the task of forging a personal identity that will support her ambition as a writer, an identity not defined for her by any political commitment, radical or conservative. The way one discovers the potency of one's self is through power-giving love—a truth Bianca has learned in her friendship with Trudy. However, Deutsch's ability to imagine such an intimate, mutually empowering relationship between adults was circumscribed by her assumption that the only possibility lay in heterosexual love and marriage. Accepting marriage and mother-hood as the natural and unavoidable course of life, Deutsch pro-ceeds to redefine them in a way that contributes to a woman's pursuit of her own goals of growth and achievement.

Deutsch's wishful depiction of such a liberated marriage is unfortunately somewhat vague. Bianca's husband is drawn one-dimensionally as simply an agreeable man who puts his wife's novel-writing above his own interests, even sacrificing his dreams of a career in the theater in order to support a family. If Deutsch was too casually optimistic in depicting the male component in a liber-ated marriage, she plunged more deeply into the question of how a woman's revolutionary consciousness could emerge from an equi-table marital arrangement. In a revealing scene, Bianca, jostled on the street by the crowds celebrating the armistice, tries to place her own creative ambition in proper relation with the masses in whom, for the radical, political power resides: "Never, never will you be greater than they until you suffer them to be what they are, not letting them hurt you, loving them even . . . You would be less than they, because of your consciousness. . . ."[19] This is an insight possible only to the powerless in search of empowerment. Bianca wishes to assert her own power of creativity without resorting to hierarchical thinking, which requires one person's success to be at the cost of another's. She wishes to escape the grip of dominance and submission, as symbolized by a new and equal kind of mar-riage, and not merely to exchange her position for that of the dom-inant. Love is the true opponent of oppressive power. But love is known only in terms of personal relationship—women's sphere, where it is kept carefully confined so as not to interfere with the free exercise of power. Thus, the challenge of leaping from the personal to the political becomes acute.

Deutsch resolves the dilemma in the novel's climax with the birth of Bianca's first child. On the most literal level, the wrenching pain of childbirth identifies Bianca with all human suffering, and she achieves the sense of unity with humankind that she has failed to find in radical activism or social theory. As a well-dressed do-gooder of the affluent classes, her sympathy for the embittered, half-starved workers' wives in their rags was only a mockery. But as a woman suffering in common with all women, she is free of the differences created by the power structure. On a symbolic level, childbirth signifies the birth of herself, the birth of a consciousness that is truly revolutionary in its opposing power with love; and it epitomizes social change in bringing into being a new life out of the old. It is noteworthy that this radicalizing of a woman's consciousness does not arise from the love-relationship between a man and a woman, but from the woman's unique capacities and experience. The man, though a necessary adjunct, is merely an agent.

To say all this is doubtless to spell out more than Babette Deutsch intended consciously in *A Brittle Heaven*. But the novel is especially interesting because it gropes very deeply on an intuitive level toward perceptions that the author had no way of formulating in terms available to her at the time. It is all the more remarkable for its very imperfections and blind spots, always at its best when its insights become luminous beyond consciously held ideas, as Deutsch attempts to find a voice for the silences. The childbirth sequence, for example, suddenly shifts to a vivid stream-of-consciousness narrative, away from the unconvincing marital relationship to a self-contained female point of view. Candid descriptions of childbirth had long been avoided in fiction as an offense to propriety, and Deutsch's is one of the earliest to appear. It is significant that she scrupulously avoids a similar realistic treatment of sexual relations, even though this was considered the frontier by most other writers, and instead comes to grips with women's biological role, transforming the burden of the oppressed into a symbol of liberation and revolt. Childbirth does not pull her down into the unconscious physical realm assigned to women—it awakens a new female consciousness.

The title of the novel, *A Brittle Heaven*, taken from Emily Dickinson, suggests, however, the fragility of Bianca Ernesti's success in reconciling the revolutionary and the traditional. Deutsch was realistically aware that forces are always at work to destabilize one's vision, which could never be attained once and for all. And indeed Deutsch was not able to sustain the impressive advance she had started to make. Her incipient feminism became a casualty of the political conflicts of the 1930s, when painful choices had to be made. A gradual shift in Deutsch's thinking toward the conservative end of her spectrum—already foreshadowed in her desire to find a compromise between the old and the new—began probably as early as 1924, after she had spent five months in the Soviet Union with her husband, the literary scholar Avrahm Yarmolinsky. She had come away disappointed by the aftermath of the revolution that she had greeted with such hope in 1917. Then, the red flag had stood for the expansive promise of her own youth:

> This flag a nation takes, to stud
> The battle-fields with beauty . . .
> Color of dawn and of your own heart's blood . . .[20]

In subsequent years Deutsch and Yarmolinsky became increasingly disillusioned and strongly anti-Stalinist. Yarmolinsky published *Literature under Communism: The Literary Policy of the Communist Party of the Soviet Union from the End of World War II to the Death of Stalin* in 1960, a study of what he described as "a nightmarish page in the history of letters."[21] Not only had the revolution been betrayed by a return to tyranny, but reactionary opposition to change had gone the same way, culminating in Nazism and fascism, leaving only a soft, undefined middle ground of doubtful tenability. Today, feminist political theory recognizes the need to escape the terms set by the battle between left and right and to pursue a new politics of opposition to the patriarchal structures that have generated that battle in the first place. But lacking that insight then, and finding her revolutionary commitment usurped by a dogmatic, oppressive male radicalism, Deutsch was left without a coherent political position. Like Kay Boyle, she developed what might be called a politics of compassion, defending the victims of oppression wherever they might be, guided by moral feeling rather than doctrine or ideology. Thus she might seem either profoundly radical or profoundly conservative, depending on one's point of view. Admirable though it was, her position had lost its original initiative and had become essentially defensive.

The same ambiguity of commitment pervades Deutsch's status as a poet and literary critic. The idea of her creativity as essentially a form of rebellion was very deeply rooted, a recognition of her position as a woman, whether or not she framed it in feminist terms. An undying resistance to oppressive authority, a determination to bring the new into existence, were the theme and driving force of her most ambitious work, the book-length poem *An Epistle to Prometheus* (1931). The stealing of fire from the gods must have appealed to Deutsch on some unspoken level as an image of women's daring to appropriate the language and poetic forms of men. At the same time, *An Epistle to Prometheus* broods on the rampant destructiveness that always attends any revolutionary advance in human thought, and questions the future safety of the planet. In her mature years, Deutsch grew more inclined to shrink from violent change and to emphasize the continuity of cultural tradition, for fear of losing civilized life altogether.

The balance Deutsch increasingly sought between a valued past and a radically innovative future indicates that she was unable to resolve the dualism within herself—the acceptance of patriarchal authority on the one hand, a woman's revolt against it on the other. Gradually her politics became almost completely divorced from her poetic voice as she drifted toward the conservatism of the Great Tradition, with its core of male elitism.

It is easy to understand how this could occur. The modernist movement in poetry, at first a kind of anarchic revolt heading in many directions at once, as Deutsch's own rebellion had done, had begun to sift itself out after 1930 under the influence of Eliot, Pound, and Yeats. In spite of significant personal differences, these three men had arrived at a similar rationale for the salvation of Western culture whose continuity had been threatened by the political upheavals and wars of the early twentieth century. Deutsch had shared their anxiety, and now was attracted to their solution—a modern style that answered the need for innovation, along with a profound commitment to traditional values of the past. The paradoxical union of order and disorder, of authority and revolt, was precisely what Deutsch had sought in her own way. Deutsch had also needed a clear sense of self-definition as a poet—her primary need, perhaps, as a creative woman. This was provided by the modernist idea of the "pure" poet, the craftsman, the shaper, whose lofty calling placed him above politics in a class by himself. As these pronouns indicate, the artist-elite was a masculine ideal, reflecting male hierarchies of the past and revealing the reactionary character of the modernist leaders.

Deutsch could embrace the modernism of Eliot, Pound, and Yeats only by ignoring the political implications of their views for women and their direct contradiction of her own surviving radicalism. These three men had in common the belief that liberal, democratic European civilization had failed and their duty was to shore up the ruins, to take a stand for order and the preindustrial values of the past. This meant upholding the idea of a hierarchical, patriarchal, class-structured society, whose poetic culture is maintained by a traditional elite. Such societies were, in Yeats's view, "masculine, harsh, surgical," with "great wealth everywhere in few men's hands . . . an inequality made law."[22] For Eliot, speaking of an aspect of fascism which he found appealing, "Order and authority are good: I believe in them as wholeheartedly as I think one should believe in any single idea."[23] All three men had a contempt for the masses and were attracted to fascism partly because they saw Germany and Italy as the last bulwark against Communist hordes from the east. "The forces of deterioration are a large crawling mass," Eliot wrote, "and the forces of development half a dozen men."[24]

A male elite requires inferiors in order to maintain its superiority, and these were, predictably, women and racial minorities. "There will probably always remain a real inequality of races," Eliot believed, adding piously and paternalistically, like the imperial English he admired, "our moral obligation towards inferiors is exactly the same as that towards our equals."[25]* An understanding of Pound's gross anti-Semitism may not be found as convincingly in his economic theories as in the psychological need of the autocrat for a category of persons to denigrate, without which he cannot feel his greatness. Pound took the same kind of manipulative attitude toward women: he developed a theory of creativity in which male genius is literally contained in the sperm and requires depositing in an acquiescent female receptacle for the poet to father new thoughts and inventions. This echoes an ancient male belief that men are solely responsible for generating children, women being mere incubators, an attitude that Eva Keuls has called "the most fundamental cause of repression and sex antagonism."[26] It also symbolizes the male confiscation of female creativity. Throughout his life Pound appropriated women to serve the needs of his imagination. The youthful diary of his wife Dorothy Shakespeare reveals a woman confusedly searching for a great man to lead her to a vision of Truth. She wasn't sure about Ezra at first: "Oh! Ezra! how beautiful you are! with your pale face and fair hair! I wonder—are you a genius? or are you only an artist in life?"[27] It was Pound's cunning policy to head off such doubts and not wait for history's judgment, but to dictate that judgment himself: "*I* happen to be a genius."[28] The terms "great" and "genius" have traditionally been used only in reference to men, since women were automatically assigned, like Dorothy Shakespeare, to the function of support and reverence.

The modernist writers, in effect, mounted a counterrevolution

*Eliot makes a distinction here between the abstract spiritual equality of all human beings and their irremediable inequality in reality. This separation between religious truth and worldly truth is traditionally a basis for justifying the preservation of present power arrangements. It reveals Eliot's profound conservatism and the grounds for his sense of despair. The spirituality of radicalism, in contrast, always proposes a divine force active in the world to transform resistant institutions rather than preserving them, and is driven by a sense of hope. The clash between these opposing positions echoes throughout modern poetry. It can be seen, for example, in Louise Bogan's admiration for Eliot's spirituality, and in May Sarton's rejoinder (in their unpublished letters) that Eliot's spirituality lacks the true inner fire.

to the anarchic forces they believed to be destroying the fabric of European culture, and offered an alternative version of radical change: the paradox of continual experimentation in service of the values of the past. As Stephen Spender has written in his essay "Hatred and Nostalgia in Death's Dream Kingdom," "They wrote modern poetry to reject modern life."[29] Pound's *Cantos,* Louise Bogan perceptively observes, are a near-incomprehensible pastiche that gives the impression of a chaotic present, without rational order, through which shine glimpses of the idealized past. Or, in Spender's words, a "feeling that the dead had a life more living than any which is possible in the conditions in which the writer lives today."[30] The avant-garde thus became the sponsor of reactionary attitudes and values.

According to Cairns Craig, the poetic innovations of Eliot, Pound, Yeats—"the climactic image, the allusive method, the incomplete poem"—were devices "which succeeded in encompassing both the experience of loss and the sense of dynamic opportunity" brought about by the catastrophe of the war, an effort to "move dramatically forward only in order to recover the order of the past."[31] It became possible to form a paradoxical tradition of the new, to institutionalize the idea of change to the point where the always-modern could even become entrenched in the conservative academic world. Inevitably, the modernist movement fashioned a canon dominated by the figures of conservative white males, concealing its political implications under the cover of "pure art" and developing critical concepts that effectively shut out the work of women and minorities.

The ebullient outburst of female creativity that occurred between 1915 and 1930 as an important aspect of the original modernist impulse was repressed and brought to an end by the elimination of women from serious consideration, particularly under the influence of the New Critics, whose critical methods were an analogue of their conservative politics. Eliot praised the Southern Agrarians, the group from whom the New Criticism emerged, for their opposition to industrial encroachment upon the South: "The old Southern society, with all its defects, vices and limitations, was still in its way a spiritual entity."[32] The idea of a self-contained, hierarchical social order, lighted from within by its own spiritual flame, resistant to disruptive outside forces, and changing only according to its own inner laws, found its equivalent in the New Critics' concept of the poem as a timeless organic entity complete in itself and needing no external references to determine its meaning. Thus the poem was isolated from the restless emotional and political context so important to all writers who found themselves excluded from the white male hierarchy. Because of these unspoken political assumptions, the act of writing a poem served entirely opposite purposes for men and women: for men, it was an assertion of the permanent, a defense against possible intrusion and loss of power; for women, it was a connecting with the fluid forces of the world in order to establish a presence there. Deutsch's autobiographical heroine in *A Brittle Heaven* sees the need for women to escape powerlessness by giving a voice to their experience: "If you could write a poem about it, you would escape. It was the only way to conquer life. Any experience that you could set down in black ink on thin strong paper."[33] The male modernist dogma, which even today is accepted as inviolable truth, that a poem cannot be "about" anything but itself, effectively excluded women and other unvalued groups whose need was for an art of communication and connection. By selective application of this dogma, the politically inspired work of leftist poets could be deplored as a violation of artistic integrity, while the reactionary views of equally political poets like Yeats, Pound, and Eliot could be silently overlooked, even when flagrantly present as in the *Cantos*.

By eliminating considerations of gender, and treating the poem as an impersonal object or artifact, the product of male intellectual discipline, male critics could conveniently dismiss poetry by women that struck them as displaying a feminine consciousness. The method of defining women out of the canon is revealed unabashedly in John Crowe Ransom's essay "The Poet as Woman," in which he takes Edna St. Vincent Millay as the archetypal woman poet and proceeds to reduce all women to a subintellectual level, incapable of doing a man's work in poetry. Millay's shortcoming, he says, is "a deficiency of masculinity."[34] To Ransom, women are essentially naive, childlike, and earthy, and their poetry tends to be a nonintellectual expression of immediate personal feeling. Millay's poetry "fascinates the reviewer but at the same time horrifies him a little too. He will probably swing between attachment and antipathy, which may be the very attitudes provoked in him by generic women in the flesh, as well as by the literary remains of Emily Dickinson, Elizabeth Barrett, Christina Rossetti, and doubtless, if we had enough of her, Sappho herself."[35] The view of women as a "horrifying" natural force, to be excluded from the rationally controlled male sphere, puts women in the same disruptive class with revolutionaries and others whose self-assertion threatens male power. Ransom's linking of the revolutionary poet Wordsworth with women makes this clear.

Here it must be noted that the women poets who flourished in such numbers after 1915 were not motivated by the pessimistic Pound/Eliot/Yeats view of a collapsing civilization: they were filled with hope and a desire for freedom, the exhilarating promise of expanding opportunity. One need only compare Babette Deutsch's Class Day poem, with its affirmation of "Something . . . in us to answer the thrill/ Of things untried" with Eliot's youthful exhaustion and malaise—"Do I dare?"—to realize that what appears as beckoning possibility to the oppressed seeking freedom is frightening to the reactionary clinging to his security.

The clash between male conservatism and burgeoning female power, essential for understanding the modernist period, appears quite early, in a skirmish between Ezra Pound and Harriet Monroe in 1914, over her slogan for *Poetry* magazine, borrowed from Whitman: "To have great poets there must be great audiences too." Pound, outraged, immediately had visions of the rabble being invited to dictate to the elite. "Humanity is the rich effluvium," he wrote to Monroe, "it is the waste and manure and the soil, and from it grows the tree of the arts. . . . The Lord of the Universe sends into this world in each generation a few intelligent spirits, and these ultimately manage the rest. But this rest—this rabble, this multitude—does not create the great artist. They are aimless and drifting without him."[36] Monroe, however, could not be budged from her own vision of a pluralistic democracy in which all voices must be heard and no authoritative elite dictated the values. In this she provided, whether consciously or not, a political basis for women's creative work. Monroe's refusal to acknowledge the supremacy of the modernist movement has been attributed to various shortcomings on her part. But it seems rather a woman's resistance to the attempt to build a hierarchical, elitist canon dominated by white males, and her favoring instead a kind of open literary society in which women, minorities, and all classes can realize their equally valued identities. Women and minorities, who constitute powerless segments of society, have no problem with the idea of pluralistic values, since they already survive by virtue of a double or multiple consciousness. It is the powerful who insist on imposing oneness. From women's standpoint, a central elitist tradition, shored up by schools of criticism, occupying the English departments of universities, and controlling awards, prizes, and honors, appears to be a tyranny rather than the preserver of culture.

Babette Deutsch could not easily transform the reactionary views of an elitist male tradition into a suitable vehicle of expression for a woman. Indeed, she herself was transformed in the attempt, even contributing to the definition of the modernist canon that minimized—virtually excluded—women, in her critical survey, *Poetry in Our Time* (1952). Eliot, Pound, and Yeats were now firmly established as its triumvirate of heroes. Deutsch (in her 1963 revision) gives thirty pages to Eliot, twenty-eight to Pound, and twenty-six to Yeats, besides numerous additional references. Only 16 percent of the poets dealt with are women, the majority of them mentioned in only a line or two. The renaissance of women's poetry between 1915 and 1930, to which Deutsch owed much of her own impetus, has all but vanished from her picture, and is treated as passé. The women most highly regarded are Edith Sitwell, Léonie Adams, H.D., and Marianne Moore—all poets who, in various ways, were acceptable to men. Even so, the women are faulted for being overly "fastidious" and reluctant "to confront things ugly as things lovely."[37]

none of them as strong as the more intellectual males—typical male criticism of women.

Deutsch also accepts the New Critics' dogma that art and politics don't mix, that the poem exists by its own internal laws. She is scornful toward the "vulgarity" of leftist sentiments intruding upon the poem, while treating Pound's virulent anti-Semitism with surprising tolerance. Deutsch cannot avoid mentioning the towering figure of Langston Hughes, but seems to feel that ethnic consciousness weakens art. His technique is "simple," in contrast to "so scrupulous a craftsman" as Elizabeth Bishop, some of whose " 'Songs for a Colored Singer' are more telling than some of Hughes' intimate Negro songs."[38] Margaret Walker, winner of the Pulitzer Prize in 1942, and Gwendolyn Brooks, winner in 1950, are not mentioned at all, nor are any other prominent black poets. Deutsch promulgates the modernist myth that the poet stands apart from gender, race, or social circumstances in a class by himself, that art is pure, and technical skill and intellectual sophistication are the chief considerations. The result is to define a modern tradition in terms of conservative white male attitudes, and to patronize women and racial minorities in a manner Deutsch would not think of doing in other contexts.

Deutsch's retreat from her youthful revolutionary spirit, her attraction to the purportedly apolitical aestheticism and spirituality of Eliot/Yeats/Pound, seems motivated in part by her reaction against Communism. (Communist or Communist-front writers were given short shrift in *Poetry in Our Time,* or omitted altogether.) It is a characteristic of entrenched power, whether in a racial group or social structure, to consider its own actions nonpolitical, while attributing political motives to those who disagree with it. The reactionary character of the modernist/New Criticism movement is revealed in its appropriating the high ground of pure art while denying artistic validity to those who offended its unspoken political convictions. The Communist movement obliged by occupying the polarized position at the opposite extreme, subordinating art to political message. Patriarchal power always functions in this way, dividing and polarizing as a way to maintain itself, and forcing the noncommitted to choose sides. Deutsch's aversion to Communism was understandably deeper than her possible aversion to reactionary power as vindicated by Eliot and Pound. The Communists had first usurped the goals of the anarchic, free-spirited radicalism on which women had thrived, and then crudely forced artistic creativity to serve the interests of its ideology. Since there was no alternative for a woman except to subside into traditional female powerlessness, Deutsch chose to align herself with the elitists who claimed the right of proprietorship of the arts.

There is no evidence, however, that Deutsch shared the anti-Communist paranoia of Eliot, Pound, and the Southern–New Critics group. A Library of Congress committee dominated by conservatives like Eliot, Lowell, Tate, R. P. Warren, and Aiken awarded Pound the Bollingen Prize in 1949, quite conscious of the political implications of their actions. Pound was then confined in St. Elizabeth's Hospital on grounds of insanity, though his incarceration appears to have been arranged by sympathizers to avoid his standing trial for treason for his pro-Axis radio broadcasts from Italy during World War II. At St. Elizabeth's he continued to write and hold court for a crowd of admirers. The committee, anticipating an outcry against giving the prestigious, government-sponsored award to a man notorious for vilifying Jews and praising Hitler during the Holocaust, issued a press release defending its action and claiming political innocence:

To permit other considerations than that of poetic achievement to sway the decision would destroy the significance of the award and would in principle deny the validity of that objective perception of value on which civilized society must rest.[39]

In the ensuing public uproar, Eliot, writing to Léonie Adams, hinted that sinister pro-Communist elements were probably behind opposition to the award to Pound. The excitable Robert Lowell apparently also believed that anyone who objected must be either a Communist or an unknowing dupe of Communist manipulators. A few months later, Lowell went on to lead a witch-hunt against "hideous perversion"[40] by possible Communist influences at Yaddo, where he was a guest. Allen Tate perhaps contributed more than anyone else to the atmosphere of defensive hysteria, perceiving the opposition as an attack on the whole New Critical movement by its leftist enemies. The committee was dominated by a point of view sympathetic with the reactionary tendencies of Pound—the mind-set which views itself as the chosen guardian of culture against the vulgar mob, surrounded by evil, conspiratorial enemies, but noble in its defense. The pure poem had attained its political expression as the McCarthy era dawned, its ultimate divorce from moral feeling; and the idea was promulgated that the pure poet himself was above political responsibility.

Since male modernism was a kind of club to which women were seldom admitted, it is not surprising that Deutsch has been relegated like so many others to the sidelines. She was haunted toward the end of her life by the conviction that she had been undervalued as a poet and critic. Ironically, the very men she honored and strove to equal probably refused to take her quite seriously because she was a woman. While the struggle for recognition of a Joyce or a Pound has been sentimentally suffused with an aura of heroism, the more urgent, lonely, and compelling struggle of women like Deutsch, trying to hold together in one beleaguered center the creative forces of their lives, has gone unacknowledged.

Babette Deutsch's marriage exemplifies the skillful balance of opposites that was her nearest approach to an achievement of wholeness. She and her husband, Avrahm Yarmolinsky, constituted a kind of harmonious professional partnership, each producing in a long lifetime a shelf of several dozen books. Some of the volumes were translations on which they collaborated, he providing the literal sense of a Russian poem, she the form and grace of English. They met, in fact, when a friend brought them together with the idea of their translating some Russian symbolist and nineteenth-century poets. Yarmolinsky, chief of the Slavonic Division of the New York Public Library, and an immigrant from the Ukraine, was not at first approved by Deutsch's Berlin-Jewish parents, who considered his background beneath that of their daughter. Their opinion was irrelevant. Deutsch found in Yarmolinsky a gentle, bookish man who respected her creative originality without jealousy or a desire to control. The success of their mutual support is demonstrated in their immense productivity and continual development over the more than half-century of their marriage.

The dual role of poet and mother, however, was never worked out to Deutsch's satisfaction. Her son Adam Yarmolinsky has remarked that she felt she was "not cut out to be a mother." The two sons spent their childhoods in the care of full-time nursemaids, a costly procedure for a couple with only a moderate income who also gave generously to humanitarian causes. It is probable that Deutsch felt more guilt and pressure in failing to live up to the conventional image of a mother than Yarmolinsky did as a semi-absentee father. In the gently rueful judgment of their son Adam, both were "more successful as literary people than as parents."[41] In *An Epistle to Prometheus* there is a note of exasperation at having to carry the burden of domesticity while wrestling with the major intellectual questions of the age. Unlike Dante in the dark wood of his mid-life crisis, Deutsch wrote,

> my life is rather
> a clutter of furniture and books and children,
> the confusion of a cramped and crowded room.[42]

Deutsch maintained a firm and disciplined grip on her work through a lifetime of challenges and distractions. She had written poems almost as precociously as Hilda Conkling—two appear in her *Collected Poems*—and had published before the age of ten. In advanced old age, bedridden following a series of strokes and surgery to remove two blood clots from her brain, she continued to compose poetry even though she was unable to write letters or make entries in her checkbook. Deutsch never relaxed her resistance to the fears and discouragement that threaten to silence all creative women. In her poem "Quandary", she puts her finger precisely on the problem of a woman to sustain her creative will:

> How to sustain the miracle
> Of being . . .[43]

Rhetorical questions abound in Deutsch's work, their very frequency and form indicating a refusal to accept subjugation. This must be kept in mind when dealing with Deutsch's ambivalent acceptance of the male model of the poet-craftsman and the goal of success in a male world. Her unstated aim seems not to have been "male identification" (a term of doubtful validity in any case), but the assertion of a woman's strength in the face of the charge of female weakness.

Lola Ridge expressed the subtlety of gender interaction in her poem "Russian Women":

> You swing of necessity into male rhythms
> that at once become female rhythms . . .

Ridge went on to say,

> Yet in you there is no peace,
> But infinite collisions . . .[44]

Deutsch did not always find it easy to keep the upper hand on the tensions and conflicts generated by the terms of her creative life. In her later years, after a mastectomy in 1963 and the death of her husband in 1975, she suffered periods of extreme depression. "Hell is not far below," she wrote in "Damnation." It is not a place one enters permanently or avoids: "You come and go. . . . And when you go/ You do not lose it . . ."[45] When the visitations of black despair became overwhelming, she submitted to electric shock treatments. Still, she kept up a stream of letters to Congresswoman Bella Abzug and others, protesting injustices, and continued contributing money to those whose misfortunes aroused her compassion. When Kay Boyle was in financial difficulty in 1978 because of illness, Deutsch, at eighty-three and herself ill, arranged assistance for her from PEN and other sources. She had turned a deaf ear to Boyle's radical-spirited poetry, caught in the modernist dualism that called propaganda what it couldn't accept as pure art; but she did not let that affect her friendship. When Boyle heard of the shock treatments Deutsch was undergoing so late in life, she cried out in words that ring with more truth than she perhaps realized, "Are you being punished for being a strong, courageous, and enduring woman, poet, and friend?"[46]

SEVEN
The Quest for an
Alternative Vision

* **T** * HE PRICE paid by women who sought to negotiate a compromise with patriarchal power, as Babette Deutsch did, was quite different from that of women who declared themselves outlaws and challenged male sexual dominance unequivocally. The deep, internalized pain of Deutsch, shared by so many creative women, was repudiated by militant radicals like Genevieve Taggard and Lola Ridge: They were willing to suffer the consequences of a fight, but not the stifled bitterness of subordination. It is curious that they should be among the most neglected and undervalued of all the women poets of their time, "part of the buried history within the buried history," as Louise Bernikow has written, "banished from contemporary consciousness."[1] This cannot be explained by their extreme left-wing political views alone, for male artists have been forgiven greater sins. The reason appears more likely to be their alarming discovery of authentic power and self-determination; this threatened not only the entrenched privilege of conservative males, but also the patronizing sympathy of liberals, at whom Lola Ridge could snarl, "to hell with all their pity."[2]

Genevieve Taggard's development into a poet-rebel was actuated by certain harsh lessons of her childhood and youth. She was born in Waitsburg, a small town in southeastern Washington, in 1894, daughter of a schoolteacher who had married the school's principal. Mrs. Taggard, like Edna St. Vincent Millay's mother, was powerfully gripped by a thirst for education and culture, "a hard-working, high-handed, generous, and handsome girl," Genevieve wrote. "She never set limits to what she could do . . . she was in rebellion against small-town sterility, determined to go to college . . ."[3] The grand hopes of Genevieve's mother were frustrated by a lack of money and the unenterprising mildness of her husband, on whom she was forced to depend financially. Nevertheless, they saved two thousand dollars and were preparing to escape when her husband's brother arrived from the East and asked for the money to buy an apple orchard.

"My father loved my uncle with an unnatural simplicity," Genevieve wrote. "The money went of course to John, college plunged into inaccessibility, and my mother was in the usual trap and, I am sure, as bitter as any modern woman about it."[4] The series of three children had begun to arrive, and her mother's defeat at the hands of a man she relied on seemed complete.

Still, another avenue of flight opened up. The Taggards, last in a long line of pioneers, made the ultimate move westward: they pulled up their shallow roots and sailed to Hawaii in 1896 when Genevieve was two to run a missionary school. Genevieve remembered the Hawaiian years as "our garden of Eden; our newfoundland." The children turned brown in the tropical sun, and money seemed to be of little importance, for there was always an abundance of tropical fruits and friendly neighbors, "the Portuguese, the Filipinos, the Puerto Ricans, the Japanese, the Chinese, the Hawaiian Chinese, and the hap-a-haoles."[5] The easygoing multiracial life was based on mutual respect, personal freedom, and enjoyment in a spectacularly beautiful setting; the serpent that betrayed other paradises, the ruthless competition for money, property, and power, was seemingly absent. Genevieve's passive, gentle father could tend his students, his mangoes, and papayas in peace, and her mother could paint oil pictures of "red hibiscus and pink cane fields, and lavish festoons of fruit."[6]

In this retrospective version of her childhood, Genevieve Taggard had shaped her memories to fit the South Seas myth—a heaven of natural sensuality, perfect equality, and individual freedom from social controls. As Elvi Whittaker shows in her study, *The Mainland Haole: The White Experience in Hawaii,* the mythic, paradisal Hawaii is a compensatory projection of the Western consciousness upon the Third World, "the product of puritanism, guilt, constrained sexuality, unrewarding labor, malignant surroundings, and racial threats."[7] The myth of a peaceful, innocent way of life could have consequences in either of two directions: into exploitation and ruin, or into radical idealism, a hope of fulfilling what the myth promised. To Genevieve Taggard, it was the latter. She believed she had actually experienced an ideal, alternative way of life, and so never stopped fighting for it.

The conquest of paradise, for good or ill, so deeply imbedded in the Protestant-Puritan-pioneer consciousness as its ultimate goal, also had an inevitable tragic, final act: the fall from grace, the failure to retain possession of its Eden. This lesson in realism, too, was not lacking in Taggard's experience. In 1905 Genevieve's father developed lung trouble and the family were forced to return to Waitsburg. Unable now to bear the harsh, dreary, small-town life, they hastened back to Hawaii the next year. But in 1910 her father's ill health obliged them to leave Hawaii and to throw themselves on the mercy of now-prosperous Uncle John and his unsympathetic wife. What occurred then determined Taggard's attitudes about the evils of power and money for the rest of her life: John refused to pay back the two thousand dollars because the loan had never been put in writing. Instead, he offered his brother a job helping with his pear orchards. The family, humiliated, near poverty, settled down to make the best of it, no longer gathering mangoes that fell unsought from the trees. Genevieve hated the small town and its inhabitants with restrained fury. Thirty years afterward she still vented her scorn:

These people, these white people, were barbarous! They thought it was a lark to go down to see the noon train come in! They waited with great tension in a room full of tobacco spit for the mail that consisted of a mail-order catalog. They screamed out the news if a neighbor had a haircut. They told each other how many overalls they had in their washtubs last Monday. They didn't know how to live at all.[8]

The lust for profits, justified by a narrow self-righteousness, was the ugly spirit of a white America whose people preyed on one another, who "didn't know how to live," who lacked beauty and wholesome sensuality and kindness. Taggard became unwavering in her vision of races mingling in harmony, of respect for personal freedom, of generosity and enjoyment of life. She often felt that a brown-skinned playmate had been right in telling her, "Too bad you gotta be Haole [white]."[9] Never forgetting her mother's fate, Genevieve determined to forge a life for herself unmolested, if possible, by the forces she hated. Although the family was able to return to Hawaii in 1912 for two more years, the interval in Waitsburg could not be forgiven.

In 1914 Taggard was able to enter the University of California at Berkeley with money given her by friends in Hawaii. Her mother and her father, now an invalid, moved to Berkeley with her. Genevieve and Mrs. Taggard ran a boardinghouse for students in order to support the family, a necessity that forced Genevieve to take five years to graduate. Witter Bynner was teaching at Berkeley then, and encouraged her to develop her poetic talent seriously. At Berkeley, too, she became a close friend of another student and disaffected rebel like herself, the future novelist Josephine Herbst. The two sampled the radical life, joining in talk sessions with San Francisco writers and newspapermen. Taggard and Herbst nicknamed each other "Tandy," after a story in Sherwood Anderson's *Winesburg, Ohio* in which a young girl is deeply stirred by a man's words: "Out of her defeats has been born a new quality in woman. . . . I call it Tandy. . . . Dare to be strong and courageous. That is the road. Venture anything. . . . Be something more than a woman. Be Tandy."[10]

After graduation in 1919, Taggard moved the next year to New

York, where she was employed by the avant-garde publisher B. W. Huebsch. She found a place among the Greenwich Village radicals, with their experimental love affairs, and continual analyzing of painful relationships. Edna St. Vincent Millay was the brilliant focal point of the group's enchantment with the "new" woman, who acted out her feelings in public view instead of diffidently concealing them as women had done their bodies. Taggard admired her both personally and for her work: "She's the only girl that's at all like us,"[11] she told Josephine Herbst. Women's emotional freedom and sexual self-determination were revolutionary and were at the heart of the rebellion of Taggard, Herbst, and others, as well as being the object of such distaste to reactionary males like Ransom and Tate. Taggard rapidly established her reputation as a poet and in 1921 joined Padraic Colum and Maxwell Anderson in founding *Measure: A Magazine of Verse*.

While Taggard's career unfolded in much the same way as that of other women poets of her generation—the early promise, the struggle against a restrictive background, the move to New York, the acceptance into a lively subculture of writers and artists—her marriage plunged her into her own unique and lonely crisis of female power in relation to men. Genevieve Taggard had fallen in love with Robert Wolf, an aspiring novelist and contributor to radical publications, almost as soon as she arrived in New York. She described her affair to Josephine Herbst as "my broken-edge love . . . beautiful and frail . . . the realest most exquisite thing that ever happened to me . . ."[12] Still approaching life with romanticized hopes, and accepting the bohemian idea of life as passionate experimentation, Taggard married Wolf in March 1921 in spite of their frequent clashes and at least one separation.

Genevieve confided the private, inner story of her marital experience, which taught her the meaning and extent of sexual antagonism between men and women, in letters to Josephine Herbst. Herbst, her "dear one,"[13] had become an indispensable friend, drawn into intimate sharing by Herbst's own problems in love. In 1920 Herbst had become involved in an affair with Maxwell Anderson, a conventionally married man trying somewhat desperately to act out the free-love scenario of the young radicals. Herbst became pregnant, and was cheerfully willing to bear the child. But Anderson, horrified, persuaded her to have an abortion as the only way to save himself from unthinkable complications. Herbst told no one about it except Taggard, who supported her through the ordeal.

There were many parallels in the encounters of these two women with men. Both were forceful and self-reliant, both believed in women's sexual freedom, and both were attracted to sensitive men who tended to be tortured in their relationships with women. There is a clue here, perhaps, to the reason why the women poets were so attracted to the Romantics, especially Keats: a sexually ambivalent sensibility combined creative masculine power with a feminine capacity to be in touch with emotion; and yet the effort was doomed by burnout or early death, reflecting the frustration women also felt in trying to assert the power of their unexpressed selves. After reading about Keats all one day in February 1921, Genevieve Taggard wrote to Herbst, "We are his sisters, Jo. He felt and saw as we do, and he was much more in the dark, much more unfinished. Everything he wanted was denied."[14] The most appealing men were those who, in spite of their problems, seemed to share women's experience, rather than the males who dogmatically assumed superiority over women. Taggard's relation to the latter kind is amusingly revealed in her acquaintance with Mike Gold, whose stereotyped attitudes toward woman have already been noted:

Mike is writing at last & cigar in mouth pronounces as many bromides about women & Art as he once did about communism . . . one can be very fond of him, but never get any comfort from him of an intellectual sort. He is to me that emotional thing that he despises women for being.[15]

Taggard and her husband enjoyed a brief idyllic period in the first weeks of their marriage, living in a cabin on a Connecticut farm with their grey-and-white kittens named Sheats and Kelley. In striving to realize gender equality and demonstrate it to the world, they experimented with blending their names together: Genevieve Taggard Wolf, Robert Taggard Wolf. The practice was abandoned almost immediately, because each felt invaded by a foreign identity.

Wolf, besides, had to retreat in the face of embarrassment before his male friends, who were incredulous at the idea of a man's assuming a woman's family name, even in the innocuous middle position. Their playing at perfect union was soon threatened by an unexpected complication: Taggard became pregnant only a week after the wedding. They were dismayed at first by the prospect of having their writing careers interrupted by the burden of a child just when they were starting out. But they quickly accepted the idea, and Taggard, romanticizing her biological role, loved her "beautiful, full feeling"[16] and wrote a poem, "With Child." They made plans to spend two years in California, and headed west late in the year. But it seemed prudent to stop in Chicago with a cousin of Wolf's and wait for the birth of the child, whom they were alternately calling "Eric" and "Mary Jean." The child, born on December 13, 1921 after thirteen hours of labor, was at first named Mary Alta. (Her name continued to fluctuate for two years.) The idea of living with "an actual baby" "scares me to death,"[17] Taggard told Herbst, no longer romanticizing childbearing. Childbirth was the most demanding experience a woman could face, she thought; after successfully handling that, nothing else could seem quite so threatening again.

The inexperienced Taggard was too optimistic, however, about the effect a child would have on her husband, on their marriage, and on her own writing career. The next few years were a kind of hell from which she emerged only slowly. Wolf was concentrating desperately on writing a novel and had soon become querulous, moody, and uncooperative, anticipating his mental instability of later years. Taggard was already familiar with the "frightful Wolf temper,"[18] intensified now by his fear that the baby would continually interrupt his attention to his novel and that lack of money would force him to seek work and lose valuable time. He felt that the baby was chiefly Taggard's responsibility, regardless of the limits it placed on her own capacity to write.

They moved on to California in April 1922, settling into a primitive cottage in San Juan Bautista, a picturesque small village, quiet and isolated, in the hills south of San Jose, green and muddy in the spring, brown and sunbaked in summer. When Wolf's novel got stuck and wouldn't move, he would lash out at her and she would fight back, determined not to be swamped by marriage. "He's a boy you know Joe," she wrote Herbst, "& very easily upset and the baby does that . . . because he has hallucinations he'll never finish the novel."[19] Taggard took on the double responsibility of mothering "those two fragile things—the book and the baby." But her pioneer spirit began to flag after a few months:

When you struggle for weeks with stoves & mud & diapers & canned food, and hardly have time to wash your face, your attitude to Robert as an artist, to yourself as an artist, changes. You have a wooden determination to be one, and iron determination to make it possible for Bob, but all that grimness is a joke in the face of endless attempts to be practical.[20]

In the fall they moved to a friend's apartment on Russian Hill in San Francisco, with an improvement in physical comfort and the renewed pleasure of old friendships. Taggard found employment teaching the wealthy matron Mrs. Sigmund Stern and her friends about poetry, and lined up a job at Mills College in Oakland for the spring semester. "Oh Joe," she cried. "If I didn't have this terrible financial burden I could be such an artist now . . . But how can I when Mary's whole existence and Bob's single chance at self-realization depends on whether I work hard enough to earn $250 a month!"[21] Robert Wolf was still the central problem, with his insistence that his novel take precedence over everything else. Living together had become almost impossible because of his continual moodiness over any interruption of his work. In mid-December of 1922 he rented a cabin on the Marin County coast at Bolinas where he went to live by himself. They decided they would be happier meeting occasionally as lovers than living in grim union. Taggard cleaned and decorated the place for him, planting flowers, and with a measure of relief settled down to her own separate life. As she wrote later, "It is better to work hard than to be married hard."[22]

Nevertheless, one more unanticipated crisis rose to threaten her, this time reducing her to a fury against all society. Earlier, after their arrival in California, Taggard had felt morning sickness and believed she had become pregnant again. A visit to a San Francisco doctor to seek an abortion left her disturbed and uncertain:

Of course the horror of [pregnancy] was intense. You can understand—the fear of hurting Mary—the lack of money—the feeling that I'd done the last thing to Robert to break him and the book—there was too much suffering. It made me feel I'd lost all my carelessness & bravery about life—I was caught and two others would suffer. Well after that the doctor said I wasn't pregnant! I didn't believe him because he was one of those men who think women ought to suffer. He said we shouldn't have intercourse if we weren't willing to take the consequences—and said, My mother raised nine! with a finger pointed at me.[23]

Here, encapsuled, is the essential story of sexual oppression: the woman "caught," assigned to do the body work while men detached themselves from it for the transcendent labor of the mind. It lay at the heart of Taggard's rebelliousness, for she had always rankled at the victimization of her mother, whose talents and force of character had been wasted by the family role she was obliged to play. While Robert Wolf possessed his creative solitude, removed from the daily pressure of family responsibilities, Taggard had reason to feel depressed:

I am very low now, because I must have another visit to the abortionists. It is very hard to keep one's spirits up, with that physical consciousness. I am coming to hate this world Jo with a bitter hatred that goes on intensified by these compromises for money.

Having to sacrifice the potential life of a child, she lashed out at society, which "I would tear to pieces like a wild beast if I were out of its power." She hated even the "so-called radical poets and friends around here. They are all deluded, smug, hard silly second-raters . . ." A lighted candle, placed before Bob's picture on Christmas Eve like a shrine to the romantic love that struggled to endure, "shows such a face of dark unflinching suffering. I burn it and feel that way too. Don't think, Joe, that loving Bob is all radiance. He is what you see in the picture . . ."[24]

This time Taggard found a doctor who would perform the abortion. Then the pressure eased, for the job at Mills College

The ardor of most revolutionary women pales in comparison with the fire of Lola Ridge, who in another time might have been canonized as one of the great militant saints. Indeed, the word "saint" was sometimes used by contemporaries to describe her, not because of pious behavior (which she would have scorned) but because of the spiritual violence that drove her. Emanuel Carnevali tried to identify what distinguished her from other women poets: she was "virile," she had none of their "weakness" or "sweetness." Her socialist convictions, he felt, were also in a class apart:

> It is not a matter of politics, it's a matter of such damning hatred and love as would turn a modern city to ashes. . . . I think she is one of the most beautiful signs we have of woman's emancipation and independence. . . . This rebellion of hers is pure beauty, it is sanctified. . . . It is an eternal thing, the thing that caused Prometheus to be bound. It is the fire of heaven burning in this wonderful woman's blood.[41]

Ridge knew that her anger, her restlessness, her blunt force burned with the same fire as her spiritual aspiration and were inseparable from it. She differed perhaps from other women in not being fearful of these tendencies or dutifully trying to repress them, but seeking instead an individuation that would encompass the totality of herself. Ridge was fascinated to trace the origins of her own fiercely rebellious nature by poring over her childhood: the private awakenings that set her apart from others, the clash between a child's amoral, inquisitive thirst for knowledge of life and the repressive admonitions of adults who seemed bent on stifling a small girl's natural development. Her long poem "Sun-Up" (1920) is a set of remembered fragments of childhood in Australia, presented with psychological immediacy and a remarkable lack of sentimentality.

> You look in the eyes of grown-up people
> to see if they feel
> the way you feel . . .
> but they hide inside themselves,
> and so you do not find out.[42]

The child quickly builds a store of incommunicable private experience that becomes a valued treasure because adults have tried to suppress it. The child's defiant, forbidden thoughts have often to do with violence:

> But I like the picture of the Flood
> and the little babies getting drowned . . .
> If I were there I would save them,
> but as I can't save them
> I like to watch them
> getting drowned.

She is not a "nice" little girl. She sticks pins in flies and pulls off their legs, interested that they continue to buzz. Nero did the same thing as a child, Mama warns her, "and nobody loved him."[43] Because badness is unlovable and is continually condemned, the child carries a burden of self-disparagement that will erupt in further expressions of violence. When she strikes her mother, her mother withdraws love:

> though you rub your cheek against mama's hand
> she has not said darling since. . . .
> Now I will slap her again . . .
> I will bite her hand till it bleeds.

The same drama is enacted with her doll: "Sometimes I beat her/ but I always kiss her afterwards."[44]

At night there are sometimes terrifying nightmares and the presence of shadows, the projection of her own blackness:

> there is a shadow
> that is not the shadow of a thing . . .
> it is a thing itself.
> When you meet this shadow
> you must not look at it too long . . .
> it grows with your looking at it . . .

But instead of fleeing the shadow with fear and condemnation, as adults do, she offers it the love that the inner blackness craves and is always being denied:

> See—I've no light in my hand—
> nothing to save myself with—

> yet I walk right up to you
> if you'll let me
> I'll put my arms around you
> and stroke you softly.
> Are you surprised I'd put my arms around you?
> Is it your black black sorrow
> that nobody loves you?[45]

Ridge's conquest of fear, her unflinching self-acceptance, over-turned the psychological mechanisms by which women have been kept under patriarchal control. She overtly rejected the female obedience and powerlessness that her mother had settled for, the fear of stepping out of line:

> When you tell mama
> you are going to do something great
> she looks at you
> as though you were a window
> she were trying to see through,
> and says she hopes you will be good
> instead of great.[46]

Lola Ridge was a small, thin woman, whose weight often fell well below a hundred pounds, and who was besieged most of her life by ill health: tubercular lungs that would never completely heal, shattering migraine headaches that she called "blind attacks," and digestive ailments that sometimes forced her to spend days in bed. Her long, pale, thin face with aquiline nose, and dark hair pulled back, gave her a gaunt beauty that served at one time to get her a job as an artist's model.

Ridge was born in Dublin, Ireland in 1873, but remembered little of her very early childhood there, or her absent father, for her mother soon emigrated to Sydney, Australia where there were relatives. In a few years her mother moved on to New Zealand, where she married a miner and where Lola grew to maturity. The awakening of Ridge's creativity came as a "call" when she was about thirteen, living with her mother and stepfather "in that bare, small, mean sordid hut in the New Zealand bush." Her "coarse, honest, violent kind Scotch stepfather, a runaway sailor, deserted to that worked-out diggings," sometimes punctuated their life with "raging drunken sprees when he would smash every stick of furniture in the three-roomed shack—until we had to rely for seats on the big wooden boxes holding five-gallon cans of kerosene we used in the tiny lamp with which we lit the three rooms." Yet he recited Shakespeare to her on occasion and "impersonated Macbeth with a great deal of passion and power," and would tell her stories from Homer.

One summer evening after dark the three sat silently, Lola working at problems in arithmetic, "when something stopped me like a touch on my heart." In the stillness and isolation, she suddenly heard the sound of the trickling creek some fifty feet below, a sound "so long docile, unnoticed . . . endlessly vociferating, separating itself from all the other noises of the night—Suddenly talking in sweet clamor to my ears alone." It was the inner voice of herself, impinging on consciousness for the first time. "An ache fell upon me and I looked at my mother . . . the pure pale cameo of her face—unmoved, disdainfully still sadness . . . She did not hear my waters trebling." Her stepfather, "brooding and staring at the log fire," heard nothing, "but as though I touched him he glanced up at me . . ." His eyes expressed the defensiveness of a small animal at the mouth of its burrow, his habitual stance. Then his look softened, and he "said in a low grave voice, 'I am thinking of my dead sister Jessie.' " These unexpected words struck her like an impact from some realm of invisible being.[47]

Then without warning, my whole being shivered and I felt as though something had struck and passed through me, leaving behind it some of its terrific power. I turned back to my copy book as one picks himself up after an earthquake has flung things on the ground.

But I did no more arithmetic. Instead I wrote what I believe now was my first real poem. . . .

I showed it to my mother (I recall my big scrawled lines filled one page of my copy book).

My mother turned to me—an attention in her face—the Easter-lily face I was to see slowly wither—"There is something it does—a poetic image."

"Which image? It's a—a—" I groped for the word I thought of afterward as theme, but could not get it—"It's about one thing." The residue of the passed power yet in me, I thought, I am a poet, one of them. Doesn't mama see it." I felt surely, certainly, as I was sure I was alive, there was some great thing to be done and that I was to do it, that I had been called, that I should be called again, that my life was for it.

Lola Ridge at first thought of herself as much an artist as a poet. After growing up in New Zealand she had, in 1895, married the manager of a gold mine. When the marriage proved miserable, she left him and returned to Sydney where she studied art, though continuing to write poetry. In 1907 she sailed to San Francisco, using an assumed name and birth date in order to prevent her husband from tracing her. After a year on the West Coast she moved on to New York, where she eventually abandoned art and wrote for popular magazines, supporting herself in the hand-to-mouth fashion that was typical of most of her life.

When the Ferrer Association was formed in New York in October 1910, Lola Ridge found a focus for the passionate radicalism that had grown out of her experience of poverty and alienation. The group took its name from the Spanish anarchist Francisco Ferrer, who had been executed by a firing squad the previous year on dubious charges that linked him to terrorist acts. The real threat that Ferrer posed to established authorities, however, was his school in Barcelona, the Escuela Moderna. Ferrer was a freethinker whose stated aim was to teach children to resist dogma and think for themselves. The unconventional, coeducational Escuela Moderna was a model for the libertarian Free School movement, and as such was feared by the Church and state as a threat to their hegemony. Ferrer's death foreshadowed the similar fate of Sacco and Vanzetti and the wave of right-wing repression that accompanied World War I and its aftermath, setting the terms of battle between despotism and liberty that preoccupied Ridge throughout her life.

The driving spirit of the Ferrer Association of New York was Emma Goldman, whose courage and generosity Ridge admired immensely—Ridge contributed poetry to Goldman's magazine *Mother Earth*—though she found Goldman's powerful personality difficult to work with. Indeed, one of the chief problems of an association of anarchists was the clash and disorder of so many willful individualists all wanting to have their own way. Ridge later described the Ferrer Association's weekly meetings as a kind of exciting free-for-all:

Every new measure had to be put to a vote, and I had to fight hostile forces inside that mob of three hundred—mostly foreigners and all wild unkempt spirits, haling from one another by its hair that wonderful doll, Liberty.[48]

Within a few months, the Association opened a Sunday school on the model of the Escuela Moderna. Ridge, with her conviction that children's minds needed to be freed from adult tyranny, was actively involved in the organizing effort. Within a year, it had expanded to become a full-time day school, and the center had become a lively gathering place for lectures and other events, attracting not only committed anarchists and socialists but artists, writers, and all kinds of unclassifiable free spirits including, on occasion, Theodore Dreiser, George Bellows, Man Ray, and Eugene O'Neill. Lola Ridge suggested the idea of publishing a magazine, *The Modern School,* and became its first editor. She seems to have served a variety of functions as a key person in holding the organization together. Rion Bercovici, a student at the Ferrer School, remembered her from a child's point of view as someone who "fulfilled the specialized function of frying banana fritters and telling charming stories."[49]

At the Ferrer Association, Ridge met David Lawson, a man some twelve years younger than she, who became a close friend and then lover. They lived together for half a dozen years before marrying in 1919. The anarchist milieu promoted equality between men and women and abolished in principle, if not always in fact, traditional gender roles. Lola Ridge's relationship with David Lawson, which lasted for nearly thirty years until her death in 1941, was a remarkably successful attempt to put their anarchist-feminist ideals into practice. Romantic love was not the basis of their marriage, as it supposedly was in conventional patriarchal unions, where it served chiefly to submerge a woman in a man's life, as Genevieve Taggard had learned to her regret. Rather, their marriage depended on love defined as respect for one another's uniqueness and freedom, and was a voluntary commitment intended to promote individual development instead of stifling it. Such a relationship, with all good intentions, however, still requires a natural balance of temperaments. Lawson's rather prosaic personality, his steadiness and durability, were an effective foil for Ridge's mercurial, driving, excitable force. They could clash and differ, live apart, contemplate separation without tragedy, and always maintain toward each other a deep affection. Through much of his life Lawson was a civil engineer who worked for various state and municipal agencies in the New York City area. He seems to have looked up to Ridge as a great genius whom it was his privilege to serve. He performed secretarial work when needed, as well as quietly smoothing countless irritating small problems, for Ridge in her headstrong enthusiasms was prone to be forgetful and careless in keeping trace of personal things like medicines, reading glasses, books, pens, and papers. She always asked him first for his critique of her new poems, and even referred to publication decisions as "ours," made jointly.

Ridge and Lawson lived and traveled away from New York for five years after 1912. By the time they returned in 1917 the Ferrer School had moved to New Jersey and their connection with it was never reestablished. Emma Goldman was to be deported to Russia in December 1919 for her radical activism, silencing one of the major feminist voices of the period. Ridge celebrated her greatness in contrast to the little men who had hounded her out of the country:

> How should they appraise you,
> Who would walk up close to you
> As to a mountain . . .
>
> Only time
> Standing well off
> Shall measure your circumference and height.[50]

Lola Ridge saw Goldman only once again, on a street in Paris in January 1932.

No, she did not see me. I turned and walked a few steps, observing her. She looks much older and smaller. I had forgotten what a short woman she is. No, I made no move to speak to her. Our ways have long since parted. . . . Well Emma has had a difficult, yet a rich and varied life. She has seldom been bored. She is not to be pitied but envied by countless women of drab and colorless lives.[51]

On hearing of Goldman's death in June 1940 she wrote in her diary that Goldman was

the warmest woman I have ever known. She was intelligent, kind, of an unwavering purpose. I liked her well. We parted spiritually—in silence—neither speaking of that which had parted us. It was only that she could brook no independence of action in any associate—indeed she did not want associates but disciples—and realized sadly I was no disciple.[52]

In 1918 Ridge published her first volume of poems, *The Ghetto and Other Poems,* which electrified reviewers and readers with its free-verse snapshots of the city, its easy command of the style popularized by Sandburg and strongly identified with "tough" masculinity and gritty realism. "Flotsam," for example, presents an old man and woman huddling together on a cold park bench at night, "Slovenly figures like untied parcels,/ And papers wrapped about their knees . . ."[53] New York is a raft on which gathers "flotsam of the five oceans." Although there is nothing attractive about these derelicts, except perhaps their pathetic clinging to each other, the poem is nevertheless a kind of compassionate embrace of rejected and alienated people.

Ridge's love of the poor and outcast was free of any condescension, for she felt she had come from among them. And although she seldom made a point of it, she was keenly conscious of being Irish under oppressive British rule, proud of the resistance of "my shackled country."[54] Like Yeats, she wrote a poem on the Easter Uprising of 1916, though less sedately:

> My heart is like a lover foiled
>   By a broken stair—
> *They are fighting tonight in Sackville Street*
> *And I am not there!*[55]

Her bond with an oppressed people stirred her to empathize with the Jews of the ghetto, whom she depicts as bursting with the force of life, colorful, not to be contained there for long. Ridge displays none of the sentimentality of liberals who see oppressed people in terms of helplessness, of needing to have good done to them: she visualizes their freeing themselves by their own innate power. Perhaps she always bore in mind the impression made upon her as a young child by her mother's remark, "The Jews are good people. You must always be very nice to them."[56] In any event, "The Ghetto" is a challenge flung at the pervasive anti-Semitism of the literary world of Ridge's time.

Ridge did not voice her rebellion against patriarchal power in the guarded, indirect way familiar in earlier poetry written by women. The overt force of her defiance is revealed in "A Toast," in which she mocks the patriarchal god of the Christian churches,

> A being to pander and fawn to,
>   To propitiate, flatter and dread
> As a thing that your souls are in pawn to,
>   A Dealer who traffics the dead;
>
> A Trader with greed never sated,
>   Who barters the souls in his snares,
> That were trapped in the lusts he created,
>   For incense and masses and prayers—

The Christian martyrs, "anointed of heaven," are to be pitied because they "died for evil,/ Believing the evil was good." Ridge's toast is not to them, but

> To the Breakers, the Bold, the Despoilers,
>   who dreamed of a world overthrown. . . .
> —To the Outlawed of men and the Branded,
>   Whether hated or hating they fell—
> I pledge the devoted, red-handed,
>   Unfaltering Heroes of Hell![57]

After the success of *The Ghetto and Other Poems*—Ridge was nearly fifty—the emphasis in her life shifted from activist work to authorship. The golden age of anarchism had come to an end, symbolized by the deportation of Emma Goldman. In the 1920s anarchism, with its opposition to state-sponsored violence and its championing of individual liberty, was attacked and driven out of almost every country, including Russia, where Goldman remained only briefly. Lola Ridge ultimately abandoned any hope for anarchism as a political movement, but continued to hold it to be "the philosophy I'm closest to and shall always be . . . It is indeed the one ideal (social) that for being unrealizable must always remain an ideal. But that is *not* to say it must not be taught and striven for all the same—woven about the illusive essence of liberty it is the only one that surrounds this even for a moment."[58]

Ridge became the social center of a fluid, shifting group of poets who met in her apartment for the evenings of stimulating talk and mutual criticism so warmly remembered by William Carlos Williams, Marjorie Seiffert, Kay Boyle, and others. Ridge worked with Alfred Kreymborg on the short-lived but influential little magazine *Others,* and in 1922–23 as American editor of the international magazine of the arts, *Broom.*

Ridge's connection with *Others,* and her arrival at the center of the new poetry scene, brought her on a lecture tour of the Midwest in 1919. In her lecture, Ridge bypassed discussion of new directions in the "poetry renaissance," the province of popular publicists like Harriet Monroe, Jessie Rittenhouse, and Amy Lowell, and went directly to a much deeper level in considering revolutionary change. Her talk was entitled "Woman and the Creative Will."[59] Had the times been more receptive, Lola Ridge might have emerged as the chief feminist theoretician and spokeswoman for the women poets who otherwise lacked sufficient consciousness to constitute a movement. A decade before Woolf's *A Room of One's Own* and half a century before the flowering of radical feminism, Ridge conducted a wide-ranging exploration of concepts still basic to considerations of women's creativity.

Ridge began by attacking male claims "that woman has NO creative will—except the physical urge to continue the race." She dismissed the biological argument for women's supposed inferiority as an idea imposed on women's natural function by patriarchal males in order to justify their dominance. "The biological difference between the sexes is directly responsible for the social, political and intellectual disabilities that have crushed women for centuries. But it is not responsible for her deficit in the basic quality of creative art—the quality men call genius—for that deficit does not exist." Ridge proposed an androgynous, non-gender-based theory of creativity, uniting intellect and intuition, the qualities traditionally separated on sexual lines and therefore lopsidedly developed by both men and women. Great male artists have been free to correct this imbalance and to develop the "female" intuitive aspect of themselves, thereby reaching the heights of creative expression; but women have been prevented by men from developing the "male principle [of] mental order—the power of correlated thought," with the result that their creative energy has been "squandered . . . in the arduous years of childbearing."

Ridge seemed to imply that the male/intellect–female/intuition polarity is not necessarily a fixed attribute of sexual differentiation, but rather the result of historical development. She believed that the dualism was potentially present in every individual, and that its ideal expression was a kind of androgynous blending that promised real equality and an end to sexual antagonism between men and women. She touched briefly on homosexuality—a natural manifestation of the complex mixture of male and female in creative persons, she felt—but dismissed it as an issue made important only by men seeking to justify their own superiority. Ridge repeatedly urged that women's creative will should not be viewed simply as that of men's in female clothing. In appropriating "masculine" intellect, women were only reclaiming aspects of themselves that men had usurped. Her quest was for the wholeness women had been denied. "Woman is not and never has been man's natural inferior," she concluded.

She has been and is still suffering from arrested development; and considering the mental and spiritual strait jacket within which she has had to grow, she has not made such a bad showing . . . in a society, moreover, that denied her all means of perfecting her expression.

Now these equal opportunities are hers, and every year more and more women are expressing themselves in art. . . .

I see a great future for women in creative art.

But the creative artist must approach life not with braggadocio—for braggadocio is only fear ashamed—but without fear. The women of the past were dominated by fear. Even now we are a little like children who have been made afraid of the dark, and in whom fear still works through a thousand obscure impulses, whose source we can no longer trace. We [must turn] an even bolder front to the shadows.

Women have the greater part of the essential genius of the race. And when they have realized these two things—that art must transcend fear, and that thought is a spiritual substance to be molded like clay—they too will be the masters of dreams.

Lola Ridge planned to expand her lecture into a book to be called *Woman and the Creative Will*, and worked on it at intervals for a decade. The projected contents, according to her biographer and editor Elaine Sproat, included "chapters on Woman's Creative Past, The Nature of Aesthetic Emotion, Man's Conception of Womanhood as the Rib, Puritanism and Art, The Bisexual Nature of Genius, The Inner Room [a discussion of woman's suppressed will and the art of concealment], Sex Antagonism, Motherhood and the Creative Will, and Woman's Future in Creative Art."[60] Some of her topics are prophetic of concerns not developed by literary feminists for nearly half a century. Ridge produced a ten-thousand-word chapter, but after her editor at Viking held it for two years only to tell her that "he could not bring out a book written in this way as not more than three hundred people would buy it,"[61] she severed relations with Viking in 1929 and abandoned the project.

Ridge recognized that through personal relationships women's possibilities were focused and made real; and it was in friendships with women that she brought to bear her conviction that women should infuse one another with a sense of worth. Ridge seems to have had a special affinity for tormented and misunderstood women like Elinor Wylie and Evelyn Scott, disregarding their reputation for outlandish, "hysterical" behavior and finding under the surface a dignity and creative genius to be respected.

Evelyn Scott was only twenty-six, and Ridge forty-six, when they met in 1919. The young poet-novelist from a small town in Tennessee had already crowded a lifetime of experience into a few years, having eloped with a married man and spent several unhappy seasons on a failing ranch in Brazil before being transported to the bohemian literary life of New York, where she flaunted sexual promiscuity and professed the most scandalous opinions with a sardonic smirk at false morality. Ridge understood Scott's hectic behavior and exposed nerves to be her response of horror to the biological objectification of women. Not long after meeting Scott, Ridge wrote "To E. S.":[62]

> You inevitable,
> Unwieldy with enormous births,
> Lying on your back, eyes open, sucking down stars,
> Or you kissing and picking over fresh deaths . . .
> Filth . . . worms . . . flowers . . .
> Green and succulent pods . . .
> Tremulous gestation
> Of dark water germinal with lilies . . .
> All in you from the beginning . . .
> Nothing buried or thrown away . . .
> Only the moon like a white sheet
> Spread over the dead you carry.

Evelyn Scott was cynical about friendship between women, cautiously approaching Lola Ridge somewhat as Genevieve Taggard did Josephine Herbst, with a put-down of most other women for "feminine underhandedness" and dishonesty. In a poignant letter she ventured forth from her defenses to offer herself in friendship:[63]

I was thinking that if I had known there was somebody like you in the world a few years ago, some of my conclusions about the universe would have been modified and I would have been a good deal happier. When I was a lot more of a kid I wanted a woman friend tremendously, but the mystical kind of idea I had of a bond which would be a recognition of a common defeat was something I had hardly articulated and nobody else understood—and of course I never found the woman. Then I thought I would rather have a daughter than anything else. I had a son instead and

I am glad, for the other would have been too cruel a luxury. My experience with women has always led me to a deeper conviction that they are too thoroughly without faith (due to several centuries of experience) to attempt honesty without insuring themselves against the consequences with sexual weapons. . . . I was so sure of this that I said to myself once and for all, I don't want any women, ever, ever. I want to live. I want to be strong. And I want to indulge myself in my own particular vanity which is to despise evasions. . . .

Well, as I say, I had thoroughly made up my mind that it was impossible for *two* women to be honest in the same room—.

I'm not sentimental either, and I'm not insisting that we shall throw ourselves into each other's arms with cries of rapture which we don't feel. You're even a very different kind of person from me, and probably from your point of view, better. From my point of view of course, you aren't. But I do respect you. Just as I know myself worthy of respect, I feel very deeply that you are. I want to be your friend. Sometime when you are better I want to talk about myself, and I shan't apologize for doing it.

The subterfuges and betrayals of women toward one another were, as Scott saw, the product of male sexual manipulation, and a woman could not truly be the friend of another unless she recognized this and could avoid it. Ridge must have been deeply moved by this courageous self-exposure and the risks it entailed. She remained Evelyn Scott's closest friend for the rest of her life, providing the kind of acceptance and reliable affection that Scott desperately needed.

Ridge, for most of her life in New York, served as a center around which others clustered, a person who provided the spark of fire that released their energies and made things happen. Evelyn Scott wrote to David Lawson, "Going up your stairs is like mounting Jacob's ladder with the angels. And I wish this were the whole world—what I find when I get there. Where every human value that makes life exists in pure. You and Lola make me feel as people would feel in a church if religion weren't fear worship and god really divine intelligent love . . ."[64] The demands of others, however, were a heavy drain on Ridge's time and frail health. By the late 1920s—she was now in her mid-fifties—Ridge's tuberculosis began to flare up. She was also under serious financial strain, a perennial problem, since, though frugal and indifferent to luxury, she never bothered to think about earning money. Concerned friends collected money for her, handling it as delicately as possible, for she resisted accepting help.

This difficult period was intensified into spiritual crisis by the profoundly disturbing Sacco-Vanzetti case. Sacco and Vanzetti had been anarchists like herself, brothers in a cause, and to her they embodied the spirit of free thought which the state had tried to murder by killing them. Ridge had been arrested in Boston in 1927, along with Edna St. Vincent Millay, for protesting the impending execution of the men. Their deaths plunged her into a profound reconsideration of the violence out of which the defiant, creative spirit always seemed to have been born or renewed. In 1929 she completed a long, impassioned poem in nine parts on the death and resurrection of Christ, each section written from a different participant's point of view. The title, *Firehead,* signified the fire of the divine spirit in humanity, burning fiercely, destructive to complacency or to the entrenched powers that resist it. The creative spirit, in bringing into the world something new and valuable, was itself not innocent of violence.

Ridge had completed the poem in the summer of 1929 while a guest at Yaddo, a place she found surprisingly congenial and restful, for she had a congenital dislike of institutions. She was in poor shape both physically and emotionally, having spent most of the spring in a hospital bed. Under so many pressures she was alternately depressed and elated over her work and assailed by digestive problems which she tried to resolve by swallowing bottles of castor oil. She felt that *Firehead* could not have been completed without the support she received from Yaddo, and so she dedicated her book to the place. Certain portions of the book were especially difficult, "cerebral and expository . . . This is how men beat women in creative work," she wrote her husband, "Davy," "—just by doing such things as this and doing them well. It requires a mental discipline women are only beginning to get—and as you know I did not get even that poor help!"[65] At times her concentration broke down, and she felt herself swept by intense psychic storms. When an actual rainstorm burst over Yaddo, whipping the trees, she saw a spruce "with long green hair . . . the most feminine looking thing you ever saw,"[66] as an image of herself, a woman surviving the disastrous assaults of life, trying not to bend her back.

Firehead was not a final statement, but opened Ridge's imagination to the possibility of an even grander conception, the great work she had felt herself capable of in her youth. She began to envision an entire cycle of poems, "Lightwheel," on the fire of the spirit manifesting itself in certain significant periods of civilization, as in the pre-Columbian cultures of America or in Europe at the time of the French Revolution. She started to plan and do research in 1930 for the first segment, on Babylon. It was not enough, however, to meditate on information in libraries and museums—she felt compelled to visit the archaeological site of Babylon itself, where important excavations had been done in the 1920s, to absorb the spirit of the land. With insufficient money and uncertain health, unable even to see how she could succeed, she sailed from New York in mid-May 1931 for London, where she planned to work at the British Museum before traveling on eastward.

Two weeks in London proved to be costly and not as rewarding as she had hoped. Following a recommendation that Corsica offered a quiet, cheap place for creative work, and a step in the direction of her goal, she left England for the Corsican coastal town of Ajaccio. But Ajaccio turned out to be expensive and she soon ran short of money, having to send desperate appeals for help to Davy. She could not speak French, the weather grew brutally hot, and she injured herself in a fall. Nevertheless, she wrote Davy, "Do not think that I regret the step I have taken—I'd do it all over again tomorrow. I feel deep down in my own consciousness that *this* is *right,* that great work will come of it—My poem is living in me. . . ."[67] Before the summer was over, she felt trapped and desperate to get out, though the lack of money forced her to remain. The visiting British snubbed her for being both shabby and Irish, and she could barely communicate with the Corsicans. "I feel more and more my place is with the outlaws and outcasts of the world. The thing is I've got soft. I shrink from dirt and poverty. But I'm not going to give in to it. I'm going to try to harden myself more."[68]

In late August Ridge was finally able to leave Corsica for Nice, where she stayed more economically for two months and even began tentative work on the poem. "My poem started of itself—this morning as soon as I woke up,"[69] she wrote one day in early September. As she felt herself moving under the influence of some guiding hand that steered her destiny, she experienced a series of powerful, prophetic dreams. In one of them, she saw her suitcases being carried on board a ship, and a door opening, letting in a flood of sunshine. Although she had been planning to wait until mid-November before sailing to Beirut, she woke one morning with a sense of having received a message to leave on October 21. She obeyed as nearly as she could, and arranged a sailing on October 25. As she stepped onto the deck of the *Angkor,* she saw the luggage being carried, a door opening to the sun, just as she had dreamed it: "I stepped through on the very deck of my dreams."[70] Such visionary experiences were evidence to her that she was successfully following her "call."

Lola Ridge pursued her flame with the tenacity of Captain Ahab, only invigorated by problems and deterrents, more resolute than ever in the grip of her excitement.

I'm facing life and my work *stripped*—and perhaps this is good and necessary. I will get helped and looked after, for it is ordained that I am to do this work. I was born for it when I was an infant in my cradle, this work that I am to do was already forecast. Firehead was the first—all before that goes for nothing, it was only a preparation.[71]

Wearing always the same shabby clothes, crowded in a room with three other women, seeing rats running on the deck, Ridge exulted in her separation from the affluence and orderly life of powerful, dominant countries like America and Britain. She astutely observed the British dealing with the "natives" from their pinnacle of imperial superiority and soon found herself in tune with the subjected people.

Ridge made her way adventurously overland to Damascus and Baghdad, settling into the Ritz Hotel, making friends with her Chaldean servants, whose dignity was "so profound and untouched, they wait on one with a chieftain-like air."[72] "The Arab people are beautiful," she declared, "the more I see them the better I like them."[73] She even thought of leaving New York, where the "atmosphere [is] bad to do creative work in,"[74] and moving to a French-speaking eastern country like Lebanon.

Baghdad was not easy: Ridge choked on the dust clouds always blowing in the city and heard rumors of pneumonia, cholera, and typhoid fever. But in spite of delays, illness that forced her to bed, her weakened lungs, and the constant threat of failure, she managed to visit the sites of Babylon and Ur. The flayed landscape, the merciless light on sand and stone, seemed the right dwelling place for the fire of the spirit whose first lesson was total disregard of human comfort or self-interest.

Ridge also studied collections in the national museum in Baghdad, which had been founded by Gertrude Bell, an Englishwoman who earlier in the century had, like Ridge, been magnetically drawn to the East. She spent most of her life there, loved and respected by the Arabs, dying in Baghdad in 1927, a remarkable woman of personal force who rebelled against Victorian restraints. Bell was doubtless a model for Ridge of what a woman of strong character could accomplish. How deeply she felt the connection with Gertrude Bell is indicated by her seeing a vision or apparition of Bell in her hotel room, stretching forth a hand for Ridge to shake. They might have been friends, Ridge thought. However one understands it, this experience of psychic union with Gertrude Bell marks the symbolic consummation of Lola Ridge's pilgrimage: a woman seeking the divine creative fire that men had always claimed was theirs alone, joining in spirit with another woman bent on the same quest, confirming one another.

Ridge returned to New York slowly, by stages, partly because of money problems—her trip had been financed largely by piecemeal gifts from friends and admirers—partly by her reluctance to be immersed again in New York literary life. She sailed from Beirut to Trieste, thinking, as she neared Italy, of Carnevali's saying, "O do not kick me away, great shoe,"[75] the words of another outcast. She had left Baghdad with a sore chest, afternoon fevers, and night sweats; but she felt, "Nevertheless, I love Baghdad, it nearly killed me, but my heart, as long as it beats, will feel its pull. . . . I felt a quickening of all vital forces and an intense intellectual and imaginative activity."[76] It seemed to her that she had been "helped by the world-spirit."[77] "I'll get out my book—only death will stop me and I don't believe it's going to—yet."[78]

Ridge arrived in Paris at Christmas, 1931, found cheap lodgings, and began to work on her book, wracked by illness and spells of depression. In March she finally sailed for New York, having made a strong start; "I find I've gone a lot deeper into life since I wrote Firehead."[79] Thinking of all she had been through, she remarked, "You know I am strangely hardy."

The great work Lola Ridge hoped to write took a somewhat unexpected turn away from her usual free verse: "The stately rather weighty content seems to demand the sonnet form,"[80] she decided. For the next two years she struggled to fit her theme to the confines of archaic language and an unaccustomed form.

Threads of shining power raying into me as from the sun and I with hardly enough strength to gather and weave them together. But what I want to do is bring all the forces of our age into this—all the frightful tensions in a sort of shiva dance—into that resolution that only art can achieve for more than a moment.[81]

The result was a vanishing of the Babylonian subject matter into a sequence of twenty-eight sonnets, "Via Ignis," on the general subject of the life-fire as it manifests itself in perpetual destruction and renewal. Ridge's purpose had never been a study of history, but a pursuit of the source of power and the reasons why it manifests itself in violence—a projection of the core of her own experience that had preoccupied her since childhood. Believing that she lived in one of the great transformative, violent periods of history, she wished to penetrate to the spiritual center of her age as one might a hurricane, and glimpse its meaning by letting its currents flow through her. *Dance of Fire* was published in 1935, with the sonnet sequence and a collection of additional poems more or less related to her theme.

Ridge was awarded a Guggenheim Fellowship in 1935, and received as well two other cash prizes for her poetry. Although tired and ill, she took advantage of the windfall to travel to Santa Fe and Taos, New Mexico, where she planned to work on a project that had been in her mind for several years, a probing spiritual autobiography. In her usual way, she moved restlessly from one lodging place to another, making friends, having to find doctors, observing the social life and antics among the writers and artists with detached amusement. She began to feel cramped by the small-town atmosphere, possessed again by the rage to do a great work. This meant another travel-quest, like the heroic pilgrimage to Baghdad, perhaps this time to Australia and Ireland to recover the threads of her own past. But she "felt suddenly that I was not interested a bit in myself or in treating creatively my past life."[82] Instead, she turned to the large-scale idea of the "poem of Mexico."

Or rather, as it seemed, the idea of a poem on Mexico began to assert its grip on her, as Babylon had done. She felt "at a turning point in my life, but with it a strange driving power—in fact an enormous sense of inner power and tranquility. Cortez must have had it and everyone who, for good or evil, for accomplishment or disaster, has gone forward, refusing to be deflected, toward some large goal."[83] Davy had appealed to her to return to New York, but "No," she insisted, "I can't work there much and cook, clean, and all the petty details of housekeeping that litter the mind more than a straight day's office work."[84] She was annoyed that Davy and other friends were always solicitous about her, trying to discourage her from trying the great schemes that gripped her, for fear of the consequences.

A powerful dream shook her to the roots, dramatizing her life as perhaps no dream or vision had previously done. She stood before a curtain, filled with a fearful sense of menace and foreboding. Hands pushed her forward, but she shook them off, saying she would step up to the curtain of her own free will. When she did so, a hand thrust out with a knife: "I did not flinch and it was driven right into my belly, striking deep and then sweeping in a downward curve." As the knife withdrew, she felt her bowels spilling into her hands.

With one hand clutching her open wound, she was led by Davy up some stairs, then up a ladder, until finally they faced a sheer precipice where two ropes hung. As she seized one, it fell loose in her hand, leaving a way for only one of them to ascend. Hand over hand she struggled up the rope to the top of the cliff, where she looked over the edge in awe: "Before me was a strange country. High mountains rose like towers, sheer and towering into a sky so dark blue it seemed black, there were blazing stars, the land was desolate—no sign of man or man's petty little structures." In the center of the sky blazed a huge ring of light, "as though a moon had been hollowed, leaving only the ring," with distant stars showing through and other stars trailing outward from the ring like rays, burning "with a terrible power." She was too weak to draw herself up over the edge. "There was no hand to help me and there I hung—forehead to the stars, feet over the abyss and a wound in my middle." [85] The dream imagery suggests the plan of the vast work gestating in her imagination, the visionary Firewheel. But her vision of the wheel of light seems also to be a mandala-like symbol of integration and wholeness of the self, of spiritual realization, threatened, however, by the extreme difficulty of the task and by her ill health.

In mid-October 1935 she left the distractions and aimlessness of Taos and Santa Fe for Mexico City, where she felt that "in some strange way the Mexican land and all its forces (invisible forces of earth mountains) are with me." [86] The quest that took her to Baghdad and now Mexico was in some sense a search for a place of ultimate peace within herself, the inner citadel beyond the storm of fire that filled all life with violence. "This stillness, I believe it is in more or less degree in each of us—the creative worker has to get himself in contact with it—or rather identify himself with that core of quiet that can only be reached by the serene inflowing rather than by the upstarting and conscious will. Anyhow it is in that inplace of us that things are resolved and happenings sifted until we get at their reality." [87] The quest seemed unending, the peace she craved, elusive. "I am too fierce and imperious, there is too much capacity for destruction in me, too little tolerance . . . too much pride. I notice that if I have a flower in my hand I tear it to pieces—and that is what I do with life."[88] The way to peace and serenity seemed paradoxically to lie through violence, the dance of fire, not only for herself but for all humankind; to embrace the negative principle without fear in order to pass beyond it. Her own life was an enactment of that inescapable crucifixion all life had to endure: "I wish only I could take all the pains of the whole world and bear them. I know my vision has gone far beyond anything related to any benefit to myself—I'm indifferent."[89]

When Nazi Germany militarized the Rhineland in March 1936, Ridge thought, "It has commenced, the Dance of Fire. . . . What to do?" The firebath she had long anticipated was about to occur. It reminded her of the beginning of World War I: "The dance goes on and the capering, gibbering death-mask dancers . . . in this book I'm going to express it, I think. Yes, to be strong, to do the thing you conceive in spite of all . . . then go down with your wounds . . . asking no pity—to hell with all their pity. But the dance . . . I must do the dance."[90] Ridge was no pacifist. She did not feel sentimental about the bulls or horses in the bullring; they had a final opportunity to go down fighting. As Ridge studied the Aztec gods of fire in Mexico City's museums, she thought, "To me fire has no suggestion of a conscious will—it destroys, incidentally, out of a burning innocence—the need to consume in order to strive."[91] Watching a May Day parade, she raised her clenched fist in a salute to the contingent of young Communists, whose handsome, uplifted heads and purposeful eyes filled her with admiration, symbols of the defiant underdog. "Internationalist that I am," she declared to Davy, "I am now more Mexican than anything else."[92] American tourists, oblivious to the general strike that greatly interested Ridge, were "the most uncomprehending, the most oblivious people in the world . . . manlets and manletettes each so gutless and so exactly like the other, one can hardly tell them apart. Of course, I try to be nice to them. However I note most of them look more or less askance at me after a day or so. I despise them and contempt is not easy to dissemble."[93]

Ridge remained in Mexico until March 1937, two years away

from New York and from Davy. She was reluctant to return, because of her precarious health and the damp cold of New York winters—"I've coughed heartbreakingly for six months"[94]—but also because she could not endure the prospect of domestic life. She proposed that it might be better for them to live apart. With his small salary and her negligible earnings they could not afford a woman to clean or cook, and it was assumed those responsibilities would fall on her. She put off the decision, driving to Laguna Beach, California with two women she met, and with not enough money for a bus ticket to New York: "No money whatever, no health—only my head full of vast dreams and my consciousness full of a deep and terrible knowledge of life. I know I have a great work to do—my greatest—but I'm a poor manager of life—it depends on money and T.B."[95]

The Mexican trip, though it seemed to her the climax of her life-quest, did not result in a clear plan of the book she wanted to write. Furthermore, she continued to be deflected by the desire to write an autobiographical novel as well as by the hope of writing other fiction in order to earn some money. But her will was still unshakable: "I care absolutely nothing for life and glory in standing alone."[96] She left Los Angeles by bus for New York in early May 1937, returning to Davy, for she needed help. In August she was in a convalescent hospital, "The House of Rest," in Yonkers. Her weight had dropped to eighty-three pounds.

Lola Ridge was able to complete only a little of her vast projected work during the few remaining years of her life. The two-hundred-line draft of a "Prelude" points toward a concept of the fiery life-force as female, suggesting that she was in the process of finding the spiritual integration she sought:

> O sacred way of the shining, as of thunderwinds, sunbearer
>   of an
> Infinite fecundity, more than the sea or woman; you of
>   unimagined contour,
> Containing all forms and embryos of forms . . .

This female power is greater than man's logical thought, which strives to compute and measure but "cannot live, there, between the fiery/

Frontiers of the last stars and your periphery . . ."[97] The triumphant finality of this concept may be compared with an earlier poem,
"Theme," in *Dance of Fire* (1935), in which the woman who struggles for transcendence is only filled with an indigestible heaviness,
paralyzed by the effort: [98]

> She has eaten of the locusts,
> Bright, pale-dry, scab-thin,
> Drifting like a manna—unaware
> This bounty had a delicate sting.
>
> Twixt weighted lids (though she surmise
> Deficiency of bright) she strives to hold,
> Against the gradual dark, the rose
> Of morning, cut-off and pressed tight.
>
> But her wings . . . flutter without peace:
> Not yet stiffened to a formal curve
> In static pattern of flight (as arms
> Too long upraised, take root amid the air,
>
> Transfixed on their own gesture), yet they beat
> As they would soar with that which cannot rise,
> Buoyant, to the remembered light.
>
> For having fed on that
> Which she can neither assimilate nor reject,
> she lies
> On the field of the locusts,
> Heavy with waste.

The nearness of death filled Ridge with a surge of resistance, an
affirmation of herself that was increasingly feminist. There were
episodes of serious friction between her and Davy during the last
year of her life, often arising from her increasing impatience with
her role as housekeeper, which she had come to thoroughly detest
but which she believed he expected of her. She alluded to more
serious reasons for disagreement, too, and her outbursts of anger
would cause him to retreat into silence, sometimes for the entire
day. "How depressing to sit at dinner [which she had prepared]
with a person who will not speak." It was a relief when he flung at

her the accusation that she was "cruel and . . . would destroy any-one near enough to be hurt by me . . . that I am destructive in my relationships," for this was better than "sullen and glowering silence." She reviewed herself, the problem of woman's fire and man's resistance, deciding that she did indeed expect too much of others and could not help retaliating when feeling injured; but that she truly "did not wish to destroy, but to save."[99]

The outbreak of World War II fulfilled Ridge's long-standing prophecy of the furious dance of fire to be visited on the world in her time. But with the integration of herself around the female divine principle, Ridge's political thinking took a new turn: war was "pri-marily a male urge . . . Helen, a lovely scapegoat."[100] She contin-ued to develop the idea of male aggression as the cause of wars:

Nazism or National Socialism or new brand Republicanism here in our America—or what you choose to label it—it is the "Everlasting Return"—the throwback to the old pattern cunningly disguised as the new. The old Caesarean design for conquest and material power—the war for the war's sake—the ancient primal *Male Dance*—from which woman is shut out save as a chattel, a breeder of warriors or the industrial hand maiden of war-riors. To take her dead man's place. Beware. . . . *There may be a woman dance.* . . ."[101]

The impersonal fire-force, in Ridge's conception, tended to dichotomize and thrust in opposing directions—one, the male bent toward conquest and control, fixing power in the hands of tyrants; the other, female in nature, resistant, even to the point of violence if necessary, in order to restore justice and peace. This rebellion and reconstruction was the place in the dance from which women had been excluded. As she caught the vision of the primal male dance and the countering female dance, she also experienced a mystical vision of the heart of life as a garden, renewing and restoring, a refuge from the violent play of the fire, the place from which crea-tivity emanated. It was Ridge's deepest wish throughout her life to serve the immeasurable spiritual power that brought humankind its intolerable wound but also the promise of a peace scarcely to be imagined. The way lay through suffering, through sharing human suffering with love:

While there is one hungry in the world, I shall know, though obscurely, I am not fed; while there is one bound I am not free. His words shall irk me in a deep place. I shall feel his spirit drawing at my spirit. The infinitely delicate currents between us, vibrating to his need. Oh multitudes, ye drawing me from all sides! How shall I endure you? . . . There is an endless trickle from my heart. My heart, too, is wounded beyond all healing.[102]

Lola Ridge's health deteriorated throughout 1940, and by spring 1941 she was confined much of the time to her bed. She died on May 19, 1941 at the age of sixty-seven, the scope of her ambitious, unfulfilled dreams known only to a few. Nevertheless, she had proven that women bore in them a capacity to shatter the patriarchal mold and penetrate to the heart of sacred power, claiming it as their own. For this, she stands at the center of women's development in the twentieth century. Such a spiritual revolution is profound and sweeping in its consequences; as Peggy Reeves Sanday has written, "give women access to sacred roles and much else will change."[103] Ridge viewed her work as an instrument of transformation, impossible for one person to finish, spreading its ripples far beyond the limits of her own life.

One of Lola Ridge's last poems was a lyric to be included in her unfinished long poem, serene in its acceptance of death and sure of the continuity of the spirit whose voice she had been, who would revisit the earth to complete her work in a more perfect form:

> O perishing light, though thou confound
>   This blood . . . and chill it at the source,
> The song, rising from the ground
>   Shall not be swerved from its course. . . .[104]

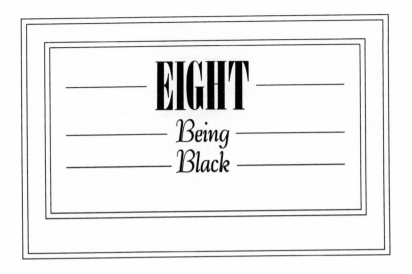

EIGHT
Being
Black

* T *HE GARDEN that appeared to Lola Ridge in a vision,
promising peace and the uninhibited flowering of imaginative beauty, is Eden restored, the place of Eve without
blame. It is a power-giving image of a woman's reconciliation with
femaleness, with the free and full expression of her true self. Those
women who understood most profoundly the nature of their
oppression were the most energized by the mythic potency of that
image. Even in many women's poems on the theme of restraint,
such as Amy Lowell's "Patterns" or Sara Teasdale's "The Garden,"
the garden is an oblique metaphor of female self-realization. But it
reaches greater consciousness among creative black women, whose
psychic survival has demanded a deep drawing on sources of symbolic self-redemption. Alice Walker's essay "In Search of Our
Mother's Gardens" points toward the centrality of the image. Its
richest expression, however, is achieved in the life and poetry of
Anne Spencer, a black poet whose garden in Lynchburg, Virginia
was the actual, physical place where she labored to unify earth and

spirit, to create herself. She would often work late into the summer evenings, sometimes by moonlight, with a diligence and inward preoccupation that were far in excess of any perceived necessity. Her intention was not merely to make a showpiece; for although the beauty of her garden was widely admired, it was her gardening itself that was amazing. Her husband built her a small house there, where she could meditate and write. She called it "Edankraal," a combination of their names, Edward and Anne, with the southern African word for a native village, suggesting also the Garden of Eden, man and woman unfallen. References to her garden appear in a fourth of her poems and perhaps figure indirectly in many others. Some lines written when she was ninety-two specifically link her garden with the creation of poems: turning up a worm, she observes, "And the curly worm, sentient *now*/ Will *light* the word that tells the poet what a poem is."[1] She probably did not have Eden's snake in mind, but the image has reverberations of sin and death being lifted from the dark unconsciousness—under a "shaly rock"—into the light, where they can be redeemed by love and creativity. One poem declares, "Say your garden at dusk/ Is your soul . . ."[2]

Anne Spencer was born on a plantation in Henry County, in the southwestern corner of Virginia, in 1882. Her mother, proud of having been born free right after the Civil War, nevertheless felt that slavery had "left its scent . . . on all of us."[3] Anne's mother was the illegitimate, unacknowledged child of a slave woman and an heir of the Reynolds tobacco family, and so internalized an irreconcilable conflict between the elite and the oppressed. On the one hand, she claimed her right to an aristocratic heritage, aspiring to the manners, the dress, and the sense of superiority of a lady. On the other, she was flung into the struggle, the lack of education, the closing of doors in her face, of a disfranchised people. At sixteen she married Joel Cephus, a man of mixed black, Seminole Indian, and white descent, born a slave in the early years of the Civil War. He was fiercely independent and proud, vowing he would never spend his life working for a white boss. He was able to save enough money to start his own business, a saloon in Martinsville, Virginia that was patronized by working-class white men.

Joel Cephus enhanced his own self-respect by a demeaning attitude toward females. He brought his small daughter, Anne, to his saloon, where she walked prettily up and down the bar, showing off, and the men tossed pennies to her. He and Anne's mother quarreled continually over this practice, until one day she marched into the saloon, where she had been forbidden to go, and tried to remove her daughter forcibly. Joel seized his wife, pulled up her skirts and spanked her in front of the silent patrons, while Anne cried. For over a year after that humiliation, Anne's mother earned her own money by sewing, since Joel would not permit her to have a job, and obtained some additional funds secretly from her brother, until she had saved enough to leave her husband. With her six-year-old child she departed for Bramwell, West Virginia, a mining town, where her brother lived. Joel did not stay long in Martinsville after that, but moved on to Illinois and then California. Neither Anne nor her mother ever saw him again, though they kept in contact from time to time.

Anne's childhood was spent in a racially mixed community, where her closest friend was a white girl. Anne's mother refused to live among poor mine-worker blacks, even her own relatives, boarding first with the only black doctor in town, and then the barber, both respectably middle-class. A "poor downtrodden snob," Anne called her many years later. Anne was an attractive, self-assertive, impudent child whom her mother always dressed in the most expensive clothes she could afford. Only later did Anne discover that self-assertive qualities considered engaging by whites in a child were rudely discountenanced in a black adult.

Anne was verbally precocious, with a surprisingly large vocabulary for a child, all the more impressive because she could not read or write. Her mother refused to send her to the black public school, not in resistance to racial segregation, but because she did not want her daughter to associate with lower-class black children. She too was illiterate, managing to conceal the fact adroitly, and so could not tutor Anne herself. Private schooling was a financial impossibility. The child picked up somewhat uneven reading skills with help from Mrs. Dixie, the barber's wife with whom they lived. When Anne was eleven, however, her father threatened to take her with him to Illinois if she was not given formal education. "[I] was the battleground on which they continued to fight out their distaste for one another,"⁴ she later wrote. Under that pressure, Anne's mother managed to arrange her admission to the Virginia Seminary in Lynchburg, Virginia, with ten dollars a month provided by Joel.

The Virginia Seminary was not an ordinary school. Its faculty was drawn from among graduates of excellent northern universities, who, led by an enlightened president, defied the idea that the education of blacks should be limited to practical manual skills, a policy designed to keep black children from entering the ranks of the elite. The Virginia Seminary taught both classical and modern languages—Anne studied Latin, French, and German—as well as mathematics and science, even psychology. The school was subsidized in part by the white National Baptist Convention, who occasionally sent inspectors, not so much to certify that the quality of education was high, but that it remained appropriately low. At such times the faculty hid their textbooks and brought forth tools and sewing machines. They were once caught off guard, however, and the president's salary was severely docked for allowing Greek to be taught to those presumed not yet ready for high culture.

Anne Spencer emerged from the Virginia Seminary in 1899, at age seventeen, as one of the school's brightest readers, with a good knowledge of literature, a lively self-respect, a conviction that no one could stop her from doing her own will, and a level, self-assured gaze that dishonest people would have difficulty facing. When selected to present a speech at graduation ceremonies, she prophetically chose the topic of black power, enlarging on de Tocqueville's statement in *Democracy in America,* "If ever America undergoes great revolutions, they will be brought about by the presence of the black race on the soil of the United States." Anne asserted, "If any disposition is to be made of the Negro, we will make that disposition."⁵ To her delight, the black students and their families occupied the main floor of the church where the ceremonies were held, while visiting whites were relegated to the balcony. Her speech, "Through Sacrifice to Victory," was the opening gun in a lifelong confrontation with racism, rising out of what she called her "colossal reserve of constructive indignation."[6]

Anne Spencer perceived that, unlike her mother, she could not live with a divided identity, reaching futilely for a world that only political force could place in her hands. Although three races were mingled in her, the potential of her creativity was defined by being black: her triumph was inseparable from the triumph of color over its desecration by whites.

Anne married Edward Spencer, a fellow student at the Virginia Seminary, in 1901, when she was nineteen. They settled in Lynchburg, Virginia, where they lived for the remainder of their lives in the home on Pierce Street that was the site of her famous garden. Ed Spencer offered the needed alternative to her father, in that he was not driven to prove himself a master of women. Anne called their marriage a rare and singular friendship. In her thinking, friends signified a spiritual union that went beyond considerations of race, sex, or power, a relationship of free spirits based on truth. As she wrote in "Black Man O' Mine," "All your loving is just your needing what's true."[7]

Ed was much darker skinned than she, a fact in which she took deliberate pride, in contrast to upwardly striving blacks who were extremely conscious of the "color line," valuing the shades of lightness closest to white. Even Langston Hughes, who asserted racial pride as Anne Spencer did, set forth in his autobiography the distinguished whites in his family tree that placed him in the mainstream. Spencer, however, suppressed all mention of her Reynolds forebears during her lifetime. She reversed the assumption that black ancestry was humiliating by considering her favorite poet Robert Browning a kind of black brother because he had a Creole grandmother. Many of her poems touch on the theme of a higher spiritual revelation hidden within what is dark, unvalued, or disregarded.

Edward Spencer's character had a core of pride and iron resistance, like Anne's. He had dropped his middle name and replaced it with "Alexander," after Alexander the Great. His homage to the truth Anne represented took the form of supporting her in the freedom she needed for her slow and arduous self-development, with the same kind of respect for personal dignity that she gave him. The world being what it was, they created their own world, and guarded it. Outside, however, there was no artistic culture to excite and guide Anne's imagination, like that which young white women could find even in provincial cities such as Chicago and St. Louis. There were no models of professional success to follow, not even a black Emily Dickinson to be unburied. Spencer made do with Browning, whom she had rendered black in order to form a bond of fellowship. She did not even think of finished poems as her objective, but rather the formulation of words and phrases in an endless process of continual self-development. She stayed up late at night, slept late, spent hours bathing and combing her hair, unceasingly busy at her mental work, which became most intense during her gardening. Women were hired to help with cooking and housework. "You write," she said, "because you can't stop writing." The words came from somewhere and had to be jotted down, or they would go away. She would even scrawl them on a bedroom wall at night in the dark on her way to the bathroom, odd Joycean phrases like "Go berserk in the widow's grey pasture,"[8] which held some nugget of meaning that might later be extracted and thought about. She covered the wall with scribbling until persuaded that it really ought to be painted over. A painter friend overlaid it with a mural, depicting, on Anne's instructions, a display of phony sophisticated people sipping drinks, entitled "The Cocktail Hour," to remind her to remain grounded in genuineness.

Over the years Anne Spencer filled innumerable sheets and odd scraps of paper with bits of sentences, paragraphs, and poetry in a process of letting the unknown depths of her mind churn up their truth, precipitated into conscious fragments of language. To display herself in formal poetry in the hope of being admired required the possibility of a publisher, an audience, a milieu in which an artistic persona could develop. Lola Ridge, in the New Zealand bush, could know that she was "one of them," because her culture and her race contained that possibility. Anne Spencer, in Lynchburg, Virginia, simply could not envision her future in such terms, despite her great gifts. The words nevertheless tumbled out as from a fountain impossible to still. Amused by the struggle of an advertising copywriter to achieve a single acceptable sentence, she said, "We have sentences all over the place."[9]

Even without the expectation of an audience, Anne Spencer did complete a few poems in the first decade or so of her marriage. Most of her finished poems, however, seem to inhabit formal structure against their will, beginning in the middle of a train of thought and breaking off with a suggestion of much still to be said. A kind of crabbed, Browningesque concentration seemed needed to force her words into even that much form. She occasionally resorted to conventional rhymed stanzas, but usually preferred clusters of irregular and asymmetrical lines, in a diction that ranged from the traditionally poetic to the contemporary conversational, emphatic with condensed restlessness. When a friend later suggested she might like Gerard Manley Hopkins, she read his work with delight and classed him with Browning as another poet who had a love of gnarled language similar to her own. But it was not until 1918, when Spencer was thirty-six, that she was stimulated to think of herself publicly as a poet rather than as a woman who played with words for her private purposes.

James Weldon Johnson, already a published novelist and poet when he became field secretary for the National Association for the Advancement of Colored People, came to Lynchburg in 1918 to help establish a local chapter there. Anne and Ed Spencer had been active on a Lynchburg committee to improve conditions for blacks and invited Johnson to stay in their home, as they regularly did visiting blacks because of Jim Crow restrictions on hotel accommodations. Anne's poems and poetic fragments lay about carelessly, as usual, and Johnson read some of them, surprised at the quality of her talent. He persuaded her to let him take several manuscripts to show to H. L. Mencken. As she recalled, Mencken said, "Tell that women to put beginnings and ends to her poems; I can't make heads or tails of them—but they're good."[10] (Mencken's taste in poetry was limited to the polished lyrics of Lizette Woodworth Reese and Sara Teasdale.)

Mencken wrote Anne what seemed rather cool and disheartening criticism of her forty-line poem "Before the Feast at Sushan," an elliptical study of a male-female relationship derived from the book of *Esther* in the Old Testament. Queen Vashti refuses the summons of the Persian King Ahasuerus to come forth and show off her beauty; he is outraged: "Every woman will come to know what the queen has done, and this will make them treat their husbands with contempt." (*Esther* 1:17) In Spencer's poem, the royal garden is second only to Eden as a place of sensuous beauty. The king is trembling with sexual desire and expects women to satisfy him at command. But to Vashti, love is a sacrament, she a "prophet come to teach a new thing." The "new thing" is the idea of woman as an independent spiritual being who will respond to love only as a respected equal. The furious king, reiterating that he is "thy lord . . . thy master . . . thy King," compares her to the wine he drinks when thirsty, the meat he eats when hungry: "Love is but desire and thy purpose fulfillment."[11] Spencer had to explain the meaning of the poem even to the sympathetic James Weldon Johnson: "Many times the King and Queen must have been together in the beautiful garden; this particular time Vashti *tried* to tell the old beast what love really meant . . ."[12] "Before the Feast at Sushan," though rejected by Mencken, became Spencer's first published poem when Johnson arranged its printing in *Crisis,* journal of the NAACP, in February 1920. Spencer's first poem states her lifelong preoccupation with sexual violence as the central experience of black women, and suggests her shrewd assessment of the political power behind it.

The contact with Mencken proved to be not only useless, but chilling in its long-range consequences. He advised her to write prose rather than poetry, and Johnson pressed her to acquiesce, in the interest of getting published by a man of national importance. Spencer tried her hand at several articles, but Mencken rejected those as well, perhaps because of their outspoken radicalism. With what seems to have been only one additional attempt, Anne Spencer never

having fallen so low as is possible under civilization, may be nearer
to art, closer to the universal creative spirit, than we. . . ."[21] Similar remarks were made in a later issue of *Poetry* about the Irish:
"The Irish have that tenacity of primitive feeling and understanding
of life, that depth which makes culture possible."[22] (James Joyce
was then about to publish *A Portrait of the Artist as a Young Man.*)
James Oppenheim saw the same qualities in Russia at the moment
of revolution: "Nowhere else is there a people who are so intuitively profound, so emotionally quick. They are not held back by
cleverness, and success, and organization, and intellectualism."[23] Carl
Van Doren, addressing a gathering of emerging young black writers in 1924, said, "What American literature decidedly needs at the
moment is color, music, gusto, the free expression of gay or desperate moods. If the Negroes are not in a position to contribute
these items, I do not know what Americans are."[24] The black
renaissance had hardly begun to manifest itself when it was met
with an effort by whites to appropriate it for their own cultural
salvation, the cleansing of self-disgust, a release from illness of the
spirit.

White patronage did benefit some black (male) writers by opening doors in the publishing world and starting a vogue for black
culture that established reputations and helped make further development possible. Black attitudes ranged from bitter resentment at
white interference to philosophical acceptance and gratitude, even
in some cases, like that of Jean Toomer, to a complete crossing over
to a white identity. Friendly white support, however, was almost
never free of a residual paternalism and demeaning racial stereotypes. Carl Van Vechten, perhaps the leading white promoter of
the Harlem Renaissance, who moved with unprecedented acceptance in black circles, described a Harlem cabaret in his novel *Nigger Heaven* (1926) as a primeval scene: "Jungle land. Hottentots and
Bantus swaying under the amber moon. Love, sex, passion . . ."[25]
Marjorie Seiffert reported in 1929 that she "went to one of [Van
Vechten's] colored parties and had loads of fun,"[26] the latest new
thing for sophisticated whites to do. Louise Bogan, attending a
party of the photographer Berenice Abbott in 1933, was defensive

and resentful toward lesbians and white intellectuals, but was put at ease by the "natural, happy and unaffected Negroes."[27] Nancy Hoyt, younger sister of Elinor Wylie, in a family memoir that dwells inordinately on bibelots, decor, and fashionable dinners, provides a glimpse of wealthy whites enjoying a taste of black soul:

> There were tea times and hours after dinner at Blanche and Alfred Knopf's, listening to spirituals and piano music from a gleaming, smiling colored singer in a dinner jacket, the quieter older Rosamund Johnson [James Weldon Johnson's brother] at the piano, lovely music filling the friendly room lined with the bright bindings of first editions, Van Vechten kind and witty as he leaned against the mantelpiece . . .[28]

Even Babette Deutsch, in her loving, well-intentioned poem "Small Colored Boy in the Subway," draws on the stereotyped imagery of the exotic other:

> A slight-boned animal, young. What jungle fruit
> Droops with such grace as you in your subway corner,
> In your Saturday suit?

The child is described in terms of food that tempts one to eat him: plums, aubergine, coffee bean. "You are a morsel,"[29] she says, openly voicing a maternal eroticism that she was too restrained to express in poems about her own sons, and suggesting also the voracious white consciousness nourishing itself on what it desires from black existence.

Ultimately, the jungle-and-tom-tom image that inspired black pride in African origins seems inextricably entwined with the romantic primitivism of whites. Exoticism may indeed have become to some extent a reflection by blacks of what whites saw in them, for some young black poets of the 1920s tended to follow the lead of white poets most empathetic with blacks, like Lindsay and Sandburg. Langston Hughes, probably the most innovative and influential of the new generation of poets, had been "discovered" by Vachel Lindsay while a busboy at the Wardman Hotel in Washington, DC, and brought to the attention of white readers (although he had already made a name for himself in black periodicals). Hughes, unable to attend Lindsay's public reading because blacks were not admitted to the auditorium, had placed copies of three of his poems beside Lindsay's plate at dinner. The next morning he found himself in the newspaper: "Vachel Lindsay had discovered a Negro bus boy poet!" Hughes remembered Lindsay affectionately as "a great, kind man."[30] It is possible that Hughes' impassioned cry of racial pride, "The tom-tom laughs and the tom-tom cries," owes something to the popular image of blacks that had been fostered by Lindsay's "The Congo."

"The Congo" (1914), a poem that has been considered by both black and white critics as influential on the black renaissance, sums up perfectly the relationship of the white psyche to the black race. Africa, for Lindsay, was the symbolic repository of all the dreaded, repressed contents of the supposedly civilized self—violent energy, cannibalism, sorcery, "bloodlust," animalism. The projection upon another race of such elements indicates that they cannot be faced in oneself, but need to be symbolically manipulated through a surrogate at a safe distance. "The Congo" is actually, then, less a "Study of the Negro Race" than it is Lindsay's attempt at self-redemption: "Then I had religion, then I had a vision. . . ." Christian "pioneer angels" and the Twelve Apostles descend from heaven to clear out the primordial evil and create "a land transformed," a "paradise": "Redeemed were the forests, the beasts and the men. . . ."[31] Lindsay's evangelical Christian background had filled him with a desperate need of self-cleansing, and it is accomplished in this poem by evoking the myths that had justified centuries of European conquest of "savage" people: the salvation of their souls, their absorption into Christian culture, where they could represent symbolically, as for Lindsay, the split-off, rejected, and feared aspect of self, still held to be inferior but subdued and manageable. It is not irrelevant that Lindsay's much-respected brother-in-law was a missionary.

Vachel Lindsay's genuine admiration for blacks and their culture was perfectly compatible with his troubled expression of the imperialist-Christian mind-set. "The Congo" displays the mingled love and condescension of one who is deeply attracted to what he half feels contempt for. Carl Van Vechten's *Nigger Heaven* similarly presents the uninhibited, "primitive" side of black life in Harlem, appealing in its emotional vitality, yet ominously evil at the core, reflecting middle-class whites' own ambivalence about freedom and restraint. Such a vision of evil is thoroughly romanticized, failing to recognize that black violence is not a racial trait but rather a response to white power. Significantly, all the operative personae in "The Congo" are male, suggesting that Lindsay's "study" aims to exorcise the guilt that underlies white male power. White male poet and black male poet could both be attracted to the same symbol, the voice of the tom-tom: one for redemption from self-loathing, the other for redemption from powerlessness. In both cases, the symbol excluded women. Lindsay refers twice to women in "The Congo," once to "coal-black maidens with pearls in their hair . . . And bells on their ankles and black little feet," and then to the rebuking by a black preacher of a "sister for her velvet gown"—first, the sexual allure of the barbaric female, followed by her desexing and depowering, her spiritualizing on the Christian model. Lindsay could relate to women sexually only when making saints of them, to save him from sexual sin. When black women were viewed through the lens of romantic primitivism they appeared as enticing, but dangerous and forbidden, sexual exotics who had been banished by white Christianity and were metaphorized now as tropical fruits, lush vegetation, and languorous heat.

Langston Hughes' "Danse Africaine" depicts the exotic black female in the role of inspiring black male creativity, dancing to male music:

> The low beating of the tom-toms,
> The slow beating of the tom-toms . . .
>   Stirs your blood.
>   Dance!
> A night-veiled girl
>   Whirls softly into a
>   Circle of light . . .[32]

Black women poets did not trust such characterizations, as Anne Spencer's snappish reaction to Untermeyer's praise indicates. Spencer also told Hughes she disapproved of forcing the tom-tom into poetry. Helene Johnson reveals the response of a black woman who wishes to claim any symbolism that will enhance the racial image, but has reservations:

> Gee boy, when you sing, I can close my ears
> And hear tom-toms just as plain.
> Listen to me, will you, what do I know
> About tom-toms? But I like the word, sort of,
> Don't you? It belongs to us.[33]

Helene Johnson's ambivalence is a signal that black women were not handed the tom-tom, and therefore lacked an equivalent empowering symbol of poetic creativity. They were encouraged, figuratively, to lie about under coconut palms waiting to be possessed by a lover, or to stir him to creativity, not to develop poetic genius of their own. The column on the arts that the poet Gwendolyn Bennett wrote for *Opportunity* during the late 1920s was entitled "The Ebony Flute," suggesting (albeit unintentionally) a feminine alternative to the image of the tom-tom. A flute is a solitary, lyrical instrument, reflecting more accurately these black women's sense of themselves: introspective, searching to redefine love, to transmute their self-image from one of abuse and suffering to self-possession and inner spiritual beauty.

Even in the ferment of the Harlem Renaissance, black women poets labored under a kind of compression, rather than release, that is epitomized in Anne Spencer's work. "Lady, Lady," for example, a poem probably written about a laundry woman who came to her home, penetrates to the divine fire banked under the oppressive layers of both racist and sexist mistreatment and hard work:

> Lady, Lady, I saw your face,
> Dark as night withholding a star . . .
> The chisel fell, or it might have been
> You had borne so long the yoke of men.
> Lady, Lady, I saw your hands,
> Twisted, awry, like crumpled roots,
> Bleached poor white in a sudsy tub,

Wrinkled and drawn from your rub-a-dub.
Lady, Lady, I saw your heart,
And altered there in its darksome place
Were the tongues of flame the ancients knew,
Where the good God sits to spangle through.[34]

By capitalizing "Lady," Spencer ironically but compassionately evokes an image of aristocracy, perhaps remembering her own mother, or, in conjunction with the religious references, a suggestion of Mary, the divine mother.

Anne Spencer's sense of sisterhood anticipates the powerful role it has played in recent black women's creativity as an answer to male oppression. Spencer in fact participated occasionally in a small circle of black women poets who were attracted during the 1920s to the home of Georgia Douglas Johnson in Washington, DC. The group included Angelina Weld Grimké and Clarissa Scott Delaney, both teachers at Dunbar High School in Washington, and Alice Dunbar-Nelson, former wife of the poet Paul Laurence Dunbar. It would perhaps be more accurate to say that Johnson was simply the mutual friend they all had. Johnson's literary gatherings were apparently fluid, and probably seldom of women alone, forming a kind of Washington locus of the Harlem Renaissance. (Johnson had planned to write a memoir about the black writers of the 1920s she knew, and the story of Washington literary society, but left behind at her death only a mass of unorganized manuscript material.) Although Washington never became the legendary home of black soul that Harlem did, it was a thriving center of black intellectual activity and political leadership, second only to New York. Georgia Douglas Johnson's salon stood at the crossroads for all visiting notables from north and south, and the chance to meet and talk must have contributed greatly to the strong sense of community among black writers of the time. It seems likely that virtually every black poet either knew or was familiar with the work of every other black poet, male or female. With the flourishing of a black press, poetry anthologies, and the annual literary contests of *Opportunity* and *Crisis,* with the eager search for new, young talent, a vigorous literary culture was developing quite independently of white patronage and white expectations. The emergence of the black women poets, then, seems rather more closely involved with the fortunes of black writers generally than it was with the ground swell of feminism, in spite of the tentative movement of the women to support one another. Black male editors and critics were quick to publish and encourage female poets in the interest of promoting black achievement.

Nevertheless, the place of the women poets in the Harlem Renaissance remained peripheral and undefined, a footnote to a male-dominated movement. A major critical study of the period, French scholar Jean Wagner's *Black Poets of the United States,* gives one sentence to Helene Johnson, but not even a mention to Anne Spencer, Georgia Douglas Johnson, or any of the half dozen other black women poets publishing in the 1920s. Their search for a voice, for a poetic identity as women, was drowned in the popular acclaim for the men and for the styles men developed. Georgia Douglas Johnson's initial volume of poems, *The Heart of a Woman* (1918), was the first to be published by a black woman since Frances Harper's *Poems on Miscellaneous Subjects* in 1854. Comprising sixty-two personal lyrics about love, death, and dreams, Johnson's work echoes Sara Teasdale's and contains no overt references to race. The reluctance of Johnson, Grimké, Bennett, and Scott-Delaney to present themselves primarily as black persons in their poetry, to draw on oral traditions as Langston Hughes did, has been viewed as typical of an earlier generation of black writers, middle-class in upbringing, genteel in outlook, anxious to distance themselves, like Anne Spencer's mother, from the stigma of "low" black origins. On the whole, the black women poets did indeed resemble educated middle-class white women more than they did the mass of poor blacks. Clarissa Scott-Delaney, a graduate of Wellesley College, was the daughter of Emmett J. Scott, Jr., secretary of Howard University; her husband, Hubert Delaney, a lawyer, was later prominent in New York City politics. Georgia Douglas Johnson was a graduate of Atlanta University, as was her husband, a recorder in the US Treasury Department. In the 1920s, her two sons were studying law and medicine, and she herself served for nine years as a conciliation

commissioner in the US Labor Department. Angelina Grimké, as
noted earlier, was the daughter of an eminent civil-rights leader and
diplomat. Her play, *Rachel,* depicts sensitive, loving relationships
within a refined middle-class family who are singled out for suffering for no reason other than skin color. When Johnson, prodded
by black critics who accused her of having "no feeling at all for the
race,"[35] turned to racial themes in her second book, *Bronze* (1922),
she voiced the bitter sense of unfairness felt by a person of mostly
white lineage who is forever stigmatized because of a trace of black
blood, as in "The Octaroon":

> One drop of midnight in the dawn of life's
>   pulsating stream
> Marks her alien from her kind, a shade
>   amidst its gleam;
> Forevermore her step she bends insular,
>   strange, apart—
> And none can read the riddle of her wildly
>   warring heart.[36]

These earlier black women poets, with the notable exception of
Anne Spencer, seemed determined to establish an image of ladylike
refinement, of a delicate poetic sensibility in search of beauty and
crying out for recognition, suggesting that their ordeal as women
took precedence over the question of racial identity. Georgia Douglas Johnson preferred to write "without regard to propaganda," to
keep poetry to "the dreams and longings of the heart . . . Somehow one suffers twice when you connect racial with world sorrow—one cross enough, is a policy I adopt. Whenever I can, I
forget my special call to sorrow and live as happily as I may . . .
It seems to me an art to forget those things that make the heart
heavy. If one can soar, he should soar, leaving his chains behind."[37]
"Let me not hate,"[38] Johnson says, in order to avoid corruption by
a hatred toward her tormentors; "The best way to overcome evil is
to do good."[39] Love builds a positive sense of identity in answer
to the curse placed upon blackness. But most importantly, the desire
for ladylike dignity, the quest for a realization of inner spiritual

beauty, seems a response to the sexual stereotype of black women as coarse and sluttish. The genteel aspirations of the black women poets can only be understood as conditioned by the doubly vicious assault of racist and sexist antagonism. Virtually no white person writing about black women has been exempt from it. Gertrude Stein's story "Melanctha," for example, heralded by Van Vechten as "perhaps the first American story in which the Negro is regarded as a human being," depicts Rose as "real black, tall, well built, sullen, stupid, childlike . . ." Although raised by white people, she is an unchangeable primitive, "careless and lazy," and has the "simple, promiscuous unmorality of the black people."[40] Rose gives birth to a child but thoughtlessly abandons it to die. The depiction of black women as bad mothers is particularly offensive, given the powerful tradition of black maternal strength and wisdom, and the deep concern of some of the black women poets for the fate of children born to a life of undeserved suffering in a white world. Georgia Douglas Johnson included a number of poems on that theme in *Bronze*. "Maternity" is an example:

> I cannot say with surety
> That I am happy thus to be
> Responsible for this young life's embarking.[41]

In "Black Woman" she turns back the soul of a child pressing to be born:

> You do not know the monster men
> Inhabiting the earth,
> Be still, be still, my precious child,
> I must not give you birth![42]

The first wave of black women poets were understandably cautious in submitting themselves to any myth of black womanhood that might perpetuate the lingering "scent of slavery," as Anne Spencer's mother had put it. Spencer herself sometimes sat in her garden cottage ruminating on the institution of slavery, contemplating the wall she had covered with original slave posters—sales, auctions, rewards for runaways, and the like. The one she especially singled out—"One can't say 'favorite,' " her son observed—announced the raffle of a horse and a mulatto girl (the daughter, obviously, of some white "gentleman"), tickets $1.00 each. The enormity of the violation of black women—Spencer herself was the granddaughter of a woman raped by her owner—had to be continually remembered.

Georgia Douglas Johnson was the only one of the black women poets of the 1920s to produce a voluminous output and to publish a book of her poems (actually four volumes in all, between 1918 and 1966). Clarissa Scott-Delaney, looked to as one of the brightest promises among the younger poets, died of kidney disease in 1927 at the age of twenty-six and was widely mourned in the black literary community. Angelina Grimké published a moving elegiac tribute to her. The fortunes of the black women poets seemed to crest with the Harlem Renaissance in the late 1920s and then fade. Virtually all of them were silent from the early 1930s on, their work buried in periodicals and a few anthologies of black writers' work, never collected to give a coherent picture of their achievement. Clarissa Scott-Delaney's death appears, in retrospect, symbolic of their short-lived season.

Gwendolyn Bennett, of the same generation as Scott-Delaney, was trained in art rather than poetry, and perhaps never seriously intended a career as a poet. Born in Texas in 1902, the daughter of a lawyer and a schoolteacher, she grew up in Washington, DC and New York City, attended Columbia University and Pratt Institute, and spent a year on a scholarship studying art in Paris. She served on the editorial staff of *Opportunity* from 1926 to 1928, publishing most of her poetry in those years, while writing her column, "The Ebony Flute." Bennett's free-verse, impressionistic work expresses the moody, unsatisfied yearning typical of other black women writers like Scott-Delaney, Grimké, and Helene Johnson. Some of her poems voice the search for an image of black womanhood to express beauty and power rather than ladylike refinement:

> I love you for your brownness
> And the rounded darkness of your breast . . .
> Something of old forgotten queens
> Lurks in the lithe abandon of your walk,—

And something of the shackled slave
Sobs in the rhythm of your talk.[43]

In "Heritage," she wants "to see lithe Negro girls/ Etched dark against the sky . . ."[44]

In the summer of 1926 Gwendolyn Bennett joined a group of young black writers, including Zora Neale Hurston, in attempting to found an avant-garde magazine called *Fire*, "the idea being," according to Langston Hughes, "that it would burn up a lot of the old, dead conventional Negro-white ideas of the past, *épater le bourgeois* into a realization of the existence of the younger Negro writers and artists, and provide us with an outlet for publication not available in the limited pages of the small Negro magazines then existing. . . ."[45] The magazine folded in a desperate financial crisis after one issue, and the remaining stock was, ironically, destroyed in a fire. The new voice that Hughes hoped to establish was the sound of street talk, the rhythm of the blues, an expression of black soul "without fear or shame," rather than the genteel dignity of an older generation anxious to obtain the respect of whites. *Fire*, whose single issue was almost uniformly excoriated by the black press, was ahead of its time. Yet the voice Hughes was introducing was essentially a male voice, an expression of black male experience in male language. It did not touch the deeply painful and sensitive areas of black women's self-knowledge. Among the women poets, only Helene Johnson attempted, occasionally, to cultivate the colloquial style, and then only in poems addressed affectionately to men, as if echoing their language. Her poem "Futility" notes the gap between genteel femininity and the realities of the street:

It is silly—
This waiting for love
In a parlor,
When love is singing up and down the alley
Without a collar.[46]

But usually she wrote in the manner of the traditional lyric, even on such subjects as the beating to death of a black woman prisoner by a white guard for picking a flower in the prison yard ("Fiat Lux," 1928):

> And like her Father
> On the holyrood, whispered, "Forgive."
> And in her eyes there shone a Candlemas light.[47]

If there seems to be a breathtaking gulf of inappropriateness between the underlying emotional violence and the lyrical surface of so much of the poetry of black women in the 1920s, it is because of the prodigious demand of their task—to emerge with self-respect from a history of brutal victimization by white male power, uncertain of their own voices and lacking a strong circle of mutual support.

The poignance of the need for an ideal of womanhood, an image of self as spiritually beautiful, can be seen especially in Angelina Grimké, who never attempted to publish her sheaf of love poems addressed to women, written over a period of years to, probably, a number of different people. "Rosabel," for example, plays on the name "Rose,"

> whose soul unfolds white petaled,
> Touch her soul, rose white,
> Rose whose thoughts unfold gold petaled
> Blossom in her light,
> Rose whose heart unfolds red petaled
> Quick in her slow heart's stir
> Tell her white, gold, red my love is;—
> And for her,—for her.[48]

There are tormented poems of crises in relationships, poems of loss, poems of painful yearning, all seemingly written only for her own eyes. There are sensuous poems, like "Mona Lisa," ending in self-obliteration:

> I should like to creep
> Through the long brown grasses
> That are your lashes . . .,[49]

and "deeply drown" in "the leaf-brown pools/ That are your shadowed eyes." "I dream of you all night," she says to "A Woman." A late-written, untitled poem recalls scalding memories,

The hot night
Hot whispers
Hot arms
Hot lips . . .
My old wasted body
With my wrinkled hands
  On my lap
  Hot, hard tears
  All because of you . . .[50]

Grimké also wrote at least one poem on black female suffering that anticipates a later generation:

  I am the laughing woman with the black black face
  I am living in the cellars in every crowded place
    I am toiling just to eat
    In the cold and in the heat
    And I laugh
  I am the laughing woman who's forgotten how to weep
  I am the laughing woman who's afraid to go to sleep.[51]

Angelina Grimké hints at the later emergence of a black lesbian sisterhood, a powerful source of pride, self-realization, and resistance to the denigration of black women. The scholar Gloria Hull, in fact, sees evidence of a black lesbian network among clubwomen in the Washington, DC area in the 1920s.[52] However, it is doubtful that Grimké was involved in it. Her poems, as Hull finds, express the stifled loneliness of a woman without a way to fulfill her emotional nature.

If there is an element lacking in the work of the pioneering wave of black women poets compared to that of a later generation, it is perhaps righteous anger. Although they wrote out of a rejection of the role in which they had been unjustly cast, they tended to seek peaceful solutions, transformation by idealized love and forgiveness. Anne Spencer stands alone among them in her "colossal reserve of constructive indignation." Cultivating her garden was her symbol of building an alternative life, with her own place, her man, her family, an answer to the brutalization of black people. It would have been tempting to withdraw into her Eden, as other poets did into their idealism, fearful of the destruction that could easily have swept them away had they ventured to fight, insufficiently armed. Perhaps their genteel upbringing did unfit them for struggle, even as it gave them opportunities. But Anne Spencer balanced her private life with a vigorous and fearless public one.

Anne Spencer is now remembered in Lynchburg, Virginia with pride, and her home, preserved as it was during her lifetime more meticulously, perhaps, than that of any other poet, has been designated an historical landmark. But for over half a century she mercilessly prodded the conscience of the community, unafraid of taunting the gods in spite of the warning to other women in her poem. She scandalized the proper citizenry by wearing pants, symbolic of male power, at a time when such garb was unthinkable for a woman. At the public appearance of a white politician who was trying to garner black votes, she asked pointed questions, and not getting straight answers, snorted, "Shit," and walked out. It was a matter of principle never to humble herself or attempt to ingratiate herself with anyone. She refused to ride the buses, and walked on all her errands through the town rather than sit in Jim Crow seats. Once, with a friend, and too tired to walk, she boarded a bus and seated herself defiantly in the white area. The angry driver found her too formidable to dislodge and simply drove on. She made herself a figure too towering, too fearsomely honest, too uncompromising to be tampered with, and maintained a steady pressure against racist policies and attitudes of the community, whether it involved politics, schools, or business. She was unperturbed when the FBI investigated her, pointlessly, for possible secret Communist affiliations.

Virtually all black intellectuals and political leaders of national stature made pilgrimages to the Spencer home, where they were given a place to sleep and treated to good food and lively conversation. Anne said she ran an "overground railway." Subservient to no one, however important, she clashed with such prominent figures as W. E. B. DuBois and George Washington Carver, who seemed to her to be arrogant elitists rejecting a sense of oneness with blacks in spite of their great work on behalf of black people. DuBois, she thought, had a streak of white meanness in him. When forced to meet people with whom she had little patience, she "stiff-armed" them in the formal living room and would not permit them access to the private areas of her home. But when young people gathered around her in her later years, she allowed them into the back room, where she sat enthroned in her comfortable chair and entertained them with her stream of wonderful talk. Sometimes she and her closest friend, a high-school French teacher named Bernice Lomax Hill, sat talking until two or three o'clock in the morning. As is the case with so many important friendships between women, the details, the meanings, have not been recorded.

Anne Spencer was "no saint," her son has insisted. The terrible force in her could rock the community and make enemies, with no regret on her part. It is that force, coiled in her poems, that makes every word count, even though she wrote so few. She understood the demonic, ravenous nature of white male power that strives to absorb everything, willing or not, into itself, and answered by exposing it, defying it with a power of her own. Her poem "White Things" (1923) unveils a vision of the world outside her garden with a devastating truth and playful irony that redeem centuries of enforced silence: [53]

> Most things are colorful things—the sky, the earth,
>   and sea.
>   Black men are most men; but the white are free!
> White things are rare things; so rare, so rare
> They stole from out a silvered world—somewhere.
> Finding earth-plains fair plains, save greenly grassed,
> They strewed white feathers of cowardice, as they passed;
>   The golden stars with lances fine
>   The hills all red and darkened pine,
> They blanched with their wand of power;
> And turned the blood in a ruby rose
> To a poor white poppy-flower.
>
> They pyred a race of black, black men,
> And burned them to ashes white; then,

Laughing, a young one claimed a skull,
For the skull of a black is white, not dull,
    But a glistening awful thing;
    Made, it seems, for this ghoul to swing
In the face of God with all his might,
And swear by the hell that siréd him,
    "Man-maker, make white!"

"We are saturated with memories of each other," she said of the black and white races in America, "making us both reluctant to let go. This I think is love—and often it is, psychologically, love raised to the point of hatred."[54]

At the age of ninety, Anne Spencer had begun to work on a number of ambitious projects in both prose and poetry, as if she had found confidence in her ability at last, releasing her creative powers. She had long hoped to write a study of the institution of slavery that had appalled and fascinated her all her life. But because of failing eyesight, she abandoned the project to concentrate on a poem of epic proportions in five cantos, "A Dream of John Brown: On His Return Home." She managed to write several hundred lines before ill health and near blindness finally brought an end to this attempt to circumvent the fate of silence. She died in a nursing home on May 8, 1975 at the age of ninety-three, "with, as Bethel [her daughter] said, a look of 'pleasure, satisfaction, and triumph.' "[55]

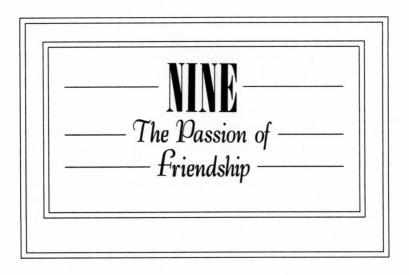

NINE
The Passion of Friendship

* **T** * HE "POWER TO BE," the power to create in the face of discouragement, has its source in love: in a passionate involvement that releases the powers of its participants to become their fully human selves. Anne Spencer learned this not from theology or theory, but from the ceaseless study of herself. Her son, Chauncey Spencer, has said, "There couldn't have been an Anne Spencer without an Edward Spencer."[1] She herself would probably have included a few others, for empowering friendship need not be exclusive or limited, in spite of its intense intimacy. It implies community as well as personal connection. James Weldon Johnson was also such a friend, with "personal gifts of sense-perception, humor, genius, and sheer human goodness,"[2] she wrote. His death in an automobile accident in 1938, just after visiting her, was a devastating shock. Anne's affection had always embraced Johnson's wife Grace as well, and in 1967, at the age of eighty-five, she wrote to Grace Nail Johnson avowing the meaning of their friendship of almost fifty years:

This is a love letter to you from one who is completely unworthy, actively, in *that* area—her spirit cares *deeply* and *daily* recalls your image as among the last so close ties of this strange world—nor is she unmindful that to you and yours is due the emergence of whatever enjoyable identity now aids the solace of her age.[3]

The kind of love that fosters the "emergence of enjoyable identity" occurs irrespective of sex, a fact of immense importance in view of the rigid gender assignments that support the power of the patriarchy. The women poets between 1915 and 1945 were moved by a groping recognition that empowering, liberating love—friendship in Spencer's sense—was the necessary root of their creative development. Indeed, the possibility of empowering friendships between women seems to have been everywhere latent and ready to flow into consciousness, as the evidence reviewed here has suggested. Even when repressed, undervalued, unmentioned, or misinterpreted, supportive relationships among women appear to have been indispensable in the phenomenal wave of female creativity. But even though the women poets experienced the stirring of a sense of community, with its nexus of loving personal relationships, they had no conceptual grasp of their need, no language for acknowledging and defining it. Their emerging consciousness was everywhere overridden by the assumptions of the patriarchy, forcing them to deny or to echo apologetically the male scorn for relationships that did not acknowledge men as the only beings worth relating to.

Women's passionate friendships had been allowed to flourish in Victorian times only as long as they remained segregated and nonthreatening. But with the rise of women into professional competition with men, power-giving unions between women became a cause of alarm. Hence the readiness to brand them as abnormal or psychopathic, in order to squelch at its source women's challenge to male dominance. Women therefore tended to suppress any overt reference in their poetry to the underlying stratum of emotion that often powered their creativity and made their work possible. A few poems here and there tell of the awakening and discovery of self through another's presence. But often that level of feeling remains hidden, attested to only in letters or in countless unrecorded con-versations and telephone calls. What does emerge in the poetry is a kind of massive resistance to traditional heterosexual love, a back-lash against romantic feeling—sometimes openly flippant and ironic, more often anguished, voicing suffering or tragedy.

Nevertheless, in order to overcome the insidiously reiterated imputation of worthlessness, women needed not merely to resist, but to see reflected back an idealized image of themselves as valu-able, potent, redeemed—the mirror men seldom held up to them. Searching among the ruins of romantic love for that possibility did not provide the electrifying charge that sometimes came with the sudden appearance of a new woman friend, arriving as a kind of goddess, the desired self made real and visible. "For me, the Muse has always been a woman,"[4] May Sarton has said, and has observed that the image of a particular woman has often provided the focus of concentration around which a poem takes shape.

Sara Teasdale, whose name is synonymous with love poetry, presents romantic love as a treadmill of suffering in most of her work. But the few love poems she wrote in a wholly positive, lib-erating spirit were inspired by women like Marion Cummings and Eunice Tietjens. Her youthful infatuations with male lovers seem curiously ritualistic, like the bobbing dances of mating birds. The genuine unpracticed awe, the disconcerting loss of normal self-possession, that attend the entrance of a god—or goddess—seem to have been felt only toward other women and were experienced as an exhilarating release. Such women were models, guides, pro-tectors, inspirers, divinities who could show her the way. One of the early recipients of her adoration was Lillie Rose Ernst, a high-school teacher who fairly bristled with professional vigor and integ-rity, much loved by the Potters, the young women's club to which Teasdale belonged. "When first I saw you—felt you take my hand," Teasdale wrote in a sonnet, "To L. R. E.," "I could not speak for happiness."

> I love you, and I crave
> A little love that I may be more brave
> Because one watches me who knows and cares.[5]

Commonly belittled as adolescent "crushes," or viewed as substitutes for more advisable emotions, such ebullient outbursts of affection were a signal of Teasdale's need for redemption of her deeply wounded femaleness. Her stricken powerlessness as the obedient daughter of a prosperous, magisterial businessman surfaced in chronic undefined illness, physical lassitude, and morbid self-doubt. She fretted incessantly over the propriety of her public image and would collapse in nervous exhaustion whenever the strain of anxiety became too great. Her life seems to have been such a continual fight against depression, so blighted by psychic misery, that one is surprised by her sustained productivity as a poet, by her clarity and force of mind. Her suffering is the kind for which the victim is often blamed, as if she were indulging in histrionics rather than paying a price exacted by male supremacy. Teasdale tried to keep inviolate a small corner of herself by cultivating a guiding interior image of realized womanhood, the powerful and beautiful Aphrodite, the sublime artist Sappho, the competent, self-assured professional woman of her own day, rather than the saintly, servile mother, bowing before her lord, that she had been taught to revere. It is ironic that Teasdale's reputation is that of the quintessential poet of heterosexual romance when in actuality conventional love was the cause of her suffering and passionate friendship with women the potential source of relief.

When Sara Teasdale's marriage was crumbling in the late 1920s, and she had accustomed herself to the idea of slain emotions, of paying for her mistakes by living in a kind of frozen anomie, a young woman walked into her life and made her feel miraculously revived. Margaret Conklin had written Teasdale a fan letter in the summer of 1926 from a small town in central New York, asking for a photograph to give to her former high-school English teacher, who had taught Margaret to love poetry. Margaret knew many of Teasdale's poems by heart: "I would walk to and from school with an open book in my hand."[6] Teasdale was traveling alone in New England that summer—she and her husband rarely traveled together—and Ernst Filsinger had been instructed to throw away, as usual, all fan letters and bothersome requests. But a note of intelligence and sensitivity in Margaret Conklin's letter caused him to forward it to Sara anyway. Somehow touched as well, she answered it, and a correspondence began. "I sent her a box of wild flowers," Margaret said, "packed roots, dirt and all, and arranged more or less as they grew."[7] Margaret was about to transfer to the Connecticut College for Women in New London that fall for her final two years, a move that brought her close enough to New York for them to meet. Teasdale arranged for her to stay at the Martha Washington Hotel for women and invited her to her apartment on Central Park West for an evening in October. When the door opened to reveal a shy, large-eyed young woman, Teasdale experienced a rush of emotion she had not expected to feel again. She was forty-two; Margaret, twenty-three. What she saw was the resurrection of herself:[8]

> You had only
>   To open the door
> To bring me the self
>   I was before.
>
> I thought I should never
>   See her again;
> I thought she had hidden
>   From women and men.
>
> Her eyes had been bright
>   As the sun on water,
> She sang as blithe
>   As an elf-king's daughter.
>
> I had hoped, and then
>   I had stopped hoping,—
> The years ran downward
>   Still and sloping.
>
> But on that autumn night
>   I knew
> The self I was
>   Came in with you.

"The really strange accord which was so much a part of our friendship," Margaret Conklin said, was evident from the moment I saw her. Of course I idolized her, and the whole thing was like a dream—the first wonderful thing that had happened to me. All my shyness . . . disappeared. We talked about books, about what I wanted to do with my life, and a bit about the way she wrote, i.e., paper and pen by the bedside. Rough drafts polished and repolished.

There were striking similarities in their early family relationships. Both felt estranged from their mothers: "My mother was a very difficult person," Margaret felt; "I had no companions of my own age, because young people might disrupt the perfection of her home. . . . I don't think that Sara was afraid of her mother, but I was terrified of mine." Margaret was many years younger than her half sister and half brother, as Sara had been, and grew up a lonely child. "I, like Sara, adored my father, but saw all too little of him." Margaret believed that her mother's irritable temperament drove her father to take positions as an institutional physician, enabling him to stay away from home for long periods. Margaret, trapped, as she felt, in a suffocating relationship, and continually monitored—"If I got home from school . . . five minutes late, she always thought the worst"—had dropped out of the University of Rochester after two years in order to work at a hospital for tubercular children, following her father's pattern of escape.[9] When Margaret met Sara, she was for the first time far and free from her oppressive homelife, and dazzled by an idolized older woman who seemed to offer all that she felt she had missed in her relationship with her own mother.

There was an important difference, however: Margaret Conklin was a far sturdier, more enduring woman, who was prepared to work hard for a living, while Sara Teasdale had been sheltered and indulged like a helpless infant until almost thirty. Margaret earned her freedom to attend Connecticut College by waiting on tables, typing students' papers, tutoring, and picking up odd jobs. Sara telephoned her often, and sometimes descended royally for a visit, staying in a nearby inn. Margaret would see that she was given the best room, and, though she could scarcely afford it, arrange for flowers and candies to be waiting. She kept the visits secret from her friends, for Sara did not wish to be bothered by importunate admirers. Teasdale was excruciatingly cautious in opening herself to intimacy, as if a relationship had to be continually tested before she dared to place any weight on it. She introduced Margaret by degrees to most of her friends, in order to obtain their opinion of her. When Margaret "passed," as it were, she allowed herself greater liberties, offering small gifts, often with a poem enclosed—a travel clock from Tiffany's with her initials engraved on it, a pair of slippers for Easter 1927, for "my proud young love."

The first year of their friendship, the period of discovery, in spite of the curious arm's length Sara held between them, was remembered by Margaret as probably the best of the six and a half years they had before Sara's death. The high point came in the summer of 1927 when Sara took Margaret to England and Scotland for ten weeks. She was trying to repeat for Margaret the most magical experience of her own life, the summer of 1912, before the disaster of marrying, when as a young woman she had traveled to Italy with Jessie Rittenhouse: two women together, in quest of beauty. This time she was the older woman mothering a bedazzled younger one with a keen, thirsting imagination to be awakened. They stayed at an inn in Lynton, Devon that had once been a monastery, and walked on the cliffs above the sea, among wildflowers. Sara wrote "On Devon Cliffs":

> Oh your fingers, oh your darling fingers
> Picking sea-pinks in the silver English sun,
> How can these wild cliffs ever forget you
> Or so good a day be done?
>
> Oh that your young heart, proud as a sea-gull,
> Need never grow tired or baffled by pain;
> Oh that my mind might keep forever
> Your look in the sun-shot rain.[10]

Both women were aware that a need to restore the damaged mother-daughter bond lay at the base of their relationship. "She told me and wrote Aline Kilmer (who later gave me the letter)," Margaret said, "that I was the daughter she and Ernst would have wanted. Certainly her feeling had much of the maternal in it, but also warm, congenial and devoted friendship. She was a very affectionate person under the surface coolness, and I was, I suppose, looking for a mother as well as a friend. I had had very little affection in my life." Sara asked Margaret for a picture of herself as a child, and kept it, framed, on her mantel.

Mother-daughter relationships are not perfect and idyllic, however, especially when consciously intended to be. "She often treated me as a child," Margaret said. Not surprisingly, Margaret found in Sara a trait that sounds rather like the mother from whom she was trying to escape:

> [Sara] was a perfectionist in every way—and expected perfection in those around her. Once at her apartment, I told her of my irritation at something minor that had happened at the office, and she literally sent me home, saying that I needed rest to get back my equilibrium. Another time, when she had one of the little cottages at Cromwell [Connecticut] and asked me for a weekend, I was sent home because I said something she didn't like. I don't think it could have been very bad, because I was always on my best behavior with her.

Once while at college Margaret was "punished" for some remark, Sara saying "she would not be in touch with me for a couple of weeks."[11] Margaret Conklin may have underestimated her own tendency to hypersensitivity, to blurt out frank, sometimes blunt or caustic, remarks when disturbed. Even on the English trip the two women had to be painfully circumspect and wary in order to avoid offending the other's overreactive sensibility.

On Margaret's graduation from college in 1928, Sara Teasdale arranged a job for her in the Publicity Department at Macmillan—Sara's publisher—in New York. She worked under Harold Latham, the legendary editor who had the foresight to sign up *Gone with the Wind,* and soon was writing jacket blurbs, meeting trains and boats, and setting up parties for visiting authors like Yeats, Masefield, G. B. Stern, and Elizabeth Bowen. Though she protested she had no creative talent of her own, she was quick in her critical grasp of it in others, and Latham put her to work reading manuscripts. She was one of three or four, she said, "shut up in a room for weeks"[12] and given the job of preparing the mountainous manuscript of *Gone with the Wind* for publication. According to Margaret, this involved some cutting and rewriting, although tradition has it that Margaret Mitchell's first and only work of fiction arrived, rather improbably, in perfect readiness for publication. (Macmillan's now-incomplete records neither confirm nor dispute Margaret Conklin's recollection, which, however, there seems no reason to doubt.) Margaret later edited Teasdale's posthumous volume, *Strange Victory*, and, with John Hall Wheelock, Teasdale's *Collected Poems*.

Sara Teasdale was oddly oblivious to the struggle of Margaret's daily life, the lack of money, the difficulty of finding an adequate place to live on the Lower East Side of Manhattan near the Macmillan office—partly, perhaps, because Margaret concealed the gritty aspects of her life, fearing to offend her angel of perfection; and partly because Teasdale wished to see only that with which she felt in harmony. Because she could not afford subway fare, Margaret walked several times a week from Twelfth Street and Fifth Avenue to Eighty-first Street and Central Park West, arriving exhausted and hungry after work but not daring to speak of it for fear of violating the mood of serene perfection she believed Teasdale required. Sara might nibble on the dinner sent up from the dining room—she virtually never cooked her own meals—but set it aside with her usual lack of appetite, while Margaret would look on silently ravenous for a bite that was never offered. One suspects, however, that this version of Sara is, to some extent, the projection of Margaret's awe, the mother-fear she could not easily shed, coupled with an anxiety to please.

Teasdale carefully kept Margaret Conklin from knowledge of her own personal problems, probably in order to save her from growing "tired and baffled by pain," and to cherish a vision of what she herself might have been. So strong was the need of each to see the other as the projection of an ideal, as an answer to the injured integrity of her self-image, that they could not meet on a thoroughly realistic basis.

Margaret Conklin was not even aware of the rift in Teasdale's marriage almost to the moment of the divorce in 1929. "I liked

Ernst tremendously," Margaret recalled. Sometimes she went to the opera or theater with him when Sara begged off. Margaret and Ernst shared in a conspiracy to protect and serve Sara, both dedicated to the kind of idealizing devotion that Sara seemed to find both necessary and annoying. Once when facing a move to another apartment, Sara, after much fussing, gave out and retreated to a country inn for the duration, while Margaret and Ernst did the work; Margaret "numbered each bookcase, lettered each shelf, and had slips of various colors and symbols in each book, so that when [Sara] returned every book was as she had placed it with her usual care." Teasdale contrived to divorce Ernst Filsinger while he was on a six-month business trip to Africa and Europe and could not fight back. She enlisted Margaret in a plan of elaborate secrecy, telling none of her friends but John Hall Wheelock, inventing misleading stories to explain her absence in Reno, taking a post-office box for mail, for which only Margaret had the key. Margaret loyally stood by her, but seems never to have understood why it all happened. She believed that Sara "probably should never have married. I think Ernst was the best choice, since she felt marriage was essential. Whatever Ernst did (and we have to use our imaginations there), he adored her and put up with a great deal."

In the years following the divorce, the relationship between Sara and Margaret began to show the strain of the unreality that was such an essential part of it. A second summer abroad ended in disaster in 1930 when Margaret became violently ill with an intestinal disorder on arriving in Paris, and Sara, soured with disappointment, arranged an immediate return, complaining to friends that Margaret had spoiled the trip. "She certainly made me aware of it at the time," Margaret remembered, "and I was heart broken."[13] Margaret herself was maturing and resisted being kept a child. There were jealousies: for a time Sara was captivated by a young woman student, to whom she bequeathed on her death a holograph letter of her favorite poet, Christina Rossetti, that she had bought in England. Margaret's deep affection for Marianne Moore troubled Sara too, Margaret believed. Not only was she a rival poet, but one and encouragement through trials, to use a word from Moore's spiritual vocabulary. Moore sprinkled Biblical references in her letters—"Margaret, 'cast down but not destroyed,' as the Apostle Paul says."[23] She compared Margaret's sufferings to Job's. "Kind Margaret, kind Margaret, kind Margaret," she wrote,

> my life enriched by your trust, your affection, by *things*. . . . I am like St. Paul in the shipwreck, all confusion by reason of simultaneous pressures. . . . Don't despair of me whether my face is lugubrious or my clothes are rags. I may trust you, may I not? Warrior of the most tested kind you are. ON WE GO. Or do we? I think so.[24]

"You are a brave and splendid person," Margaret Conklin told her, during the final illness of Marianne Moore's mother.

> I find—and have found for years—that when I am most troubled or sad or unpleasant things happen, I instinctively think of you. You are, for me, a sort of bulwark against fate, or, better, a talisman against hurt or pain or discomfort.[25]

Moore was deeply touched that she should be considered a help to others when desperately in need of support herself.

> Only a "seer" could think of me as a "bulwark against fate." The looming impasse, I wonder if anyone—the most confident and alert—is without it. . . . The dangers and difficulties of life seem ever multiplied to infinity— and surely only the love of God that is in us can neutralize the sternness of the fight.[26]

Margaret's phrase revolved in Moore's imagination until it emerged a year later as one of her best-known poems, "Bulwarked against Fate," and was used in the title of her book, *Like a Bulwark*, in 1956.

> I wonder if you suspect how you helped me by your phrase, a bulwark against fate;—a kind of talisman when temptation assails; as I said to my brother at the time and have said since—till finally I put it down and can't lose it through the anomalies of disability and chaos.[27]

Marianne expressed her gratitude privately to Margaret; but because "you . . . applied [the phrase] to me, . . . I couldn't explain, and

therefore let you go unthanked, by the general public."[28] Marianne
Moore's ability to be "firmed by the blast" supplied the model of
strength in adversity that Margaret Conklin required so urgently
after Sara Teasdale's surrender to self-destruction.

*

The life-struggle shared by Margaret Conklin and Marianne
Moore in doubt-shadowed determination—"ON WE GO—or do
we?"—reflects the challenge of survival, of "getting through," that
became critical for women poets after 1930. The untimely deaths of
Elinor Wylie and Amy Lowell, the suicide of Sara Teasdale, the
rapid decline in the reputation of Edna St. Vincent Millay, removed
the most prominent and productive women of the older generation
from the scene, and along with them, the atmosphere of success.
Harriet Monroe was gone; *Poetry* was edited by a man. The black
women, who had made a promising beginning, fell silent. Women
like Marjorie Seiffert, Eunice Tietjens, Grace Hazard Conkling, and
a host of other lesser-known female writers who had contributed
to the boom in women's poetry found the tide of power ebbing
away, their careers and personal growth essentially ended long before
their creative potential was fulfilled. The emerging sense of community that breathed life into women's creativity in the exciting
decade after 1915 had all but vanished, leaving the survivors to work
in relative isolation, without the sense of a goal shared by all women.
From their commanding position in the academy, male critics and
poets created the impression that modernist poetry could virtually
be defined in terms of its opposition to the bad examples set by
women, for which female nature was held to be at fault. It is no
wonder that creative women increasingly faced a crisis of confidence, an apologetic defensiveness, a crippling of the will. So thorough was the denigration of the women poets who flourished
between 1915 and 1945 that their continuity with a later generation
of women poets has effectively been destroyed; even many important names have been forgotten. (This has been the repeated experience of women writers through history—the deprivation of
ancestors whose struggle can bear no fruits, the unbridged gaps

that require the periodic rediscovery by women of themselves as creators.) The struggle of individual women for survival in a time of declining fortunes therefore reflects beyond the personal, beyond the familiar stories of anxiety, of psychoanalysis and electric shock treatment, alcoholism and self-repudiation, to the political.

The friendship of Margaret Conklin and Sara Teasdale, for example, was strained and hypersensitive because, as an attempt at mutual empowerment, it had so much negativity to overcome. Against the pressure of patriarchal sexual tyranny that divided women from one another, both women were seeking to restore the archetypal power-giving relationship of mother and daughter. Teasdale and Conklin had repudiated mothers who they felt had betrayed them by playing according to the patriarchal rules, giving up their "souls" (in Teasdale's words) in return for petty manipulation and irritable territorial possessiveness. "You must not grow like her, you must not grow like her,"[29] Teasdale told herself. Yet Teasdale, too, had been so trained to bow her head, to practice submissiveness, that the rebellious thrust of her creativity set up an intolerable conflict: "Whichever it is, when the end has come,/ I shall be the defeated one,"[30] she wrote. Margaret had idealistically looked to her for a model of triumph, and therefore her suicide nearly shattered Margaret's own confidence in survival. Such survival depended on linking herself with older women who had successfully braved the blast and retained self-possession; Margaret's profound admiration for Marianne Moore thus centered on Moore's ability to convert female abasement, through her religious faith, into a kind of tough strength.

Also contributing to the crisis of confidence were the increasing tensions of professional competition that came with the ascendancy of male modernism. Creative women tended to react to competitiveness with some degree of guilt and an inability to be satisfied with success. Sara Teasdale sought friendship chiefly among women of lesser talent or ambition than herself. It was safe to encourage young women of promise like Louise Bogan, whom she had to tea, or to sympathize with women suffering from neglect or down on their luck; but Teasdale was capable of acidulous put-downs of her chief rivals—Wylie was to her an exploitive literary climber, Millay a female Don Juan. Her reproof, however, has overtones of self-disapproval, for she felt her own success to be worthless as well. Teasdale's uneasy feeling that success was inappropriate for a woman can be explained as a conditioned response to the patriarchal demand that women be humble, serve rather than strive for prominence. While this may be true, it is not the whole truth. Teasdale had a sense of the community of women writers. To impose the system of male competition upon women was to violate a certain female integrity, to separate them from one another, from their origins in female oneness, and therefore to induce feelings of guilt and loss.

Although psychological studies of creativity in relation to gender are still speculative, certain recent models of male and female development suggest that while males in our culture form a sense of identity by separating themselves and marking clear-cut personality boundaries, women engage in a more complex interplay between separation and remaining at one with the mother. Mother-daughter love, female cooperation, would seem then to be an essential element in women's creativity. At this point, friendship takes on a political dimension: men delight to see infighting among women, for it undermines female solidarity and female power as well as supporting the male view of competition as the norm. Men with literary views as opposite as those of Lola Ridge and Marianne Moore would find it difficult to be friends, for they would take their differences as essential to their definition of themselves. Friendship, however, readily transcended professional differences for Moore and Ridge in a way uniquely possible to women. Marianne Moore typed the manuscript of *Firehead* for Ridge when she was too ill to do it herself, and distributed the notices of Ridge's death. One has only to imagine Robert Frost typing a manuscript for Wallace Stevens to realize the extent of the difference.

The first wave of women poets was released, it seems, by a breakdown in traditional male power structures in a time of fluid, even chaotic, change around World War I, when a healing sense of renewal, of women's perceived gifts for love and cooperation, seemed called for. No one knew how to describe what was happening in the arts except to say that it was "new." Gradually, however, the familiar male pattern reasserted itself, a "movement" was identified, with its conservative male heroes at the head, its critical principles for justification, and its hierarchical ranking of who was important and who was not. As in sports and politics, women were crowded to the periphery and allowed only a token presence. The effect of this historical process on individual women is illustrated with clarity and poignance in the life and work of Louise Bogan, a writer young enough to reach maturity just as the great wave of women's poetry was ebbing and male modernism was gaining ascendancy. As one might predict, Bogan felt the full brunt of the conflict between female solidarity and divisive male competitiveness.

Like Sara Teasdale, Louise Bogan suffered irreparable psychic damage in her relationship with her mother. Bogan recognized this as the probable cause of her tortured struggle to free herself from inner demons that continually threatened to throttle her creativity. She tried marriage, love with no strings attached, electric shock treatments, and writing about it, but never succeeded in permanently banishing the upwelling pressures that menaced her sanity and self-possession. Her only successful tactic was to distance herself from her own emotions with a kind of steely resolve.

Bogan's dependence on her male psychoanalyst doubtless contributed to the hardening of this division of herself. The cornerstone of analysis was the attempt to free the patient from emotional identification with the mother, in the belief that individuation could occur only through separation—a view that reflected men's perception of themselves. The mother was seen, in effect, as a voracious mouth threatening to swallow her offspring. Louise Bogan's notes on her mother suggest that she was following her doctor's prescription not merely to overcome fear and hatred toward her mother, but to avoid succumbing to the powerful pull of affection as well, to free herself by eliminating, or controlling, all feeling. Marjorie Seiffert had reported the effect of psychoanalysis to be emotional aridity, a loss of creative drive. Louise Bogan would seem to have experienced a similar result, for in periods of balance and control she virtually stopped writing. The shortest route to the castration of women was to cut the bond of empowering love between mother and daughter. Emily Dickinson's words continually reverberate: *I never had a mother.*

As Bogan tried to solve her problems by accommodation to male psychological theories current in the 1930s, so she also tried to adapt to the precepts of male modernist poetry. The horror and disgust that male critics voiced toward feminine feeling in poetry are reflected in Bogan's extreme care to avoid offense, to stand over herself with a kind of admonishing severity. Yet as Gloria Bowles shows in her study *Louise Bogan's Aesthetic of Limitation,* Bogan sought to preserve in modified form the "line of feeling" she believed central to female poetic tradition. Her poetry, like her life, was a negotiation for survival, to succeed as both woman and modernist. As Bowles brings out, the antifemale bias of modernist poetry led Bogan to internalize many of its strictures, to define woman-as-poet in terms of limitation, of what women could and could not do. This amounted to a defensive strategy for producing a body of poetry and criticism that could take a respectable place in the modern movement and not be segregated or belittled because it was written by a woman. Louise Bogan presented to the world a formidable surface of rigorous competence and austere self-discipline, so as to forestall any imputation of vulnerability.

The possibility of power-giving female solidarity did not figure in Louise Bogan's ideas about women's creativity. In fact, the prospect of passionate involvement among women made her uneasy and defensive, for it threatened the balance she had achieved at such cost. This is revealed in the tensions in her friendship with May Sarton, harbinger of a new generation that shifted from Bogan's kind of male orientation to an unapologetic affirmation of female identity.

To the young May Sarton, Louise Bogan represented what she was struggling to achieve: a perfection of her craft, "clarity, precision, the formal lyric where thought and emotion have been brought down to essence . . ."[31] Both Sarton and Bogan were working in the lyric tradition that had been closely associated with women; both saw the tradition as capable of growth and continued extension, of adaptation to modern expression. Their commitment, however, ran counter to the prevailing tendency of the male avant-garde, which viewed the formal lyric as a relic of the dead past. "As I need not tell you," Sarton wrote to Bogan in 1947, "I am utterly out of fashion. . . . It's a damned lonely business." Out of this lonely separation of creative women from one another and from the mainstream of power, May Sarton reached to Louise Bogan for help with a publisher, for encouragement, for the recognition that a younger aspirant craves from an admired master. "It would be wonderful indeed to feel that I had an ally," she said. "But I know too that it is asking a good deal." [32]

Louise Bogan was extremely sensitive to the pressure of any emotional demand, and tended to react guardedly, out of self-protection. She had barely survived her own long battle and attained a precarious peace with herself. As Gloria Bowles writes, "What Louise Bogan had faced and *gotten through* was a troubled childhood and the challenge of being woman and poet in the modernist period and the expectation of Love and Romance and the care of a child and the drain of critical work and drug therapy and a lack of recognition . . ." [33] Although she allowed her "soft" side a degree of play in her response to May Sarton, she also tried to establish a certain controlling distance, as if fearful of being pulled back into her old conflicts. This ambivalence remained throughout the years of their friendship, in spite of Sarton's repeated attempts to resolve it.

After an exchange of letters over several years, May Sarton and Louise Bogan finally met personally in November 1953. To enter Bogan's New York apartment, with its luminous atmosphere of classical order and simplicity, successfully wrested from the emotional disorder of her life, was exhilarating to Sarton: "It was as if some awful constriction and tension eased at once, and I could be myself again." [34]

It is evident from a reading of their correspondence that Sarton was not aware at first of Bogan's tendency to pull back and keep a breathing space—something she demanded in all relationships—to display cool wisdom in response to youthful enthusiasm, as if measuring out a kindness she could not afford to squander. She read Sarton's recently published volume, *The Land of Silence,* and offered criticism that reflected her own circumscribed views of a woman poet's proper mode. While Bogan praised several poems generously, "the book is *too long,*" she admonished. "Prune! Never publish more than 40 poems at a time!" In contrast to Bogan's perfectionism, the severe self-limitation that ended in silence, as it did for many women poets, Sarton tended to be prodigal, to free her tongue to speak of anything that might concern her, even if the results were not invariably up to her highest standard. Although male poets were routinely allowed such freedom, Bogan believed that women had to constrain themselves with excruciating care. "Again," Bogan told her,[35]

certain of the poems seem to be written slightly more from an *impulse toward literature* than as direct impulsions from life. This latter difficulty always must be faced, by lyric poets like ourselves; and, I fear, more drastically by women than by men. For, as Wystan Auden wrote me when *Poems and New Poems* was published, the world will take play and elaboration and things at second-hand from men more easily than from women. Women must be responsible from the beginning; and women poets are not allowed the latitude that men poets are allowed; they must go to the heart of the matter and stay there!

That is to say, Bogan accepted the no-win situation imposed on women poets: to restrict themselves to personal emotion—culture being men's province—and then to exercise rigorous self-restraint lest female emotion be embarrassingly displayed; to overachieve in order to be noticed at all.

    May Sarton was deeply grateful for Bogan's critical attention, but was gradually obliged to realize that her own tendencies were in the opposite direction, toward freedom and expansiveness, emotional candor rather than self-veiling. Sarton used the word "transparency" to describe the effect she wished to obtain. Bogan obviously did not feel she could help Sarton in a development so contrary to her own assumptions about women, but was willing to stand benignly by and encourage her to follow her own chosen path. One sees May Sarton trying, out of admiration and affection, to apply Bogan's pronouncements to herself. But it only increased the self-doubt and frustration against which she was battling. It was a matter of bitter disappointment to Sarton that over the years Louise Bogan, in her powerful position as poetry critic for the *New Yorker*, never reviewed her work, except for brief mention.

May Sarton's feeling of "being herself" upon meeting Louise Bogan resulted from the sudden focus of all her own strivings in this woman of achievement. Sarton's love was an offering of homage, and she hoped for love in return, the kind of love that circulates back to infuse the admirer with confidence and encouragement. "When I say I love you," Sarton told Bogan, "I am saying that I love poetry."[36] It is significant that Sarton associated her sense of release as much with Bogan's surroundings, the place where she worked, as with her person. May Sarton stated the experience of finding self-wholeness in a later poem, "Now I Become Myself":

> All fuses now and falls into place
> From wish to action . . .
> My work, my love, my time, my face
> Gathered into one intense
> Gesture of growing like a plant . . .
> Made so and rooted so by love.[37]

The friendship between May Sarton and Louise Bogan developed rapidly in the early months of 1954, following their meeting, filling Sarton with refreshed life and excitement: "Yours with much wonder and gratefulness," she signed one letter.[38] Sarton's reference in the poem above to her face being made one with the inner aspect of her life is an important image, indicating the unity and harmony of the true self with the front it presents to the world, a transparency, a lack of duplicity. Much has been written about the subversive strategies women poets have used to say "slant" what they have felt unable to say directly. May Sarton's work is a kind of watershed in women's poetry in its deliberate avoidance of indirection and artistic game-playing in order to overcome the incapacitating effects of gender delimitation. Sarton tried to explain to

Bogan her search for wholeness as a woman and what it implied for creative women's relations with one another—and to encourage Bogan to realize that she was truly the exemplar Sarton found her to be.

What the robin's egg room is, where every object means something and is beautiful, and all is peace and inwardness and an achieved serenity, that is your face too. That is you. You mustn't lose the sense of yourself as what you are. . . . Please accept the fact that you are beautiful and everyone must love you, each in his own way. . . . You are a central person, which is also to be centered, and that always means to be a magnet in a world where few people are.[39]

It was difficult for Louise Bogan to either understand or accept May Sarton's offering of love, for her own experience had convinced her that love only trapped two people in pain. Sarton had gently to explain, first of all, that "to confuse such love with sex is perhaps fatal, at least very disturbing." Bogan, with her Catholic background, her psychiatric conditioning, and the memory of her mother's infidelities, tended to subsume all emotional attraction between people in the heterosexual pattern. Sarton saw such an equation as typical of male nature, not female. In spite of the broadmindedness on which she prided herself, Bogan had at times expressed distaste for deviation. Reflecting the gender polarization so firmly fixed in her outlook, she explained to Sarton that she felt love required the "other," the difference from oneself, in order to attain harmony or completeness (though in her own case it had only produced conflict). Sarton readily conceded the truth of this, but knew that there was another dimension of self-fulfillment which required union with likeness. Without it, there was a danger of self-rejection. Sarton felt that Bogan's shrinking from love was a kind of denial of her own genius, of her own possibilities:

There is this anxiety I have because I think you are withdrawing too much and especially that you have not come to terms or something with being grownup. . . . There is something in you which rejects yourself. . . . You simply have no right to, for the sake of poetry, which is after all why you are on earth.

"I see some deep and flowing freedom between us," Sarton told Bogan. "You opened the very deep door that has not been opened for me for a very long time. . . . Don't shut me out."[40]

At this point, Louise Bogan became uncomfortable, for May Sarton was beginning to penetrate her carefully constructed defenses, and she felt forced to redirect their relationship onto safer ground. "Perhaps this love," she told Sarton, "is part of the process" of Sarton's own development, relatively independent of Bogan herself. "That I cannot *give back* has nothing to do with your emotional truth." From then on, Bogan tried consistently to objectify their relationship, to establish a kind of affectionate regard that left each of them essentially in emotional isolation from the other in any deeper sense. She could not handle the prospect of an emotional involvement that required her to merge herself with another, for she had sought safety in patriarchal assumptions about love, laboriously constructing boundaries and guarding against any breaching of them. Paradoxically this was her freedom; emotional involvement with others meant submitting to the tyranny of patterns. "That is to me the truth I learned when I was *ill:* break out of the pattern in some fashion, in order to grow and be free."[41] Little by little, Bogan told Sarton of her problematic relationship with her mother and of her own disastrous marriage with Raymond Holden and the consequent impossibility of intimate union with anyone. (The fact that May Sarton and Louise's mother, May Bogan, had the same first name might have created some emotional obstacle too.) The only thing she could offer Sarton was "just standing by with my hand out."[42] "Be happy, dear May, and remember that I proffer you all that I can proffer any *human being*. Which isn't, I suppose, v. much, but all of it is fresh and non-*patterned*."[43]

Louise Bogan could not comprehend a passionate friendship in terms other than the very kind of "patterned" heterosexual relationship she found too controlling. May Sarton seemed to baffle her by not differentiating between love and friendship and not identifying love with sex. Ritualized gender relations, of aggression and submission, Sarton tried to explain, do not apply to love between women, which is primarily emotional rather than sexual . . . What the woman discovers is herself *in* someone else. You break out of yourself through someone else, to find yourself. . . . It is metaphysical . . . exceedingly pure and intense, an exchange of souls. . . . One never reaches the deepest place of feeling part of the almost unconscious universe, of being *lost*. Instead one reaches a place of extreme consciousness; one is *found* as an individual.[44]

Bogan did not respond to this "essay" for weeks, and then confessed, "I must admit that I don't understand its statements. The idea of *likeness* in love *does* disturb me; it brings back too vividly my mother-attachment, that it took years and much suffering to escape from. I feel that any return to a delight in *likeness* would really give me a bad time; would really *defeat* a great deal." The struggle to separate herself from her mother "exhausted me forever. So far as closeness to the feminine principle is concerned."[45]

Louise Bogan thenceforth practiced a kind of emotional fencing, a fending off of what she perceived as invitations to feeling. Posing as a somewhat world-weary, aging survivor, she periodically counseled May Sarton to separate herself from emotion rather than to pursue it: "I keep feeling that you, like myself, should be fully emancipated from any closeness or dependence on any human being."[46] "Be calm and gay, and base not your heart on *persons*." She had survived, she said, only by giving up people, escaping their power over her. "It is a sort of amputation, I am sure; but one can manage. . . ."[47]

In spite of differences so fundamental, so directly relevant to the creativity of each, Louise Bogan and May Sarton enjoyed a surprisingly successful friendship over nearly two decades, collaborating on translations from Verlaine, talking, writing, visiting often. Perhaps the sense of a common commitment to their art, which had drawn them together in the first place, sustained them across the chasm that neither really wanted to see open between them. Survival as artists was more important in the end than an insistence on differences.

Nevertheless, there was a tragic aspect that could be neither overlooked nor exorcised: Bogan's failure to give Sarton the kind of professional encouragement and support she sought during years of self-doubt and the struggle to establish herself. Bogan had only to say a word, to give a nod; but she would not. Once or twice Sarton exploded with indignant exasperation; and Bogan would reply with bland benevolence: "I should hate to have to think that *I* have closed you [from creativity] in any way.—Surely this cannot be true, no matter how different our respective attitudes to our respective gifts may be."⁴⁸ "Be wise," she would cheerily advise. "Be happy." It seems that Bogan could not separate the demon of emotion she saw in Sarton from Sarton's work; to approve or promote her poetry would be to yield to the feared enemy. But in this stubborn refusal, or incapacity, Bogan unintentionally subverted the female cause. The withholding of love—negating the female bonding that nourishes female creativity—is the ultimate undermining of the creative woman's confidence. When love is not given as it can be, self-esteem is irreparably damaged and the artist suffers a lifelong, unhealing wound. Louise Bogan had, in the blind way of most human beings, re-created with May Sarton the tragedy of separation from her own mother rather than the empowering union they both required.

*

The unsettled question that has been pursued throughout this book comes to rest here, in a friendship. How is woman's creative will to be freed? Louise Bogan and May Sarton presented to one another the two alternative answers emerging in their time: to accept women's defensive position and work within the lines of power laid down by men; or to find a new empowerment in a woman-centered vision. The urgency of the question held them together in spite of their differing answers. May Sarton, with the advantage of youth, could anticipate the future, yet could revere those older women who strove with such courage to claim the royal name of poet against all odds.

*

SOURCE NOTES

*

FOREWORD

[1] Gertrude Stein, *Everybody's Autobiography* (New York: Cooper Square, 1971), p. 92.

[2] Nikki Giovanni, in *Black Women Writers at Work,* ed. Claudia Tate (New York: Continuum, 1984), p. 64.

[3] Helen Hoyt, special women's issue of *Others,* vol. 3, no. 3 (September 1916), p. 54.

[4] Edmund Wilson, *The Shores of Light* (New York: Farrar, 1952), p. 242.

[5] *The Letters of Edna St. Vincent Millay,* ed. Allan Ross Macdougall (New York: Harper, 1952), p. 173.

[6] Sara Teasdale, ed., *The Answering Voice* (New York: Macmillan, 1928), p. ix.

[7] *Giovanni,* p. 64.

ONE POETS AS DAUGHTERS

[1] Unpubl. diary, July 5, 1940. Sophia Smith Coll., Smith College.

[2] Unpubl. diary, January 17, 1940. Sophia Smith Coll., Smith College.

[3] Unpubl. diary, May 8, 1940. Sophia Smith Coll., Smith College.

[4] *Sun-Up* (New York: Heubsch, 1920), dedication.

5 *Sun-Up*, p. 69.

6 *The Ghetto and Other Poems* (New York: Heubsch, 1918), p. 80.

7 Unpubl. diary, August 8, 1940. Sophia Smith Coll., Smith College.

8 Unpubl. diary, September 12, 1940. Sophia Smith Coll., Smith College.

9 Donald Hall, *Marianne Moore: The Cage and the Animal* (New York: Pegasus, 1970), p. 16.

10 Margaret Conklin, personal interview, June 22, 1983.

11 Interview with Donald Hall, *A Marianne Moore Reader* (New York: Viking, 1961), p. 261.

12 Hall, *The Cage*, p. 18.

13 *Like a Bulwark* (New York: Viking, 1956), p. 7.

14 *A Reader*, p. 258.

15 *Autobiography of William Carlos Williams* (New York: New Directions, 1967) p. 146.

16 Conklin, personal interview, June 22, 1983.

17 Barbara Guest, *Herself Defined: The Poet H.D. and Her World* (New York: Doubleday, 1984) p. 295.

18 *A Reader*, p. 65.

19 Robert McAlmon, *Being Geniuses Together, 1920–1930*, rev. with suppl. chs. and an afterword by Kay Boyle (San Francisco: North Point, 1984) p. 18.

20 McAlmon, p. 40.

21 McAlmon, p. 16.

22 Edmund Wilson, *The Shores of Light*, p. 755.

23 *The Letters of Edna St. Vincent Millay*, ed. Allan Ross Macdougall, p. 82.

24 *Letters*, p. 120.

25 *Shores*, p. 760.

26 Edmund Wilson, *The Twenties* (New York: Farrar, 1975), p. 347.

27 *A Room of One's Own* (New York: Harcourt, 1929), p. 98.

28 "Imeros," *Mirror of the Heart: Selected Poems of Sara Teasdale*, ed. William Drake (New York: Macmillan, 1984), p. 9.

29 "The Kiss," *Mirror*, p. 4.

30 "Sappho," *Collected Poems of Sara Teasdale* (New York: Macmillan, 1966), p. 89.

31 William Drake, *Sara Teasdale: Woman and Poet* (San Francisco: Harper, 1979), p. 71.

32 Drake, *Teasdale*, p. 294.

33 Drake, *Teasdale*, p. 47.

34 Louise Bogan, *Journey around My Room*, ed. Ruth Limmer (New York: Penguin, 1981), p. 72.

35 *Journey*, p. 167.

36 *Journey*, p. 72.

37 *Journey*, p. 172.

38 *Journey*, pp. 28, 29.

39 *Journey*, pp. 23, 25.

40 *Journey*, p. 29.

41 *Journey*, p. 35.

[42] *Journey*, p. 27.

[43] *Journey*, p. 172.

[44] Unpubl. letter to Archibald Grimké, September 22, 1884. Angelina Weld Grimké Papers, Moorland-Spingarn Res. Center, Howard U.

[45] Unpubl. letter. Angelina Weld Grimké Papers, Howard U.

[46] Gloria T. Hull, "Under the Days: The Buried Life and Poetry of Angelina Weld Grimké," *Home Girls: A Black Feminist Anthology*, ed. Barbara Smith (New York: Kitchen Table, 1983), p. 74.

[47] Emma Toller to Angelina Weld Grimké, Hartford, Conn., October 1, 1898. Angelina Weld Grimké Papers, Howard U.

[48] *The Crisis*, vol. 21 (1920), p. 64.

[49] "Rachel," unpubl. ms. Angelina Weld Grimké Papers, Howard U.

[50] Unpubl. letter. Angelina Weld Grimké Papers, Howard U.

[51] Unpubl. diary, Angelina Weld Grimké Papers, Howard U.

[52] Unpubl. poem. Angelina Weld Grimké Papers, Howard U.

[53] Unpubl. poem. Grimké Papers, Howard U.

[54] Unpubl. diary, Angelina Weld Grimké Papers, Howard U.

[55] Unpubl. diary, Angelina Weld Grimké Papers, Howard U.

TWO FAMILIES

[1] *Letters of Edna St. Vincent Millay*, p. 220.

[2] *Letters*, p. 83.

[3] *Letters*, p. 137.

[4] *Letters*, p. 151.

[5] *Letters*, p. 164.

[6] *Nation*, vol. 125 (1927), p. 715.

[7] Kathleen Millay, *The Hermit Thrush* (New York: Liveright, 1929), p. 55.

[8] *Thrush*, p. 17.

[9] *Thrush*, p. 18.

[10] *Thrush*, p. 127.

[11] *Thrush*, p. 129.

[12] *Thrush*, p. 81.

[13] *Letters*, p. 352.

[14] Drake, *Sara Teasdale: Woman and Poet*, p. 50.

[15] "Crowned," "The Door Mat," Drake, *Teasdale*, pp. 73, 72.

[16] Teasdale, poetry notebooks. Beinecke Library, Yale U. Marginal annotation: "written in the winter of 1918–19" (at age thirty-four).

[17] Drake, *Teasdale*, p. 71.

[18] Drake, *Teasdale*, p. 102.

[19] Drake, *Teasdale*, p. 210.

[20] Drake, *Teasdale*, p. 10.

[21] Drake, *Teasdale*, p. 10.

[22] Teasdale, *Mirror of the Heart: Selected Poems of Sara Teasdale*, p. 79.

[23] Unpubl. letter to her mother, Anne McMichael Hoyt, June 12, 1903. Berg Coll., N.Y. Publ. Lib.

[24] Unpubl. letter to her mother, July 1903. Berg Coll., N.Y. Publ. Lib.

[25] Unpubl. letter to her mother, June 2, 1903. Berg Coll., N.Y. Publ. Lib.

[26] *Collected Poems of Elinor Wylie* (New York: Knopf, 1932), p. 5.

[27] Stanley Olson, *Elinor Wylie: A Life Apart* (New York: Dial, 1979), p. 42.

[28] Anne McMichael Hoyt, "The Naked Truth," unpubl. memoir. Berg Coll., N.Y. Publ. Lib.

[29] Unpubl. letter. Berg Coll., N.Y. Publ. Lib.

[30] Olson, p. 104.

[31] Olson, p. 72.

[32] Olson, p. 50.

[33] Unpubl. letter to her mother, November 23, 1911. Berg Coll., N.Y. Publ. Lib.

[34] William Jay Smith, *The Spectra Hoax* (Middletown, Conn.: Wesleyan U.P., 1961), p. 135.

[35] Smith, p. 27.

[36] Undated news clipping. Moline, Illinois Publ. Lib.

[37] College music composition book. Seiffert family papers, quoted by permission of Allyn Asti-Rose.

[38] John Pryor, personal interview, May 5, 1985.

[39] Marjorie Seiffert, *A Woman of Thirty* (New York: Knopf, 1919), pp. 81–84.

[40] Undated news clipping. Moline Publ. Lib.

[41] Anne Dunn, "Biographical Note," in Gladys Cromwell, *Poems* (New York: Macmillan, 1919), p. 113.

[42] Mary Colum, *Life and the Dream* (Garden City: Doubleday, 1947) p. 261.

[43] "The Weakling," *Poems*, p. 66.

[44] Dunn, "Note," p. 113.

[45] "The Weakling," *Poems*, p. 66.

[46] *Poems*, p. 90.

[47] "Winter Poetry," *Poems*, p. 67.

[48] "The Weakling," *Poems*, p. 66.

[49] "The Lion," *Poems*, p. 44.

[50] Dunn, "Note," p. 113.

[51] *Poems*, p. 31.

[52] *Life and the Dream*, pp. 261–262.

[53] Unpubl. letter. Berg Coll., N.Y. Publ. Lib.

[54] *New York Times*, January 29, 1919.

[55] *New York Times*, March 5, 1919.

[56] *Poems*, p. 33.

THREE OPENING DOORS

[1] Babette Deutsch, *A Brittle Heaven* (New York: Greenburg, 1926), p. 210.

[2] *Heaven*, p. 161.

[3] *Heaven*, p. 123.

[4] *Banners* (New York: Doran, 1919), p. 17.

[5] Lillian Rubin, *Just Friends* (New York: Harper, 1985), p. 167.

[6] Quoted by Carolyn Hielbrun, *Toward a Recognition of Androgyny* (New York: Knopf, 1973), p. 170.

[7] *Surpassing the Love of Men* (New York: William Morrow, 1981), p. 205.

[8] Drake, *Sara Teasdale: Woman and Poet*, p. 24.

[9] Drake, *Teasdale*, p. 25.

[10] Nathalia Crane, *Venus Invisible and Other Poems* (New York: Coward, 1928), p. 15.

[11] Drake, *Teasdale*, p. 26.

[12] "Song," *Collected Poems of Sara Teasdale* (New York: Macmillan, 1966) p. 21.

[13] Unpubl. letter to Marion Cummings Stanley, February 13, 1909. Newberry Lib., Chicago.

[14] Drake, *Teasdale*, p. 47.

[15] Unpubl. letter to Zoë Akins, n.d. [1905]. Huntington Lib., San Marino, Calif.

[16] Harriet Gardner, unpubl. diary, quoted by Ruth Perry and Maurice Sagoff, "Sara Teasdale's Friendships," *New Letters*, vol. 46, no. 1 (Spring 1980), p. 103.

[17] Gardner, unpubl. diary, quoted by perm. of Ruth Perry and Maurice Sagoff.

[18] Drake, *Teasdale*, p. 61.

[19] Teasdale, *Collected Poems*, p. 180.

[20] Unpubl. letter from Teasdale to Stanley, March 18, 1909. Newberry Lib., Chicago.

[21] Harriet Monroe, *A Poet's Life* (New York: Macmillan, 1938), pp. 323–324.

[22] *Little Review*, vol. 1, no. 2 (April 1914), p. 17.

[23] Drake, *Teasdale*, pp. 108, 109.

[24] Teasdale, *Mirror of the Heart: Selected Poems of Sara Teasdale*, p. 17.

[25] Adelaide Crapsey's nephew Arthur J. Crapsey, quoted in Susan Smith, *The Complete Poems and Selected Letters of Adelaide Crapsey* (Albany: S.U.N.Y.P., 1977), p. 6.

[26] Mary Elizabeth Osborn, *Adelaide Crapsey* (Boston: Bruce Humphries, 1933), p. 57.

[27] *Complete Poems*, p. 93.

[28] *Complete Poems*, p. 80.

[29] Nichol, quoted by Smith, *Complete Poems*, p. 11.

[30] *Complete Poems*, p. 101.

[31] Crapsey to Esther Lowenthal, February 4, 1914, *Complete Poems*, p. 15.

[32] Crapsey to Lowenthal, May 11, 1914, *Complete Poems*, p. 248.

[33] Ridge, "Adelaide Crapsey," *Red Flag* (New York: Viking, 1927), p. 85.

[34] *Poetry*, vol. 16, no. 2 (June 1920), p. 146. Quoted from the Philadelphia *Record*.

[35] Monroe, *Poetry*, vol. 16, no. 2 (June 1920), p. 148.

[36] Smith-Rosenberg, in *Disorderly Conduct* (New York: Knopf, 1985), pp. 245–296.

[37] Ezra Pound, *Selected Prose*, ed. William Cookson (New York: New Directions, 1950), p. 424.

[38] Harriet Monroe, *Poetry*, vol. 17, no. 4 (Jan. 1921), pp. 205, 208.

[39] Eunice Tietjens, *Poetry*, vol. 10, no. 4 (Jan. 1917), p. 198.

[40] Unpubl. letter to Eunice Tietjens, May 27, 1944. Newberry Lib., Chicago.

[41] Unpubl. letter to Tietjens, March 11, 1939. Newberry Lib., Chicago.

[42] Unpubl. letter to Tietjens, May 27, 1944, Newberry Lib., Chicago.

[43] Unpubl. letter to Tietjens, May 27, 1944, Newberry Lib., Chicago.

[44] Drake, *Teasdale,* p. 233.

[45] Drake, *Teasdale,* p. 120.

[46] Glenn Ruihley, *The Thorn of the Rose: Amy Lowell Reconsidered* (Hamden, Conn.: Archon, 1975), p. 23.

[47] Foster Damon, *Amy Lowell* (Boston: Houghton, 1935), p. 29.

[48] Damon, p. 29.

[49] Damon, p. 90.

[50] Damon, p. 148.

[51] Lowell, *Complete Poetical Works* (Boston: Houghton, 1955), p. 42.

[52] *The Autobiography of Emanuel Carnevali,* comp. and pref. by Kay Boyle (New York: Horizon, 1967), p. 92.

[53] Unpubl. letter to Eunice Tietjens, June 4, 1913.

[54] Teasdale, *Mirror,* p. 4.

[55] Lowell, *Works,* p. 217.

[56] Drake, *Teasdale,* p. 188.

[57] Unpubl. letter to Amy Lowell, January 28, 1918. Houghton Lib., Harvard U.

[58] Conkling, "To the Schooner Casco, Dear to R. L. S.," unpubl. ms., 1913. Houghton Lib., Harvard U.

[59] Quoted by Conkling in unpubl. letter to Lowell, December 7, 1919. Houghton Lib., Harvard U.

[60] Unpubl. letter to Conkling, December 10, 1919. Houghton Lib., Harvard U.

[61] Lowell to Conkling, July 1, 1922, unpubl. ms. Houghton Lib., Harvard U.

FOUR   MEN AND MARRIAGE

[1] Teasdale, *Collected Poems of Sara Teasdale,* p. 31.

[2] Millay, "Thursday," *Collected Poems* (New York: Harper, 1956), p. 129.

[3] Margaret Widdemer, *Golden Friends I Had: Unrevised Memoirs of Margaret Widdemer* (Garden City: Doubleday, 1964), p. 268.

[4] Wylie, "The Eagle and the Mole," *Collected Poems of Elinor Wylie,* p. 4.

[5] Teasdale, "Barter," *Collected Poems,* p. 97.

[6] Wylie, "Madman's Song," *Collected Poems,* p. 5.

[7] Adrienne Rich, *Of Woman Born* (New York: Norton, 1976), p. 29.

[8] Unpubl. letter to William Rose Benet, January 1921. Barrett Coll. #8287, Alderman Lib., U. of Va.

[9] Unpubl. letter to Benet, January 1921. Barrett Coll. #8287, Alderman Lib., U. of Va.

[10] Unpubl. letter to Benet, n.d. [January or February 1921]. Barrett Coll. #8287, Alderman Lib., U. of Va.

[11] Unpubl. letter to Benet, n.d. [spring 1921]. Barrett Coll. #8287, Alderman Lib., U. of Va.

[12] Unpubl. letter to Benet, n.d. [spring 1921]. Barrett Coll. #8287, Alderman Lib., U. of Va.

[13] Unpubl. letter to Benet, n.d. [early summer 1921]. Barrett Coll. #8287, Alderman Lib., U. of Va.

[14] Unpubl. letter to Benet, n.d. [summer 1921]. Barrett Coll. #8287, Alderman Lib., U. of Va.

[15] Unpubl. letter to Benet, n.d. [summer 1921]. Barrett Coll. #8287, Alderman Lib., U. of Va.

[16] Unpubl. letter to Benet, n.d. [1921]. Barrett Coll. #8287, Alderman Lib., U. of Va.

[17] Unpubl. letter to Benet, n.d. [1921]. Barrett Coll. #8287, Alderman Lib., U. of Va.

[18] Unpubl. letter to Benet, n.d. [1921]. Barrett Coll. #8287, Alderman Lib., U. of Va.

[19] Wylie, *Collected Poems*, p. 51.

[20] Pref. to Wylie, *Collected Poems*, p. viii.

[21] Horace Gregory, *Amy Lowell: Portrait of a Poet in Her Time* (New York: Nelson, 1958), p. 184.

[22] Louis Untermeyer, *From Another World* (New York: Harcourt, 1939), pp. 248, 249.

[23] Olson, *Elinor Wylie: A Life Apart*, p. 221.

[24] Edmund Wilson, *The Twenties*, pp. 78–79.

[25] Eunice Tietjens, *The World at My Shoulder* (New York: Macmillan, 1938), pp. 191–192.

[26] Untermeyer, *World*, p. 250.

[27] Elinor Wylie, *The Orphan Angel* (New York: Knopf, 1926), p. 45. The most thorough treatment of Wylie's identification with Shelley is found in Judith Farr, *The Life and Art of Elinor Wylie* (Baton Rouge: Louisana State U.P., 1983).

[28] *Angel*, p. 178.

[29] *Angel*, 330.

[30] *The Letters of Virginia Woolf*, vol. 3, 1923–1928, ed. Nigel Nicolson (London: Hogarth, 1977), pp. 279–280.

[31] Unpubl. letter to Benet, August 1922. Barrett Coll. #8287, Alderman Lib., U. of Va.

[32] Unpubl. letter to her mother, October 1928. Berg Coll., N.Y. Publ. Lib.

[33] Olson, p. 290.

[34] Edmund Wilson, "The Death of Elinor Wylie," in *The Shores of Light*, p. 392. Published accounts vary, but Wilson's is probably the most reliable, since he drew on both Nancy Hoyt's reminiscences and personal comments of Benet.

[35] Lola Ridge, unpubl. diary, March 29, 1940. Sophia Smith Coll., Smith College.

[36] Drake, *Sara Teasdale: Woman and Poet*, p. 112.

[37] Drake, *Teasdale*, p. 132.

[38] Margaret Conklin, personal communication to the author.

[39] Drake, *Teasdale*, p. 141.

[40] Drake, *Teasdale*, p. 140.

[41] Drake, *Teasdale*, p. 139.

[42] Drake, *Teasdale*, p. 148.

[43] Olson, p. 245.

[44] "The Conflict," *Mirror of the Heart: Selected Poems of Sara Teasdale*, p. 108.

[45] "The Conflict."

[46]"The Hawk," *Mirror*, p. 101.

[47]"Oh You Are Coming," *Mirror*, p. 74.

[48]Drake, *Teasdale*, p. 257.

[49]Unpubl. letter to Eunice Tietjens, October 1922. Newberry Lib., Chicago.

[50]Wilson, *Shores*, p. 771.

[51]Jane Stanbrogh, "Edna St. Vincent Millay and the Language of Vulnerability," *Shakespeare's Sisters*, ed. Sandra Gilbert and Susan Grubar (Bloomington: Indiana U.P., 1979), p. 184.

[52]Wilson, *Shores*, p. 757.

[53]Wilson, *Shores*, p. 778.

[54]Wilson, *Shores*, p. 784.

[55]Teasdale, "Broken Things," *Mirror*, p. 77.

[56]H.D., *An End to Torment: A Memoir of Ezra Pound* (New York: New Directions, 1979), p. 35.

[57]Quoted in Anne Cheney, *Millay in Greenwich Village* (Alabama: U. of Alabama P., 1975), p. 64.

[58]H.D., *Tribute to Freud* (New York: Pantheon, 1956), p. 12.

[59]*Tribute*, p. 22.

[60]*Tribute*, p. 25.

[61]*Tribute*, p. 76.

[62]*Tribute*, p. 23.

[63]*Tribute*, p. 65.

[64]Unpubl. letter from Marjorie Seiffert to John Hall Wheelock, February 7, 1929. Scribner's Coll., Princeton U. Lib.

[65]Unpubl. letter to Harriet Monroe, December 11, 1918. *Poetry* Magazine Papers, 1912–1936, U. of Chicago Lib.

[66]Unpubl. letter to Arthur Davison Ficke, October 1920. Beinecke Lib., Yale U.

[67]Unpubl. letter to Witter Bynner, October 2, 1918. Houghton Lib., Harvard U.

[68]*A Woman of Thirty*, p. 118.

[69]Unpubl. letter to Bynner, April 10, 1918. Houghton Lib., Harvard U.

[70]*A Woman*, pp. 4, 7.

[71]Unpubl. letter to Monroe, December 29, 1918. *Poetry* Magazine Papers, 1912–1936, U. of Chicago Lib.

[72]To Prof. Henry Pettit, May 22, 1961. Special Coll., U. of Colorado Lib.

[73]William Carlos Williams, *Autobiography* (New York: New Directions, 1967), p. 243.

[74]Unpubl. letter to Monroe, October 5, 1925. *Poetry* Magazine Papers, 1912–1936, U. of Chicago Lib.

[75]"Rebellion," unpubl. ms. Seiffert family papers, quoted by permission of Allyn Asti-Rose.

[76]Unpubl. letter to Wheelock, January 17, 1929. Scribner's Coll., Princeton U. Lib.

[77]Unpubl. letter to Monroe, July 31, 1926. *Poetry* Magazine Papers, 1912–1936, U. of Chicago Lib.

[103] Peggy Reeves Sanday, *Female Power and Male Dominance* (Cambridge: Cambridge U.P., 1981), p. 12.

[104] "Lyric," in unpubl. work. Sophia Smith Coll., Smith College.

EIGHT BEING BLACK

[1] J. Lee Greene, *Time's Unfading Garden: Anne Spencer's Life and Poetry* (Baton Rouge: Louisiana State U.P., 1977), p. 175. Greene gathered biographical information from a reluctant Anne Spencer during the last years of her life, and has published, as an appendix to the biography, virtually all of her extant poetry. Greene's invaluable work is gratefully acknowledged as the source of most of the biographical information included here, supplemented by a visit to Anne Spencer's home in Lynchburg and interviews with her son, Chauncey Spencer.

[2] "He Said," Greene, p. 183.

[3] Greene, p. 4.

[4] Greene, p. 19.

[5] Greene, p. 35.

[6] Greene, p. 66.

[7] Greene, p. 183.

[8] Information from taped interview with Anne Spencer, supplied by Chauncey Spencer.

[9] Spencer, taped interview.

[10] Greene, p. 50.

[11] Greene, pp. 195–196.

[12] Greene, p. 52.

[13] Unpubl. letter to James Weldon Johnson, April 12, 1922. Beinecke Lib., Yale U.

[14] Greene, p. 189.

[15] Greene, p. 194.

[16] Louis Untermeyer, *American Poetry since 1900* (New York: Holt, 1923), p. 374.

[17] Greene, p. 61.

[18] Langston Hughes, "The Negro Artist and the Racial Mountain," *Nation*, June 23, 1926, p. 694.

[19] George Schuyler, "The Negro-Art Hokum," *Nation*, June 16, 1926, p. 662.

[20] Langston Hughes, "Afro-American Fragment," *Selected Poems* (New York: Knopf, 1977), p. 3.

[21] Frank S. Gorden, *Poetry*, vol. 9, no. 6 (February 1917), p. 329.

[22] Alice C. Henderson, *Poetry*, vol. 10, no. 2 (May 1917), p. 105.

[23] James Oppenheim, *Seven Arts* (May 1917), quoted by Daniel Aaron, *Writers on the Left* (New York: Harcourt, 1961), p. 63.

[24] Carl Van Doren, quoted by Arna Bontemps in *The Harlem Renaissance Remembered* (New York: Dodd, 1972), p. 14.

[25] Carl Van Vechten, *Nigger Heaven* (New York: Grosset, 1926), p. 281.

[26] Unpubl. letter to Arthur Davison Ficke, November 11, 1929. Beinecke Lib., Yale U.

[27] Louise Bogan, *What the Woman Lived: Selected Letters of Louise Bogan, 1920–1970*, ed. Ruth Limmer (New York: Harcourt, 1973), p. 72.

[28] Nancy Hoyt, *Portrait of an Unknown Lady* (Indianapolis: Bobbs-Merrill, 1935), p. 154.

[29] *Collected Poems of Babette Deutsch* (New York: Doubleday, 1969), p. 131.

[30] Langston Hughes, *The Big Sea* (New York: Hill, 1984), pp. 212, 213.

[31] Vachel Lindsay, *Collected Poems* (New York: Macmillan, 1952), pp. 178ff.

[32] Hughes, *Selected Poems*, p. 7.

[33] "Little Brown Boy," in *The Book of American Negro Poetry*, ed. James Weldon Johnson (New York: Harcourt, 1931), p. 279.

[34] Greene, p. 179.

[35] Unpubl. letter from Georgia Douglas Johnson to Arna Bontemps, July 19, 1941. Harold Jackman Coll., Atlanta U. Lib.

[36] "The Octaroon," *Bronze* (Boston: Brummer, 1922; repr. New York: AMS, 1975), p. 36.

[37] Georgia Douglas Johnson to Arna Bontemps, July 19, 1941.

[38] *Bronze*, p. 22.

[39] List of spiritual maxims sent to William Stanley Braithwaite [n.d.]. Unpubl. ms. Syracuse U. Lib.

[40] Gertrude Stein, *Three Lives* (Norfolk, Conn.: New Directions, n.d.), pp. 85, 86.

[41] *Bronze*, p. 42.

[42] *Bronze*, p. 43.

[43] "To a Dark Girl," *American Negro Poetry*, p. 243.

[44] *American Negro Poetry*, p. 245.

[45] *The Big Sea*, p. 235.

[46] *Opportunity* (August 1926), p. 259.

[47] *Opportunity* (December 1928), p. 361.

[48] Unpubl. ms. Angelina Weld Grimké Papers, Moorland-Spingarn Res. Center, Howard U.

[49] Unpubl. ms. Angelina Weld Grimké Papers, Howard U.

[50] Unpubl. ms. Angelina Weld Grimké Papers, Howard U.

[51] Unpubl. ms. Angelina Weld Grimké Papers, Howard U.

[52] See Gloria T. Hull, Introd., *Give Us Each Day* (New York: Norton, 1984), the diary of Alice Dunbar-Nelson, for a valuable glimpse into Washington, DC life in the 1920s and 1930s.

[53] Greene, p. 191.

[54] Greene, p. 167.

[55] Greene, p. 174.

NINE   THE PASSION OF FRIENDSHIP

[1] Chauncey Spencer, personal interview, October 25, 1984.

[2] Unpubl. letter to Grace Nail Johnson, n.d [c. 1937]. Beinecke Lib., Yale U.

[3] Unpubl. letter to Grace Nail Johnson, February 21, 1967. Beinecke Lib., Yale U.

[4] *May Sarton, A Self-Portrait* (New York: Norton, 1986), p. 42.

[5] *Sonnets to Duse and Other Poems* (Boston: Poet Lore, 1907), p. 25.

[6] Margaret Conklin, personal communication to the author.

[7] Margaret Conklin, "Notes on M. C.'s meeting and Friendship with Sara" (unpubl. ms., written for the author, n.d. [1976]).

[8] "The Self," *New York Times Book Review*, August 26, 1984, p. 3. Repr. by perm. of Wellesley College, trustee of the estate of Sara Teasdale.

[9] "Notes."

[10] "On Devon Cliffs," unpubl. poem in Sara Teasdale's poetry notebooks. Beinecke Lib., Yale U.

[11] "Notes."

[12] Margaret Conklin, personal interview, June 22, 1983.

[13] "Notes."

[14] Unpubl. letter from Jessie B. Rittenhouse to Aline Kilmer, February 6, 1933. Kilmer family papers.

[15] Drake, *Sara Teasdale: Woman and Poet*, p. 291.

[16] "Notes."

[17] "To M.," *Collected Poems of Sara Teasdale*, p. 209.

[18] "Notes."

[19] Unpubl. letter to Conklin, February 25, 1939. Beinecke Lib., Yale U.

[20] Unpubl. letter to Conklin, March 5, 1940. Beinecke Lib., Yale U.

[21] Margaret Conklin, personal interview, June 22, 1983.

[22] I am indebted to Penny Lehman of New York City for this anecdote. Mrs. Lehman was a friend of Margaret Conklin for many years and knew Marianne Moore through her.

[23] Unpubl. letter to Conklin, October 22, 1957. Beinecke Lib., Yale U.

[24] Unpubl. letter to Conklin, May 28, 1958. Beinecke Lib., Yale U.

[25] Unpubl. letter to Moore, December 19, 1947. Rosenbach Museum and Lib., Philadelphia.

[26] Unpubl. letter to Conklin, December 21, 1947. Beinecke Lib., Yale U.

[27] Unpubl. letter to Conklin, January 9, 1949. Beinecke Lib., Yale U.

[28] Unpubl. letter to Conklin, December 17, 1956. Beinecke Lib., Yale U.

[29] Drake, *Teasdale*, p. 71.

[30] "Conflict," *Mirror of the Heart: Selected Poems of Sara Teasdale*, p. 108.

[31] Unpubl. letter from May Sarton to Louise Bogan, February 1, 1947. Amherst College Lib.

[32] Sarton to Bogan, February 1, 1947, Amherst College Lib.

[33] Gloria Bowles, *Louise Bogan's Aesthetic of Limitation* (Bloomington: Indiana U.P., 1987), p. 28.

[34] Unpubl. letter to Bogan, November 4, 1953. Amherst College Lib.

[35] Unpubl. letter to Sarton, January 4, 1954, Berg Coll., N.Y. Pub. Lib.

[36] Unpubl. letter to Bogan, January 26, 1954. Amherst College Lib.

[37] May Sarton, *Selected Poems* (New York: Norton, 1978), p. 191.

[38] Unpubl. letter to Bogan, January 26, 1954. Amherst College Lib.

[39] Unpubl. letter to Bogan, January 24, 1954. Amherst College Lib.

[40] Unpubl. letter to Bogan, January 26, 1954. Amherst College Lib.

[41] Unpubl. letter to Sarton, January 26, 1954. Berg Coll., N.Y. Publ. Lib.

[42] From a letter to Sarton, January 28, 1954, in the Berg Coll., N.Y. Publ. Lib., a portion of which has been published in *What the Woman Lived,* p. 285.

[43] From a letter to Sarton, February 16, 1954, in the Berg Coll., N.Y. Publ. Lib., a portion of which has been published in Limmer.

[44] Unpubl. letter to Bogan, March 8, 1954. Amherst College Lib.

[45] Unpubl. letter to Sarton, March 29, 1954. Berg Coll., N.Y. Publ. Lib.

[46] Unpubl. letter to Sarton, April 16, 1954. Berg Coll., N.Y. Publ. Lib.

[47] Bogan from a letter to Sarton, August 14, 1954, in the Berg Coll., N.Y. Publ. Lib., a portion of which has been published in Limmer, p. 286.

[48] Unpubl. letter to Sarton, August 14, 1954. Berg Coll., N.Y. Publ. Lib.

*

TIME LINE

*

1906   Emma Goldman begins publication of the magazine *Mother Earth* (1906–1917).

1909   Freud visits the United States to attend conference on psychiatry at Clark College, Massachusetts.

1910   Founding of the National Association for the Advancement of Colored People and the National Urban League. NAACP begins publishing the *Crisis,* edited by W. E. B. DuBois. Formation of the Poetry Society of America.

1911–   Historic shift from reticence to frankness in sexual matters
1917   takes place. Women born near 1900, interviewed by Kinsey in the 1940s, gave 1916 as the approximate date of their initiation into liberated sexual attitudes.

1912   Founding of *Poetry* magazine in Chicago by Harriet Monroe.

1913 Ezra Pound publishes *Des Imagistes,* launching a movement that will strongly influence the work of women poets.
Population of blacks in Harlem reaches 35,000. Over a fourth of all American blacks have migrated to urban centers.

1914 The *Egoist* (1914–1919) founded in London, with H.D. an assistant editor. The *Little Review* (1914–1929) founded in Chicago by Margaret Anderson.
The Great War begins in Europe.

1915 *Others* (1915–1919) founded in New York, center of a group of poets including William Carlos Williams and Lola Ridge.

1916 Founding of the *Seven Arts* (1916–1917).
United States enters the Great War.

1917 The Russian Revolution.
Suppression of the *Masses* (1904–1917) by the U.S. government for opposing the war effort. It reappears immediately as the *Liberator* (1917–1924), then *New Masses* after 1924.
Pulitzer prizes established, awarded through Columbia University, with no provision for poetry. The Poetry Society of America raises funds privately for a "Columbia Prize" in poetry. The first award is given to Sara Teasdale in 1918.

1918 Great War ends.

1919 Raids by Attorney General Palmer on aliens to suppress radical dissent. Emma Goldman deported to Russia. Treaty of Versailles sets the stage for German military resurgence in the 1930s.
Second Columbia Poetry Prize is split between Margaret Widdemer and Carl Sandburg.

1920 Nineteenth Amendment to the U.S. Constitution extends suffrage to women. Certain long-term trends accelerate in the 1920s: Divorce rate, tripling since 1900, increases still more rapidly, while fertility rate undergoes a sharp decline. Approval of extramarital sex (among intellectuals, as reflected in magazines) reaches peak between 1925 and 1929.
Nineteen pieces of major legislation expanding women's

rights and benefits are passed by Congress between 1917 and 1925, pressured by the women's suffrage movement. When women do not emerge as a political force after 1920, pro-women's legislation and political activism decline steadily until the 1950s.

The *Dial* (1920–1929) founded in New York.

1921   The Sacco-Vanzetti trial.

The *Measure* (1921–1926) cofounded by Genevieve Taggard; Louise Bogan serves on editorial board.

Broom (1921–1923) founded; Lola Ridge as American editor.

1922   *The Waste Land* is published in the first number of *Criterion*, which Eliot edits until 1939.

Joyce's *Ulysses* published.

The *Fugitive* (1922–1925) marks rise of the Southern group.

Pulitzer Prize in poetry established; first award goes to E. A. Robinson.

1923   Edna St. Vincent Millay receives the Pulitzer Prize for *The Harp-Weaver*. *Palms* founded, publishing with interruptions until 1940. *Opportunity*, journal of the National Urban League, founded in part to give "Negro authors, creative writers and artists an opportunity to display their works." It becomes the major outlet for black women poets of the 1920s.

1924   *Crisis* and *Opportunity* begin annual literary competitions for black writers. *Opportunity* receives 732 manuscripts for its first contest.

1925   The John Simon Guggenheim Memorial Foundation established for awards to writers, scholars, and artists.

Marianne Moore edits the *Dial*, 1925–1929.

Death of Amy Lowell.

1926   *Fire*, avant-garde magazine founded by Langston Hughes, Gwendolyn Bennett, Zora Neale Hurston, and others, publishes its only issue in November. The Harlem Renaissance at its crest. Amy Lowell receives a Pulitzer Prize posthumously.

1927 The executions of Sacco and Vanzetti.
T. S. Eliot becomes a British citizen.
Leonora Speyer receives the Pulitzer Prize for poetry.

1928 Death of Elinor Wylie.
Léonie Adams receives a Guggenheim Fellowship.

1929 Stock market crash begins the Great Depression.

1930 Number of books of poetry by women declines through the 1930s. Eleven poets still living in 1940, who had collectively published forty-five volumes in the 1920s, publish only sixteen in the 1930s. Although five women received Pulitzer (and Columbia) prizes for poetry before 1930, only one does so during the 1930s (Audrey Wurdemann, 1935, for *Bright Ambush*). Most of the little magazines publishing the new poets in the 1920s, with many women in editorial positions, are defunct by 1930.

1933 Hitler becomes chancellor of Germany.
Louise Bogan receives a Guggenheim Fellowship.
Death of Sara Teasdale.

1935 Lola Ridge receives a Guggenheim Fellowship.

1936 Germany remilitarizes the Rhineland, violating the terms of the Versailles treaty. Spanish civil war begins.
Death of Harriet Monroe.

1938 Germany annexes Austria. Munich "appeasement" pact. The

1939 World War II begins.

1941 Hitler invades Russia. The United States enters the war.
Death of Lola Ridge.
Ezra Pound broadcasts in Italy for the Axis powers, 1941–1943.

1942 Margaret Walker is the first black poet to be awarded the Pulitzer Prize.

1945 End of World War II.

1946 Pound incarcerated in St. Elizabeth's Hospital, Washington, DC.

1948 Death of Genevieve Taggard.
T. S. Eliot awarded the Nobel Prize in literature.

1949 Pound receives the Bollingen Prize.

1950 Gwendolyn Brooks is awarded the Pulitzer Prize, second black woman in a decade so honored.

*

THE POETS AND
THEIR WORKS

*

GWENDOLYN BENNETT (1902–   )

Bennett's work has never been collected, although it has appeared in nearly a dozen anthologies of Afro-American literature from the 1920s to the present day, including *The Book of American Negro Poetry*, ed. James Weldon Johnson (New York: Harcourt, 1922); *The New Negro*, ed. Alain Locke (New York: Boni, 1925): *Caroling Dusk: An Anthology of Verse by Negro Poets*, ed. Countee Cullen (New York: Harper, 1927); *American Negro Poetry*, ed. Arna Bontemps (New York: Hill, 1963); and *Black Sister: Poetry by Black American Women, 1746–1980*, ed. Erlene Stetson (Bloomington: Indiana U.P. 1981). Bennett's poems, considered by critics to be among the most skilled and varied of the black women poets' of the 1920s, appeared almost entirely in *Opportunity* in the late 1920s, where she was on the editorial staff. Bennett ceased publishing after 1934. Brief biographical notices appear in the anthologies above.

LOUISE BOGAN (1897–1970)

Most of Bogan's poetry was written between 1920 and 1940 and is included in *Body of This Death* (New York: McBride, 1923), *Dark Summer* (New York: Scribner's, 1929), *The Sleeping Fury* (New York: Scribner's, 1937), and *Poems and New Poems* (New York: Scribner's, 1941). Her *Collected Poems, 1923–1953* appeared in 1954 (New York: Noonday). Bogan, intensely self-critical, pared her acceptable work down to only 105 poems which she published in *The Blue Estuaries: Poems 1923–1968* (New York: Farrar, 1968). Two volumes of criticism, culled in part from her work as poetry critic for the *New Yorker*, are *Achievement in American Poetry, 1900–1950* (Chicago: Regnery, 1951) and *Selected Criticism: Poetry and Prose* (New York: Noonday, 1955). *A Poet's Alphabet: Reflections on the Literary Art and Vocation*, ed. Robert Phelps and Ruth Limmer (New York: McGraw, 1970) appeared posthumously. Ruth Limmer, Bogan's literary trustee, also compiled a volume of autobiographical writings from both published and unpublished sources, *Journey around My Room: The Autobiography of Louise Bogan, A Mosaic*, ed. Ruth Limmer (New York: Viking, 1980). A selection of Bogan's letters appear in *What the Woman Lived: Selected Letters of Louise Bogan, 1920–1970*, ed. Ruth Limmer (New York: Harcourt, 1973). *Louise Bogan: A Portrait* by Elizabeth Frank (New York: Knopf, 1985) is a definitive biography. *Louise Bogan's Aesthetic of Limitation* by Gloria Bowles (Bloomington: Indiana U. Press, 1987) relates her work to biography and to male modernist poetry. Bogan's personal papers are at the Amherst College Library. Important collections of her correspondence are at Princeton University and the University of Chicago. Her letters to May Sarton are in the Berg Collection of the New York Public Library.

KAY BOYLE (1903–   )

Although her major output has been in fiction and other prose, Boyle began her writing career as a poet, and her poetry remains an important aspect of her art and thought. *A Glad Day* (Norfolk, Conn.: New Directions, 1938) was her first volume of poetry, followed by *American Citizen Naturalized in Leadville, Colorado* (New York: Simon and Schuster, 1944). Most of that work was included later, along with new poems, in *Collected Poems* (New York: Knopf, 1962). *Testament for My Students and Other Poems* (Garden City: Doubleday, 1970) reflects her political activism at San Francisco State University in the 1960s. *This Is Not a Letter and Other Poems* was published by the Sun & Moon Press, Los Angeles, in 1985. Autobiographical writings are found in *Being Geniuses Together, 1920–1930* by Robert McAlmon, revised with supplementary chapters and an afterword by Kay Boyle (San Francisco: North Point, 1984) and in *Words That Must Somehow Be Said,* ed. Elizabeth S. Bell (San Francisco: North Point, 1985). A recent biographical/critical study is *Kay Boyle: Artist and Activist* by Sandra Whipple Spanier (Carbondale: Southern Illinois U.P., 1986). A major collection of Boyle's papers is at the Morris Library, Southern Illinois University, Carbondale.

GRACE HAZARD CONKLING (1878–1958)

Conkling found her direction under the influence of Amy Lowell, and her work evinces the imagist, impressionist, free-verse tendencies of the time, which many women found liberating. Her five volumes of poetry, all published before 1930, reflect her extensive traveling, especially in Latin America: *Afternoons of April* (Boston: Houghton, 1915); *Wilderness Songs* (New York: Holt, 1920); *Ship's Log and Other Poems* (New York: Knopf, 1924); *Flying Fish* (New York: Knopf, 1926); and *Witch and Other Poems* (New York: Knopf, 1929). Conkling translated the poems and Alice P. Hubbard the prose for *Prometheus: The Fall of the House of Limón* by Ramón Perez de Ayala (New York: Dutton, 1920). Conkling's pamphlet, "Imagination and Children's Reading," was published by the Hampshire Bookshop, Northampton, Mass. (1921), and "Steps toward the Control of the Munitions Industry" by the Women's Press (New York, 1935). Her correspondence with Amy Lowell is in the Houghton Library, Harvard University, and with Harriet Monroe, in the University of Chicago Library.

HILDA CONKLING (1910–1986)

Hilda Conkling's two volumes of childhood poetry, published at the ages of ten and twelve, are *Poems by a Little Girl* (New York: Stokes, 1920) and *Shoes of the Wind* (New York: Stokes, 1922). A selection of poems from the two volumes was published in an illustrated edition, *Silverhorn, the Hilda Conkling Book for Other Children* (New York: Stokes, 1924). Hilda Conkling is treated in depth, with original material from interviews, by Myra Cohn Livingston, *The Child as Poet: Myth or Reality?* (Boston: Horn, 1984).

ADELAIDE CRAPSEY (1878–1914)

All of Crapsey's work appeared posthumously: *Verse* (Rochester, N.Y.: Manas, 1915) and *A Study in English Metrics* (New York: Knopf, 1918). Knopf reissued *Verse* in 1922. All of her poetry, published and unpublished, has been gathered by Susan Smith in *The Complete Poems and Selected Letters of Adelaide Crapsey* (Albany: S.U.N.Y. P., 1977), with a critical and biographical introduction. An earlier biography, with material from original sources, is Mary Elizabeth Osborn's *Adelaide Crapsey* (Boston: Humphries, 1933). Crapsey's papers are at the University of Rochester, Rochester, New York.

GLADYS CROMWELL (1885–1919)

Cromwell published *The Gates of Utterance* (Boston: Sherman) in 1915. *Poems* (New York: Macmillan, 1919), with an introduction by Padraic Colum and a biographical note by Anne Dunn, appeared posthumously and included material from the earlier volume. The Cromwell sisters are known to have kept a war diary of considerable psychological interest during their Red Cross service in France, but its whereabouts, as well as that of other papers, is presently unknown.

BABETTE DEUTSCH (1895–1982)

Deutsch achieved a reputation as a prolific professional woman of letters, as a poet, novelist, critic, translator, and teacher, deeply concerned with the major themes of war, political morality, and spiritual crisis. Her first volume of poetry, *Banners* (New York: Doran, 1919), reflects her youthful radicalism and excitement generated by the Russian Revolution. Later volumes trace her concern to relate individual experience to history and philosophical questions: *Honey out of the Rock* (New York: Appleton, 1925), *Fire for the Night* (New York: Cape, 1930), *Epistle to Prometheus* (New York: Cape, 1931), and *One Part Love* (New York: Oxford U.P., 1939). Two volumes of poetry reflect on World War II: *Take Them, Stranger* (New York: Holt, 1944) and *Animal, Vegetable, Mineral* (New York: Dutton, 1954). With *Coming of Age: New and Selected Poems* (Bloomington: Indiana U.P., 1959) Deutsch began selecting and rearranging her poems, continuing with *Collected Poems 1919–1962* (Bloomington: Indiana U.P., 1963) and *The Collected Poems of Babette Deutsch* (Garden City: Doubleday, 1969). Duetsch's four novels are: *A Brittle Heaven* (New York: Greenberg, 1926); *In Such a*

Night (New York: Day, 1927); *Mask of Silenus: A Novel about Socrates* (New York: Simon, 1933); and *Rogue's Legacy: A Novel about François Villon* (New York: Coward, 1942). Her major critical work is *Poetry in Our Time* (New York: Holt, 1952), revised and enlarged in 1963 (Garden City: Doubleday). Deutsch's concern for craft and technique resulted in *Poetry Handbook: A Dictionary of Terms* (New York: Funk, 1957) with revisions in 1962, 1969, and 1974. Deutsch also wrote a number of books for children, including the prize-winning *Walt Whitman: Builder for America* (New York: Messner, 1941), and collaborated with her husband, Avrahm Yarmolinsky, on a dozen well-regarded translations of Russian writers.

H.D. [HILDA DOOLITTLE] (1886–1961)

Named "H.D.," labeled "Imagiste," and launched on a career by Ezra Pound, Hilda Doolittle was only slowly recognized as a strongly individual voice rather than the exponent of a movement. Her first volume of poetry, *Sea Garden*, was published in 1916 (London: Constable; Boston: Houghton). Then followed *Hymen* (London: Egoist; New York: Holt, 1921), *Heliodora and Other Poems* (London: Cape; Boston: Houghton, 1924) and *Collected Poems of H.D.* (New York: Boni, 1925). Two later collections have been published: *Selected Poems of H.D.* (New York: Grove, 1957) and *Collected Poems 1912–1944*, ed. Louis L. Martz (New York: New Directions, 1983). Other major works of poetry include three poems of epic scope rising from H.D.'s response to World War II, *The Walls Do Not Fall* (London: Oxford U.P., 1944), *Tribute to the Angels* (London: Oxford U.P., 1945) and *The Flowering of the Rod* (London: Oxford U.P., 1946), reprinted as *Trilogy* (New York: New Directions, 1973). Of especial interest today is H.D.'s mythologizing of female experience to create a woman-centered epic, of which the chief example is *Helen in Egypt* (New York: Grove, 1961). *Hermetic Definition* (New York: New Directions, 1972) gathers three long poems based on personal experience, including her early relationship with Pound. H.D. also wrote a series of autobiographical novels: *Bid Me to Live*, begun in 1918 as "Madrigal" but not published until 1960 (New York: Grove); *HERmione*, written in 1922 but not published until 1981 (New York: New Directions); *Kora and Ka* (Dijon: Darantière, 1934); *The Usual Star* (Dijon: Darantière, 1934); and *Nights*, written under the pseudonym "John Helforth" (Dijon: Darantière, 1935). H.D. produced two works of historical fiction with ancient Greek settings, *Palimpsest* (Boston: Houghton, 1926) and *Hedylus* (Boston: Houghton, 1928). *The Gift* (New York: New Directions, 1982) is a memoir centering on the mysticism of her Moravian religious background. *Tribute to Freud* (Boston: Godine, 1974) and *End to Torment; A Memoir of Ezra Pound,* ed. Norman Holmes Pearson and Michael King (New York: New Directions, 1979) are reflections on her relationships with Freud and Pound. Recent biographies of H.D. are Janice S. Robinson, *H.D.: The Life and Work of an American Poet* (Boston: Houghton, 1982) and Barbara Guest, *Herself Defined: H.D. and Her World* (Garden City: Doubleday, 1984). The major collection of H.D.'s papers is at the Beinecke Library, Yale University.

ANGELINA WELD GRIMKÉ (1880–1958)

Though she showed early promise, with juvenile poems appearing in the Boston *Globe* in the 1890s, Grimké never published a volume of poetry. Her work appeared chiefly in *Opportunity* and *Crisis* in the 1920s and can be found in the anthologies of Afro-American poetry (see Bennett, above). Grimké's play *Rachel* was first published in the *Birth Control Review* (September 1919). It was reprinted in 1921 (Boston: Cornhill) and in 1969 (Washington, DC: McGrath). *Rachel* is presently available in *Black Theater, U.S.A.: Forty-Five Plays by Black Americans,* ed. James V. Hatch (New York: Free, 1974), pp. 137–172. Grimké also published a few prose articles and reviews. Gloria T. Hull's essay "Under the Days: The Buried Life and Poetry of Angelina Weld Grimké" in *Home Girls: A Black Feminist Anthology,* ed. Barbara Smith (New York: Kitchen Table, 1983), pp. 73–82, finds Grimké a tragic, defeated artist. Grimké's papers are in the Moorland-Spingarn Research Center of Howard University and include much unpublished poetry, fictional sketches, family letters, and miscellaneous material.

GEORGIA DOUGLAS JOHNSON (1886–1966)

Johnson published four volumes of poetry: *The Heart of a Woman,* introduced by William Stanley Braithwaite (1918), reprinted (Freeport, N.Y.: Books for Libraries, 1971); *Bronze,* introduced by W. E. B. Du Bois (1922), reprinted (New York: AMS, 1975); *An Autumn Love Cycle* (1928), reprinted (Freeport, N.Y.: Books for Libraries, 1971); and *Share My World* (Washington, DC: privately printed, 1962). Her poems appeared frequently in *Crisis* and *Opportunity* in the 1920s. Letters and other papers of Georgia Douglas Johnson are at Atlanta University, Syracuse University, and the Beinecke Library of Yale University, though most are still privately held.

HELENE JOHNSON (1907–   )

Helene Johnson's poems appeared chiefly in *Crisis* and *Opportunity* in the 1920s and have been reprinted with brief biographical notices in anthologies of Afro-American poetry (see Bennett, above). Johnson never published a volume of her work.

AMY LOWELL (1874–1925)

Lowell was slow to mature, but once she had found her voice—her first volume of poetry was published in 1912, when she was thirty-eight—there followed an explosion of productivity lasting until her death. Lowell published eight volumes of poetry during her lifetime: *A Dome of Many-Colored Glass* (Boston: Houghton, 1912); *Sword Blades and Poppy Seed* (Boston: Houghton, 1914); *Men, Women, and Ghosts* (New York: Macmillan, 1916); *Can Grande's Castle* (New York: Macmillan, 1918); *Pictures of the Floating World* (New York: Macmillan, 1919); *Legends* (Boston: Houghton, 1921); *A Critical Fable,* anonymously (Boston: Houghton, 1922); and *What's O'Clock* (Boston: Houghton, 1925). Two additional volumes, *East Wind* (Boston: Houghton, 1926) and *Ballads for Sale* (Boston: Houghton, 1927), appeared posthumously. Amy Lowell's *Complete Poetical Works* (Boston: Houghton) was published in 1955. Lowell's major project in the last years of her life was the two-volume biography *John Keats* (Boston: Houghton, 1925). Lowell also published two volumes of critical essays: *Six French Poets* (New York: Macmillan, 1915) and *Tendencies in Modern Poetry* (Boston: Houghton, 1917). A further collection of essays was published posthumously: *Poetry and Poets* (Boston: Houghton, 1930). An important biographical source is S. Foster Damon, *Amy Lowell: A Chronicle* (Boston: Houghton, 1935). Lowell's papers are in the Houghton Library of Harvard University.

EDNA ST. VINCENT MILLAY (1892–1950)

Fame came to Millay at the age of nineteen with the publication of her poem "Renascence." Millay published poetry professionally while a student at Vassar, and by the time her first volume appeared, *Renascence and Other Poems* (New York: Kennerley, 1917), her reputation was already established. Millay's chief subsequent volumes of poetry are: *A Few Figs from Thistles* (New York: Shay, 1920); *Second April* (New York: Kennerley, 1921); *The*

Harp-Weaver and Other Poems (New York: Harper, 1923); *The Buck in the Snow and Other Poems* (New York: Harper, 1928); *Fatal Interview* (New York: Harper, 1931); *Wine from These Grapes* (New York: Harper, 1934); *Conversation at Midnight* (New York: Harper, 1937); *Huntsman, What Quarry?* (New York: Harper, 1939); *Collected Sonnets* (New York: Harper, 1941); *Collected Lyrics* (New York: Harper, 1943); *Mine the Harvest,* published posthumously, ed. Norma Millay (New York: Harper, 1954); and *Collected Poems,* ed. Norma Millay (New York: Harper, 1956). Millay also wrote four verse plays: *Aria da Capo* (New York: Kennerley, 1921), *The Lamp and the Bell* (New York: Shay, 1921), and *Two Slatterns and a King* (Cincinnati: Kidd, 1921), reprinted as *Three Plays* (New York: Harper, 1926). *The Princess Marries the Page* is a one-act play written while Millay was a student at Vassar (New York: Harper, 1932). Millay collaborated with Deems Taylor to provide the libretto for his opera *The King's Henchman,* published as a three-act play (New York: Harper, 1927). Millay's passionate protest against the Sacco-Vanzetti executions in 1927—she and Lola Ridge were arrested in Boston during a demonstration—foreshadowed her political poetry during World War II: *Make Bright the Arrows: 1940 Notebook* (New York: Harper, 1940) and *The Murder of Lidice* (New York: Harper, 1942). *The Selected Letters of Edna St. Vincent Millay,* ed. Allan Ross McDougall (New York: Harper) was published in 1952. Millay supported herself in the early 1920s by writing light sophisticated prose sketches for *Ainslee's* magazine under the pseudonym "Nancy Boyd." A collection of these articles, *Distressing Dialogues,* was published under her pseudonym in 1924 (New York: Harper). Major collections of Millay's papers are in the Berg Collection of the New York Public Library, the Beinecke Library of Yale University, and the Library of Congress.

KATHLEEN MILLAY (1896–1943)

Kathleen Millay's brief writing career saw the publication of three volumes of poetry and two novels between 1926 and 1931. Her poems are collected in *The Evergreen Tree* (New York: Boni, 1927); *The Hermit Thrush* (New York: Liveright, 1929); and *The Beggar at the Gate* (New York: Liveright, 1931). Kathleen Millay's novels are *Wayfarer* (New York: Morrow, 1926) and *Against the Wall* (New York: Macauley, 1929). Her papers are in the Berg Collection of the New York Public Library.

HARRIET MONROE (1860–1936)

Although Monroe is remembered chiefly as the founder/editor of *Poetry* and promoter of modern poetry beginning in 1912 when she was over fifty, she was a poet in her own right and continued to think of herself as "one of them," publishing her own poems occasionally in *Poetry* and in the anthology she edited. Her autobiography is significantly titled *A Poet's Life* (New York: Macmillan, 1938). Monroe privately printed her first volume, *Valeria and Other Poems,* in Chicago in 1891; it was reissued in 1892 (Chicago: McClurg). Her *Columbian Ode* (Chicago: Way, 1893), written for the Columbian Exposition in 1892, was widely praised. *The Passing Show: Five Modern Plays in Verse* (Boston: Houghton) appeared in 1903. Monroe followed with *You and I* (New York: Macmillan, 1914) and *The Difference and Other Poems* (Chicago: Civici, 1924). Monroe and her assistant editor at *Poetry,* Alice Corbin Henderson, compiled an anthology, *The New Poetry* (New York: Macmillan, 1917). Some of Monroe's critical articles from *Poetry* were collected in *Poets and Their Art* (New York: Macmillan, 1926). Monroe's papers are at the University of Chicago Library.

MARIANNE MOORE (1887–1972)

Marianne Moore's first work appeared in the avant-garde magazines *Egoist* and *Others,* and her first volume of poems was published by the Egoist Press in London, *Poems* (1921), linking her reputation from the outset with modernist experimentation. Her chief books in the following years are: *Observations* (New York: Dial, 1924; rev. 1925); *Selected Poems* (New York: Macmillan, 1935); *The Pangolin and Other Verse* (London: Brendin, 1936); *Nevertheless* (New York: Macmillan, 1944); *Collected Poems* (New York: Macmillan, 1951); *Like a Bulwark* (New York: Viking, 1956); *O To Be a Dragon* (New York: Viking, 1959); *Tell Me, Tell Me: Granite, Steel, and Other Topics* (New York: Viking, 1966); *The Complete Poems of Marianne Moore* (New York: Macmillan, 1967); and *The Complete Poems of Marianne Moore,* ed. Clive E. Driver (New York: Macmillan-Viking, 1981). *Predilections* (New York: Viking, 1955) is a collection of critical essays by Moore. Selected poetry and prose, along with an interview by Donald Hall, are gathered in *A Marianne Moore Reader* (New York: Viking, 1961). Moore also translated *The Fables of La Fontaine* (New York: Viking, 1954). *The Complete Prose of Marianne Moore,* ed. Patricia C. Willis, was published by Viking (1986). Moore was a prolific letter writer, and collections of her letters can be found in research libraries throughout the United States. The repository of her personal papers is the Rosenbach Museum and Library, Philadelphia.

LOLA RIDGE (1873–1941)

Although Ridge aimed at becoming a poet in girlhood, her first volume of poetry was not published until she was forty-five: *The Ghetto and Other Poems* (New York: Huebsch, 1918). *Sun-Up and Other Poems* (New York: Huebsch, 1920) contains autobiographical material. *Red Flag* (New York: Viking, 1927) and *Firehead* (New York: Payson, 1929) rise out of her politics of compassion, the latter her response to the Sacco-Vanzetti executions. Her last book, *Dance of Fire* (New York: Smith, 1935), evinces her deepening mysticism. Ridge's feminist thought can be found in "Woman and the Creative Will," ed. Elaine Sproat, *Michigan Occasional Paper* No. 18 (Spring 1981), in *Michigan Occasional Papers in Women's Studies,* Ann Arbor. A definitive biography by Elaine Sproat, Ridge's literary trustee, is forthcoming. The major collection of Ridge's papers, including her unpublished diary, letters to her husband, and miscellaneous manuscripts, is in the Sophia Smith Collection, Smith College.

MAY SARTON (1912–   )

May Sarton's work falls largely outside the scope of this book, in a more recent period. However, her career was well established with four volumes of poetry when she met Louise Bogan in 1953: *Encounter in April* (Boston: Houghton, 1937); *Inner Landscape* (Boston: Houghton, 1939); *The Lion and the Rose* (New York: Rinehart, 1948); and *The Land of Silence* (New York: Rinehart, 1953). Sarton had also begun her dual career as a novelist with *The Single Hound* (Boston: Houghton, 1938); *The Bridge of Years* (New York: Doubleday, 1946); and *Shadow of a Man* (New York: Rinehart, 1950). Sarton was working on the roman à clef, *Faithful Are the Wounds* (New York: Rinehart, 1955), during the first year of her friendship with Bogan described in this book. Sarton's memoir of Louise Bogan appears in *A World of Light: Portraits and Celebrations* (New York: Norton, 1976).

Of interest also is *I Knew a Phoenix: Sketches for an Autobiography* (Norton, 1959). May Sarton's letters to Bogan are in the Amherst College Library.

CLARISSA SCOTT-DELANEY (1901–1927)

Scott-Delaney's poems began to appear in *Opportunity* shortly before her death. "Solace" has been anthologized most often. (See entries under Bennett, above.)

MARJORIE SEIFFERT (1884–1970)

Seiffert's first volume was *A Woman of Thirty* (New York: Knopf, 1919). Her second was *Ballads of the Singing Bowl* (New York: Scribner's, 1927) followed by *The King with Three Faces* (New York: Scribner's, 1929) and *The Name of Life* (New York: Scribner's, 1938). Seiffert's contributions to the Spectra hoax, under the name of Elijah Hay, can be found in William Jay Smith, *The Spectra Hoax* (Middletown, Conn.: Wesleyan U.P., 1961). Seiffert also contributed satirical light verse to the *New Yorker* in the late 1920s and early 1930s under the pseudonym "Angela Cypher." The major collection of Seiffert's papers is at the University of Colorado Library, Boulder. Other important collections are at the Princeton University Library, the University of Chicago Library, and the Beinecke Library of Yale University.

ANNE SPENCER (1882–1975)

Spencer's biographer J. Lee Greene writes, "Although Anne Spencer referred to having written over a thousand poems, only about fifty items are now available as complete poems and significant fragments." Greene includes forty-two of these (about half of them previously unpublished) in *Time's Unfading Garden: Anne Spencer's Life and Poetry* (Baton Rouge: Louisiana State U.P., 1977). Some of Spencer's letters are in the James Weldon Johnson Collection at the Beinecke Library, Yale University, though she selected and edited them before allowing them to be preserved. Her diaries, poetic fragments, and other papers and memorabilia are at the Anne Spencer home in Lynchburg, Virginia, now a state historical landmark maintained by the Anne Spencer Memorial Foundation for study and research.

GENEVIEVE TAGGARD (1894–1948)

Taggard's first volume was *For Eager Lovers* (New York: Seltzer, 1922) followed by *Hawaiian Hilltop* (San Francisco: Wyckoff, 1923); *Travelling Standing Still* (New York: Knopf, 1928); *Not Mine to Finish, Poems 1928–1934* (New York: Harper, 1934); *Calling Western Union* (New York: Harper, 1936); *Collected Poems, 1918–1938* (New York: Harper, 1938); *Long View* (New York: Harper, 1942); and *Slow Music* (New York: Harper, 1946). *To the Natural World*, a selection from Taggard's work, edited by her daughter Marcia D. Liles, was published in 1980 with a valuable introduction by Liles, a note by Josephine Miles, and bibliographical notes (Boise, Idaho: Ahsahta Press, Boise State U.).

Taggard's major prose work is *The Life and Mind of Emily Dickinson* (New York: Knopf, 1930). She also edited two anthologies: *May Days: An Anthology of Verse from Masses-Liberator* (New York: Boni, 1925) and *Circumference, Varieties of Metaphysical Verse, 1456–1928* (New York: Covici, 1929). Autobiographical writings can be found in her preface to *Calling Western Union* (see above) and in *These Modern Women*, ed. Elaine Showalter (Old Westbury, N.Y.: Feminist, 1983). Taggard's personal papers are in the Taggard Collection, New York Public Library. An extensive collection of her published work is at the Dartmouth College Library. University Microfilms has published on film *The Complete Works of Genevieve Taggard*, including all uncollected articles, reviews, and poems in their chronological sequence.

SARA TEASDALE (1884–1933)

Teasdale's first volume of poetry was privately published: *Sonnets to Duse and Other Poems* (Boston: Poet Lore, 1907). This was followed by *Helen of Troy and Other Poems* (New York: Putnam, 1911); *Rivers to the Sea* (New York: Macmillan, 1915); *Love Songs,* including both reprinted and new work (New York: Macmillan, 1917); *Flame and Shadow* (New York: Macmillan, 1920); *Dark of the Moon* (New York: Macmillan, 1926); and *Stars To-Night, Verses Old and New for Boys and Girls* (New York: Macmillan, 1930). *Strange Victory* appeared posthumously, edited by Margaret Conklin (New York: Macmillan, 1933). *The Collected Poems of Sara Teasdale* (New York: Macmillan, 1938) was compiled by Margaret Conklin and John Hall Wheelock. A selection of Teasdale's poetry together with fifty-one previously unpublished poems from manuscripts in the Beinecke Library at Yale University can be found in *Mirror of the Heart: Selected Poems of Sara Teasdale*, ed. William Drake (New York: Macmillan, 1984). Teasdale edited *The Answering Voice: One Hundred Love Lyrics by Women* (Boston: Houghton, 1917; enl. ed., Macmillan: New York, 1928) and *Rainbow Gold: Poems Old and New Selected for Girls and Boys by Sara Teasdale* (New York: Macmillan, 1922). A recent biography is William Drake, *Sara Teasdale: Woman and Poet* (San Francisco: Harper, 1979). The first book-length study of Teasdale's poetry is Carol Schoen's *Sara Teasdale* in the Twayne series, 1986. Teasdale's poetry notebooks are at the Beinecke Library, Yale University. The manuscript of her unfinished study of Christina Rossetti is in the Wellesley College Library. Important collections of letters and other papers are at the Missouri Historical Society, St. Louis; the Newberry Library, Chicago; Lockwood Memorial Library, State University of New York at Buffalo; Rollins College Library, Winter Park, Florida; the University of Chicago Library; and the Alderman Library, University of Virginia.

EUNICE TIETJENS (1884–1944)

Tietjens' extensive traveling and periods of residence in the orient dominate much of her published work. Her first volume was *Profiles of China: Sketches in Free Verse of People and Things Seen in the Interior* (Chicago: Seymour, 1917), followed by *Profiles from Home: Sketches of People and Things Seen in the U.S.* (New York: Knopf, 1925). Her prose works on Asia include *Japan, Korea, and Formosa* (Chicago: Wheeler, 1924) and *China* (Chicago: Wheeler, 1930). Tietjens edited *Poetry of the Orient,* an anthology (New York: Knopf, 1928). Her two books of poetry on personal themes are *Body and Raiment* (New York: Knopf, 1919) and *Leaves in Windy Weather* (New York: Knopf, 1929). Tietjens also wrote five books for children and an autobiography, *World at My Shoulder* (New York: Macmillan, 1938). The repository of her papers is the Newberry Library, Chicago.

ELINOR WYLIE (1885–1928)

Wylie's first volume was privately printed: *Incidental Numbers* (London: Clowes, 1912). None of these poems was included in later volumes. Her next book of poetry was *Nets to Catch the Wind* (New York: Harcourt, 1921), followed by *Black Armour* (New York: Doran, 1923) and *Angels and Earthly Creatures* (New York: Knopf, 1929). *Collected Poems,* ed. William

Rose Benet (New York: Knopf, 1932) is still the standard collection of her poetry, supplemented by *Last Poems of Elinor Wylie* ed. William Rose Benet (New York: Knopf, 1942) from material left in manuscript at her death. Miscellaneous essays are found in *Collected Prose* (New York: Knopf, 1933). Wylie's four novels are *Jennifer Lorn: A Sedate Extravaganza* (New York: Doran, 1923); *The Venetian Glass Nephew* (New York: Doran, 1925); *The Orphan Angel* (New York: Knopf, 1926); and *Mr. Hodge and Mr. Hazard* (New York: Knopf, 1928). Recent biographies of Wylie are Stanley Olson, *Elinor Wylie: A Life Apart* (New York: Dial, 1979) and Judith Farr, *The Life and Art of Elinor Wylie* (Baton Rouge: State U. of Louisiana P., 1983). Wylie's letters to her mother and other family papers are in the Berg Collection of the New York Public Library. Her letters to William Rose Benet are in the Alderman Library, University of Virginia.

*

PERMISSIONS AND ACKNOWLEDGMENTS

*

Permission to use the following material is gratefully acknowledged: Letters of Louise Bogan to May Sarton from the Henry W. and Albert A. Berg Collection, quoted by permission of the New York Public Library, Astor, Lenox and Tilden Foundations, and Ruth Limmer for the Estate of Louise Bogan. A letter of Kay Boyle to Babette Deutsch from the Babette Deutsch Papers, quoted by permission of the New York Public Library, Astor, Lenox and Tilden Foundations and Kay Boyle. Personal interview with the author (June 22, 1983); "Notes on M.C.'s Meeting and Friendship with Sara" (unpublished manuscript, n.d. [1976]), and a letter of Margaret Conklin to Marianne Moore, are quoted by permission of Ruth Conklin, executor for Margaret Conklin. A letter of Margaret Conklin to Marianne Moore, quoted by permission of the Rosenbach Library and Museum, Philadelphia, Pennsylvania. A letter of Grace Hazard Conkling to Louis Untermeyer, quoted by permission of the Lilly Library, Indiana University. Letters of Grace Hazard Conkling to Harriet Monroe, quoted by permission of the University of Chicago Library. Letters of Grace Hazard Conkling to Amy Lowell, quoted by permission of the Houghton Library, Harvard University. A letter of Grace Hazard Conkling to Abbie Farwell Brown from the Grace Hazard Conkling Collection (acc. no. 8399), quoted by permission of the Clifton Waller Barrett Library, University of Virginia Library. A letter of Gladys Cromwell to Padraic Colum from the Henry W. and Albert A. Berg Collection, quoted by permission of the New York Public Library, Astor, Lenox and Tilden Foundations. Letters of Babette Deutsch to Harriet Monroe, quoted by permission of the University of Chicago Library, and Adam Yarmolinsky for the Estate of Babette Deutsch. A letter of Babette Deutsch to Kay Boyle from the Babette Deutsch Papers, quoted by permission of the Rare Books and Manuscripts Division, the New York Public Library, Astor, Lenox and Tilden Foundations, and Adam Yarmolinsky for the Estate of Babette Deutsch. Interview with author (June 18, 1985), quoted by permission of Adam Yarmolinsky for the Estate of Babette Deutsch. Excerpts from an unpublished diary of Harriet Gardner, quoted by permission of Maurice Sagoff and Ruth Perry. Excerpts from Angelina Weld Grimké's letters, diary, poems; from letters of Archibald Grimké, Sarah Stanley Grimké, Emma Toller, and H. G. Wells; and from the manuscript *Rachel* from the Grimké Papers, are quoted by permission of the Moorland-Spingarn Research Center, Howard University. Excerpt from a letter of H. G. Wells to Angelina Weld Grimké, quoted by permission of A. P. Watt Ltd. on behalf of the Literary Executors of the Estate of H. G. Wells. Excerpt from Perdita Schaffner's "The Egyptian Cat," published in H.D., *Hedylus.* Copyright © 1980 by Perdita Schaffner. Reprinted by permission of Black Swan Books, Redding Ridge, Connecticut. Excerpt from "Danse Africaine" by Langston Hughes from *Selected Poems of Langston Hughes.* Copyright © 1959 by Langston Hughes. Reprinted by permission of Alfred A. Knopf, Inc. A letter of Georgia Douglas Johnson to Arna Bontemps from the Cullen-Jackman Memorial Library Manuscript Collection, quoted by permission of the Atlanta University Center Woodruff Library, Division of Archives and Special Collections, Atlanta University Holdings, Atlanta, Georgia, and Henry Lincoln Johnson for the Estate of Georgia Douglas Johnson. A letter of Georgia Douglas Johnson to William Stanley Braithwaite from the William Stanley Braithwaite Collection, quoted by permission of the George Arents Research Library for Special Collections at Syracuse University, and Henry Lincoln Johnson for the Estate of Georgia Douglas Johnson. Letters of Amy Lowell to Grace Hazard Conkling, quoted by permission of the Houghton Library, Harvard University, and G. d'Andelot Belin and Brinton P. Roberts, Trustees under the Will of Amy Lowell. Letters of Marianne Moore to Margaret Conklin, quoted by permission of the Collection of American Literature, The Beinecke Rare Book and Manuscript Library, Yale University, and Clive E. Driver, Literary Executor of the Estate of Marianne C. Moore. "Bulwarked against Fate" by Marianne Moore from *Like a Bulwark.* Copyright © 1949 and 1956 by Marianne Moore. Reprinted by permission of Viking Penguin, Inc., and Clive E. Driver, Literary Executor of the Estate of Marianne C. Moore. Excerpts from letters of Lola Ridge to Evelyn Scott and Idella Purnell, quoted by permission of the Harry Ransom Humanities Research Center, the University of Texas. Excerpts from "Dedication (to my Mother)," "Sun-Up," "Emma Goldman," "Mother," and "(To E.S.)" by Lola Ridge from *Sun-Up* (B.W. Heubsch, 1920); excerpt from "A Toast" by Lola Ridge from *The Ghetto and Other Poems* (B.W. Heubsch, 1918); excerpt from "Adelaide Crapsey" by Lola Ridge from *Red Flag* (Viking, 1927); and "Theme" by Lola Ridge from *Dance of Fire* (Smith, 1935), are reprinted by permission of Elaine Sproat for the Estate of Lola Ridge. Letters of Lola Ridge to David Lawson; Diary, 1940-41; and the unpublished poems "Lyric" and "Prelude" by Lola Ridge, from the Lola Ridge Papers, are quoted by permission of the Sophia Smith Collection, Smith College, and Elaine Sproat for the Estate of Lola Ridge. A letter of Jessie B. Rittenhouse to Aline Kilmer, quoted by permission of Kenton Kilmer for the Estate of Aline Kilmer, and Nellie R. Valley for the Estate of Jessie B. Rittenhouse. Letters of May Sarton to Louise Bogan from the Louise Bogan Collection, quoted by permission of the Trustees of Amherst College and May Sarton. The lines from "Now I Become Myself" from *Selected Poems of May Sarton,* edited by Serena Sue Helsinger and Lois Brynes, are used with the permission of W.W. Norton & Company, Inc. Copyright © 1978 by May Sarton. Excerpts from a letter of Evelyn Scott to David Lawson and from a letter of Evelyn Scott to Lola Ridge, quoted by permission of Paula Scott for the Estate of

Permissions and Acknowledgments 3 0 7

Evelyn Scott. Excerpts from college music composition book; unpublished story, "Rebellion"; unpublished poem, "the Mouse"; "Maura," from *A Woman of Thirty* by Marjorie Seiffert (Knopf, 1919); and poems, prose sketches, and a drawing by Helen Pryor, quoted and reproduced by permission of Allyn Asti-Rose and John C. Pryor. Interview with the author (May 5, 1985) quoted with the permission of John C. Pryor. Letters of Marjorie Seiffert to John Hall Wheelock, Author Files I, Scribner Collection, Box 136, quoted by permission of Princeton University Library and Charles Scribner's Sons. Letter of Marjorie Seiffert to Prof. Henry Pettit, quoted by permission of the University Libraries, University of Colorado at Boulder. Letters of Marjorie Seiffert to Arthur Davison Ficke, quoted by permission of the Collection of American Literature, the Beinecke Rare Book and Manuscript Library, Yale University. Letters of Marjorie Seiffert to Harriet Monroe and Morton Zabel, quoted by permission of the University of Chicago Library. Letters of Marjorie Seiffert to Witter Bynner, quoted by permission of the Houghton Library, Harvard University. Excerpts from unpublished letters of Anne Spencer to James Weldon Johnson and Grace Nail Johnson; Anne Spencer's " 'Dear Langston,' " "Letters to My Sister," "Lady, Lady," and "White Things" from *Time's Unfading Garden* (Louisiana State University Press, 1977), are reprinted by permission of Chauncey E. Spencer for the Estate of Anne Spencer. Letters of Anne Spencer to James Weldon Johnson and Grace Nail Johnson from the James Weldon Johnson Collection, quoted by permission of the Collection of American Literature, the Beinecke Rare Book and Manuscript Library, Yale University. Excerpts from the Preface and lines for "Funeral in May" by Genevieve Taggard from *Calling Western Union* (Harper, 1936); lines from "Leave Me Alone a Little" and "The Quiet Woman" by Genevieve Taggard from *For Eager Lovers* (Thomas Seltzer, 1922); lines from "The Desert Remembers Her Reasons," "Galatea Again," "Chanson," and "The Quarrel" by Genevieve Taggard from *Words for the Chisel* (Knopf, 1926); and lines from "Evening Love of Self" by Genevieve Taggard from *Collected Poems, 1918–1938* (Harper, 1938) are reprinted by permission of Marcia D. Liles, Literary Trustee for the Estate of Genevieve Taggard. A letter of Genevieve Taggard to Fred Millet, quoted by permission of the Collection of American Literature, the Beinecke Rare Book and Manuscript Library, Yale University, and Marcia D. Liles, Literary Trustee for the Estate of Genevieve Taggard. Ten letters of Genevieve Taggard to Josephine Herbst from the Genevieve Taggard Papers, quoted by permission of the Rare Books and Manuscripts Division, the New York Public Library, Astor, Lenox and Tilden Foundations, and Marcia D. Liles, Literary Trustee for the Estate of Genevieve Taggard. A letter of Sara Teasdale to Ernst Filsinger from the Sara Teasdale Collection, quoted by permission of the Missouri Historical Society. Letters of Sara Teasdale to Zoë Akins, Marion Cummings, and Ernst Filsinger; "To L.R.E." and "To E.T.," by Sara Teasdale, are quoted by permission of Wellesley College for the Estate of Sara Teasdale. A letter of Sara Teasdale to Zoë Akins from the Akins Collection, Box 126, quoted by permission of the Huntington Library, San Marino, California. Letters of Sara Teasdale to Marion Cummings from the Marion Cummings Papers, quoted by permission of the Newberry Library. "Imeros" and "The Star" are reprinted with permission of Macmillan Publishing Company from *Mirror of the Heart* by Sara Teasdale. Copyright © 1984 by Morgan Guaranty Trust Company of New York. The poem "On Devon Cliffs" from the Teasdale Poetry Notebooks, quoted by permission of the Collection of American Literature, the Beinecke Rare Book and Manuscript Library, Yale University. A letter of Arthur Davison Ficke to Eunice Tietjens, quoted by permission of Jane J. Ficke for the Estate of Arthur Davison Ficke. Letters of Arthur Davison Ficke, Margery Currey, and Ethel Murrel to Eunice Tietjens from the Eunice Tietjens Papers, are quoted by permission of the Newberry Library. Excerpt from "Epitaph" by Elinor Wylie from *Collected Poems of Elinor Wylie*. Copyright © 1932 by Alfred A. Knopf. Reprinted by permission of Alfred A. Knopf, Inc. Letters of Elinor Wylie to William Rose Benet from the Elinor Wylie Collection (acc. no. 8287), quoted by permission of the Clifton Waller Barrett Library, University of Virginia Library, and Edwina Curtis Schiffer for the Estate of Elinor Wylie. Letters of Elinor Wylie to her mother, Mrs. Hoyt; excerpts from Mrs. Hoyt's memoir, "The Naked Truth," and a letter of Philip Hichborn to Mrs. Hoyt, are quoted by permission of the New York Public Library, Astor, Lenox and Tilden Foundations, and Edwina Curtis Schiffer for the Estate of Elinor Wylie. The lines from "Moth" and "The Empty House" from *The Hermit Thrush* by Kathleen Millay are used with the permission of Liveright Publishing Corporation. Copyright 1929 by Kathleen Millay, copyright renewed 1956 by Kathleen Millay.

INDEX

Teasdale, Sara (*continued*)
and motherhood, 121, 123-124; and gender conflict, 94-95; search for empowerment, 55-56, 80, 94; as love poet, 14-15, 95; and Rossetti, 13-14; on growth of women's poetry, xvii; and Bogan 16, 17, 18; and Conklin, xv-xvi, 242-251, 252, 254, 255; and Lowell, 77; and Reed, 148; and Tietjens, 61-63; and Wheelock, 95-96; and Wylie, 89, 100, 122; suicide, 44, 250, 254, 288
Tietjens, Eunice, 72, 75; and women's clubs, 69-71; and Teasdale, 61-63, 68, 96, 97, 241
Tocqueville, Alexis de, 214
Toomer, Jean, 220, 223
Twain, Mark, 26

Untermeyer, Jean, 62, 124-126
Untermeyer, Louis, 31; and son, 124-126, 133; and Spencer, 220-221, 226; and Wylie, 87-88, 89, 100
Untermeyer, Richard, 124-126
Urban League, 285

Van Doren, Carl, 223
Van Vechten, Carl, 223, 224, 225, 231
Vanity Fair, xvii
Veblen, Thorstein, 151
Venus, 55, 56
Verlaine, Paul, 264

Wagner, Jean, 229
Walker, Alice, 211
Walker, Margaret, 164, 289
Warren, Robert Penn, 165
Webster, Jean, 66
Wells, H. G., 23
West, Rebecca, 88
Wheelock, John Hall, and Seiffert, 42, 118, 119, 136; and Teasdale, 15, 95-96, 101, 247, 248
Whitman, Walt, 72
Whittaker, Elvi, 172
Widdemer, Margaret, 286
Wilder, Thornton, 146

Williams, William Carlos, 149, 194, 286; and Moore, 7; and Seiffert, 40-41, 42, 114
Wilson, Edmund, and Millay, 10, 11, 27, 105, 106, 107, 108; and Wylie, 88, 94, 273n; and women poets of 1920s, xvii
Wolf, Robert, 174, 175, 180, 182
women poets, conflict caused by male power-model, 31, 33, 50, 52-53, 90, 94, 141, 145, 168; creativity as rebellion, 144-145, 170; and self-redemption, 53, 79, 141, 211, 239, 240, 261; denigration by male critics, 160-163, 170, 254, 258; resisted by males, 54, 55, 68, 69, 80; recognition of in 1920s, xvii-xviii, 160
women's clubs, 56, 69-72
Woodhouse, Henry de Clifford, 93
Woolf, Leonard, 92
Woolf, Virginia, 103, 194; on creativity, 12; on Wylie, 92
World War I, as agent of renewal, 126-127, 145, 256
Wright, Richard, 251
Wylie, Elinor, xvii, 99, 100, 103, 106, 109, 114, 115, 119, 124, 254, 256; birth and family background, 33-36; as rebel, 35, 36, 38, 39; marriage to Hichborn, 36-37; elopement with Wylie, 37-38, 81; separation from Wylie, 81-82, 87; and Benét, 83-88, 92, 94, 99, 122; and Woolf, 92; relation to men, 39; as mother, 82, 83, 86, 122-123; gender conflict, 90-92; quest for empowerment, 88, 89; and Shelley, 88, 89-92, 122; *The Orphan Angel,* 89-92; death, 44, 194, 288
Wylie, Horace, 37-38, 81-83, 85, 87, 93, 94

Yaddo, 165, 199
Yarmolinsky, Adam, 128, 149, 167
Yarmolinsky, Avrahm, 156, 166-167
Yeats, William Butler, 71, 162, 163, 192, 246; and politics, 157-158, 160, 161
Young, Marguerite, 5

Zabel, Morton Dawen, 42, 135

FEB 2 7 1989 A